Imprint

ISBN Softcover 978-3-384-09989-1
ISBN E-Book   978-3-384-09990-7

tredition GmbH
Heinz-Beusen-Stieg 5
22926 Ahrensburg

Disclaimer

The organizing team and editors cannot be held responsible for mistakes in information in the articles or consequences relating to the use of them. The views and opinions expressed do not necessarily reflect the views of the editors as the organizing team of this project.

Contact

The Institute for a Greater Europe,
124 Avenue de la Couronne, Box 1,
1050, Ixelles, Brussels Capital Region, Belgium.

Email: Journal@institutegreatereurope.com
Website: https://www.institutegreatereurope.com/
Facebook: /InstituteGreaterEurope/
Twitter: @InstituteEurope
Instagram: Instituteforagreatereurope

Dialogue through Education- Learning between Europe and China

Publication of Submission

This project was run in collaboration between the Institute for Greater Europe and the European Guanxi. Both are youth led think tanks run by young academics and young professionals from all over Europe and beyond. Meanwhile, the Institute for Greater Europe puts a focus on the role of the European Idea on the European continent and beyond, European Guanxi searches to foster a mutual understanding between Europe and China. Together an essay competition was held from January to September 2023, which concluded with a symposium on the 23rd of September. During this project young students and young professionals from Europe and China were invited to submit their essays on the following topics:

- *How will exchange programs develop in the future?*
- *How can curiosity and enthusiasm for the other culture be awaken and strengthened?*
- *What potential does educational diplomacy have?*
- *What is the new approach to international and global education?*

The submissions of this unique academic project are collected in this publication, encompassing a wide range of authors from different interdisciplinary and intercultural backgrounds. During the symposium the ideas presented here were shared with a wider audience. The experience of this unique online event can be found on the last pages of this publication.

Partner Organizations

The **European Guanxi** is a youth-led think tank aiming for better mutual understanding of Europe and China. In the context of the *"polycrisis"* the sense of loss of identity and voice, or the Fourth Industrial Revolution, among others, it is imperative for the EU to readdress both its strategic objectives and its role in the world. Unity, consistency, and vision should guide the EU's engagement with China and more broadly, the international community. For further information please consult: https://www.europeanguanxi.com/

The **Institute for a Greater Europe** is a non-profit youth-led think tank based in Brussels, Belgium with members and interests all over Europe and Beyond. Founded in 2018, the Institute has members and writers from over 30 countries in Europe, North America, Middle East and North Africa, and Asia. The mission searches to generate challenging new ideas, bridge cultural divides and foster a community based around shared values across a wider European scale. For further information please consult: https://institutegreatereurope.com/

Foreword by the Editors

An old Chinese saying states: 三人行，必有我师 (Sānrén xíng, bìyǒu wǒ shī) – In a group of three people, there will always be one person I can learn from." Education has always served as a bridgebuilder, opening new worldviews, and fostering a mutual understanding of different cultures. Simultaneously, education is always directed to the future, preserving what has been learned from the past, meanwhile equipping learners with the skills to realize the vision of a still uncertain future. Thus, with this project we dare a view into the future of global education.

The educational exchange between Europe and China is looking back onto a long history. Especially during the early 20th century many young Chinese students came to Europe for studying such as the famous Cai Yuanpai (蔡元培), who later became the founding father of modern pedagogy in China. Others who returned back from their studies abroad became iconic leaders, shaping the changes their society has underwent. Meanwhile in earlier times, China was considered as country of academic emigration, now it has turned into a country academic immigration likewise. Nowadays in reverse many young students from Europe are travelling to China to learn more about this country, culture, and its growing influence in global politics. During the last years, the educational and cultural exchange between the People's Republic of China and the European Union has gained new dynamics, such as the inauguration of the Confucius Institute, giving an interested audience in Europe access to the Chinese culture.

Nevertheless, new challenges of globalization and a knowledge-based society are shaping the corporation between Europe and China. Therefore, we encouraged young people, students, young researchers, and young professionals to share their experiences, their innovations, and their visions for the future of educational exchange between Europe and China. We are delighted that many followed our call contributing their ideas into this project. The topics discussed are very diverse, which were structured into three sections. The section: "New Ways for Linguistic" look upon motivation for and methods to learn foreign languages. The section "Mutual Learning between Europe and China" provides suggestion how different educational systems can provide inspiration for their counterparts to innovate. The section " Educational Diplomacy through intercultural exchange" looks upon potentials for improving intercultural encounters between Europe and China. Those essays are accompanied by insights into an academic project on introducing dual degree systems in China according to German experience. Furthermore this publications gives a look upon intercultural legal education. Eventually also a bridge between Brazil and China will be built, to sum up this intercultural academic reading experience.

We would like to thank all organizers, all participants, and all speakers for their tremendous contribution, which lead to the successful completion of this unique project. Especially we would like to thank our partners form European Guanxi for their support from the first draft to the final conference. Moreover, special thanks go to the Confucius Institute Freiburg, which gave inspiration for starting this project. Eventually the hard work and commitment of our assistants in Germany and China, name Zhou Yuchen, Liu Yuetong and Li Hongyan have to be mentioned. Their commitment was of high importance for the realization of this unique educational encounter between Europe and China. Hopefully, there will be another chance of working with you in a similar way. A solid fundament for future exchanges is set.

Concluding now we wish you dear readers an insightful lecture and wish you a great learning journey between Europe and China, between language, culture, and a vision for the future.

Best wishes,

Stephan Raab   *Associate Professor Dr. LI Jie (李洁)*

Head of the Organizing Team   **Co-Head of the Organizing Team**

TABLE OF CONTENTS

I. PERSPECTIVES FROM RESEARCHERS

II. NEW WAYS FOR LINGUISTICS

III. MUTUAL LEARNING BETWEEN EUROPE AND CHINA

TABLE OF CONTENTS

III. MUTUAL LEARNING BETWEEN EUROPE AND CHINA

IV. EDUCATIONAL DIPLOMACY THROUGH INTERCULTURAL EXCHANGE

V. REPORT ON THE SYMPOSIUM:

I. Perspectives from Researchers

Lessons learned? Research on the introduction of a German dual degree system in Chinese higher education

Dr. LI Jie[1] *Stephan Raab*[2]

Abstract

Education, especially higher education, stands as the embodiment for a society to prepare its young generation towards the future. Due to unprecedented technological innovations, probably many of nowadays generation of students will work in a job, that still does not exist today. Consequently, the classical division of subjects does not fit anymore, requiring an interdisciplinary thinking for the challenges of global digital times. Therefore, following the Bologna process, Germany has introduced a system of single degree dual major studies, combining different fields such as for instance digital humanities. This paper embarks on a concise comparative journey scrutinizing potentials of introducing a dual degree system in China, following the German example. Looking upon Chinese educational reforms, the implementation of new liberal arts at the Northwestern Polytechnical University will be discussed. Taking the technological revolution foremost artificial intelligence into mind, this paper argues for more interdisciplinary and transdisciplinary thinking in education to overcome epistemic boundaries and preparing students and research for an age of increasing complexity.

Keywords Dual Degree System, Germany, China, Comparative Analysis, Future Studies

Introduction

Every society is built on a certain degree of education, inheriting lessons learned from the past, meanwhile preparing the next generation for the future. In other words, societies are built through learning from their history through a process of change before and after lessons learned. However, despite this forward looking framework of education, the Italian sociologist and president of the Italian Associazione dei Futuristi Italiani (AFI), Roberto Poli bemoans about his scientific formation: " *There was no kind of forward-looking framework, no frame where to fit in the future"* (Poli, 2019, p.1). Such criticism has been reiterated by the Chinese educationist as first director of the renowned Beijing University: "Cai Yuanpai [蔡元培] considering his academic upbringing as *"wasted"*, as Chinese education seemed reverted mostly to the past memorizing classical texts (Zhang, 1993, pp.147). Therefore, Cai Yuanpai emphasized his mission as: *"Educators are not for the past, nor for the present, but for the future"* (Zhang, 2020, p.359). Building on that, new ways of education are needed to prepare students for coping with the rising complexity of our societies. Consequently, several universities in Germany have introduced dual degrees, enabling to study and enrich their academic perspectives with combining two different subjects.

This paper will build on that issue, discussing the potentials of introducing dual degree systems in the Chinese university system. This discussion is structured as following. In the first part the Bologna process and the introduction of dual degree systems in Germany will be presented.

---

[1] Associate Professor Dr., Faculty of Foreign Studies at the Northwestern Polytechnical University (Xi'an, PRC)
[2] President and Member of the Advisory Board of the Institute for Greater Europe
This paper is supported by "the Fundamental Research Funds for the Central Universities" — 2023 西北工业大学发展战略研究基金项目（No. 2023FZY20，德国 U15 大学 "双专业单学位" 学制对我校新文科建设的破局之思）

After that the second part will show the practical implementation of this concepts into German higher education as well as presenting lessons learned. The third part will act as a connector, foremost describing the context of rising complexity. As every education is normative, embedded in a certain sociocultural context, here a general paradigm shifts in science through new scientific means will be examined. A critical understanding of the potentials and limits of this scientific innovations are essential for a suitable educational reform. Building on that the fourth part demands for thinking beyond the boundaries of one subject, explaining the differences between multidisciplinary, interdisciplinary, and transdisciplinary approaches. The fifth part will elaborate on the implementation of this system in Chinese higher education, taking the different sociohistorical trajectories into mind. Eventually, the six parts will give an outlook on the empirical results of the current educational reform in China. Eventually the last part will give an outlook on the importance of mutual learning for promoting educational diplomacy through encouraging an interdisciplinary as intercultural exchange of people and thoughts in global world.

1. The Bologna Process and the German High-Tech Strategy

Looking into the future of higher education within the European Union started at a historic spot. On the 19th of June 1999 the ministers of education from 29 countries gathered at the assumed oldest university in the world, at the University of Bologna, signing the "Bologna Declaration". Here the great importance of higher education in Europe is emphasized by the following words: "*A Europe of Knowledge is now widely recognized as an irreplaceable factor for social and human growth and as an indispensable component to consolidate and enrich the European citizenship, capable of giving its citizens the necessary competences to face the challenges of the new millennium, together with an awareness of shared values and belonging to a common social and cultural space.*"(European Ministers of Education 1999) This declaration started the "Bologna Process" searching to improve the comparability of educational systems upon the European continent. This reform came along the introduction of the Bachelor-Master System, replacing the previous diploma degrees. Prior to that reform, there were no interim degrees, only a "Vordiplom" with a "Grundstudium", acknowledging, that the students had acquired the basic skills and knowledge of the subject. After that students could specialize in their "Hauptstudium", eventually graduating with a diploma. Nevertheless, different then the Bachelor (seven to eight semesters) and Master (four to six semester) there was no restriction on semesters studied, theoretically studying undefined time. Based upon the European Credit Transfer System (ECTS), academic achievements between different European countries should be made comparable, building on a common system of measurement. Simultaneously, referring the Erasmus scheme, academic mobility should be encouraged, spending semester abroad (ibid.).

As a result, the mobility of students has increased tremendously. In comparison about 48.000 German students were inscribed at a university abroad in 1999. However, ten years after the commencement of this process, in 2009 already 115.000 German students had spent at least a semester abroad. Simultaneously the influx of foreign students had increased tremendously after the reform, reaching about 75.000 (Deutscher Bundestag, 2012, p.14.). A striking example of this reform are Erasmus Mundus Programs, where students spend each semester in another country.

The Bologna process began in the early days of what should become the digital revolution. In 2011 at the Hannover Messe CEBIT, one the biggest fairs for innovations in IT that time, the term industry 4.0. was presented to the public. Different than Industry 1.0 driven by the steam engine, Industry 2.0 driven by the conveyor belt and Industry 3.0. driven by automation, this new type of Industry 4.0 will be driven by the interconnection of humans and machines through the power of big data and artificial intelligence. After the fair a working group elaborated recommendations how to conceive a high-tech strategy for German economy. This report focused especially on six domains, foremost Industry 4.0, Smart Services, Smart Data, Cloud Computing, Digital Interconnectedness, Digital Science, Digital Education and Digital Living Spaces. (Deutscher Bundestag 2016). With the implementation of Germany's Industry 4.0

program, the German U15 university consortium [3] has gradually reformed from the characteristic of *"separate academic disciplines"* to implement interdisciplinary, integrated, and open teaching. It has taken interdisciplinary human resource training and interdisciplinary research as a feature of development in the context of the new era, and has opened up new cross-disciplines, dual degrees, and double professional degrees. Specifically, to draw on Germany's U15 University Consortium 's *"single degree with double majors"* academic system and tailor-make the university's *"single degree with double majors"* academic system for liberal arts, in order to promote academic disciplines and the development of the university's new liberal arts. It encourages preliminary cross-fertilization of disciplines, breaks down discipline and major barriers, and strives for in-depth integration of university liberal arts majors as well as embedded cross-fertilization with the university's peripheral majors of science, technology, agriculture, and medical science. The university's *"new liberal arts"* will be able to renew and revolutionize itself in the primary transition stage, with *"single degree with double majors"* as the main focus, supplemented by double degree training as the construction path.

2. Introducing dual-degree systems in German higher education

After having presented the trajectory of the Bologna process, this part will give an overview how those concepts were implemented in the German higher education. After that, lessons learned will be presented, which have to be taken into mind for the introduction in a Chinese context. Professor Bernd Eitel, President of the U15 Consortium and Chancellor of the University of Heidelberg, stated in his speech at the establishment of the Faculty of Engineering (2021) that *"through interdisciplinary dialogues, universities will facilitate the transfer of knowledge to society and contribute to breakthroughs in social change."* In the new era, the U15 consortium has made interdisciplinary talent training and interdisciplinary research the core of its philosophy and development characteristics, and it promotes interdisciplinarity and interdisciplinary development through three paths:

(1) **Establishment of a dual-major, single degree** (Zwei-Fächer-Studium): In contrast to the dual degree system, this is the system used by the vast majority of German universities in the humanities, languages, and social sciences, as well as a few science schools. At the undergraduate level, one must select at least two majors, namely a major (90-150 credits with a mandatory thesis) and a minor (30-90 credits without a thesis) and must complete a total of 180 credits for the major and minor, which is the same as for a single-major degree in general. However, the major and minor courses cannot be duplicated, and the credits are not interchangeable, i.e., duplicated courses in the course selection lists of the two majors will not be counted in only one of the major directions. After graduation, only one-degree certificate will be issued for the major direction, but the certificate will include the names of the major and minor, as well as the corresponding scores. For example, most humanities and social sciences programs at the University of Heidelberg require single-degree students to complete 75% of their major (Hauptfach) and 25% of their minor (Ergänzungsfach), or 50% of each of the two majors.

(2) **Doppelstudium**: Students are eligible for admission to two programs and enrol in two 180-credit degree programs (either concurrently or sequentially), which can be either a single or a double degree program, with credits transferred by the Prüfungsamt, the university's examination board, based on the similarities of the two programs. The total number of credits required ranges between 210 and 360ECTS, and students must complete two theses. Students receive a dual degree in both programs upon graduation. However, the duration of the dual studies is not doubled, and both degree programs must be completed within the time limit. For example, if the University of Leipzig allows

---

[3] **German U15 e.V.** is an association of fifteen major research-intensive and leading medical universities in Germany with a full disciplinary spectrum, excluding any defining engineering sciences. For more information please consult: https://www.german-u15.de/

a maximum of nine semesters for Physics and nine semesters for History, then a dual degree student must complete both programs in nine semesters (Physics and History do not have the same courses, so there is no credit offsetting) to reach a total of 360 credits.

(3) **Setting up a new cross-discipline:** A cross-discipline is the intersection and fusion of two or more disciplines to gradually form a new discipline, which, as an independent speciality, also needs to reach the 180 credits required for a general single-specialty degree and complete a thesis, and after graduation, it can be awarded a degree certificate of the independent speciality. For example, the University of Trier in Germany has recently established the cross-discipline digital humanities, which primarily focuses on the digitization of articles with humanities content as the theme, such as labelling or networking, and more on. This discipline has been constantly developed and improved, and the university has prioritized the establishment of an independent faculty.

After that overview, the following will show the benefits and drawbacks of the three major cross-disciplinary and integration paths in German U15 colleges and universities, as well as the current state of development. With the increased demand for complex and innovative talents, German colleges and universities continue to establish *"emerging cross-disciplines,"* but the development of a cross-discipline requires many years of comprehensive knowledge system construction and discipline setting experience, and the number of disciplines is often small. However, the development of a cross-discipline requires years of comprehensive knowledge system construction and discipline setting experience, and the number of disciplines offered, and number of students admitted for enrolment are frequently small, with demand exceeding supply. As a result, only a small number of students can pursue *"cross-discipline"* degrees at German universities; in other words, emerging cross-disciplines cannot meet the vast majority of students' specialisation integration demands in a timely manner. According to the 2022 report published by the Centre for Education and Academic Research of German Universities, the dual-degree system in German universities is gradually fading away, and only a small number of students choose to study dual degrees (of which dual degrees in economics, engineering, and sociology are more common), which is closely related to academic pressure in German universities. According to figures of the *"Study on Undergraduate Dropout Rates at Comprehensive Universities across Germany"* in 2022, the average dropout rate of undergraduates at comprehensive universities in Germany in the graduation year of 2020 was as high as 35%, implying that nearly one-third of undergraduates interrupted their studies, with mathematics and natural sciences having the highest dropout rate of 43%. The dropout rate in math and natural science is 51%, which is the highest, followed by the humanities (literature, history, linguistics, culture, etc.) with 50% dropout rate, which corresponds to an increase by 8% (Heublein et.al 2022, pp.5). However, here the difficult circumstances during Covid lockdowns have to be considered, probably worsening figures.

Besides those dropout rates students bemoan an increased level of disorientation. In 2000 there were about 450 bachelor and master programs, increasing to 13.000 until 2012 by either reforming previous or creating new ones from the scratch (Wissenschaftsrat 2012: 36f.). In 2021 this has increased to already close to 21.000 degrees (HRK 2021: 7). Due to that overwhelming choice often a comparability of study programs is hardly feasible, leaving students clueless. Moreover, students bemoan an increased level of pressure due to condensed curricula, often putting a four years' program into three years. Every module has to be concluded with an academic work, either a paper or exam. This comes along an increased feeling of stress and exhaustion among students. During the semester 2021 about half of students indicated a prolonged period of extensive stress burden, with 42% feeling over-exhausted by workload (BMBF 2023, p.40f.) Eventually due to the strict corset of the Bachelor- Master system a "Verschulung" (schoolification) is taking place, turning university into a prolonged school period. Especially the renowned German philosopher Julian Nida-Rümelin bemoans. the rigidity of the new system, shaped by obligation of presence ("Präsenzpflicht") as well as less leeway for creating a study program according to own interested. Consequently, a standstill in higher education is taking place. As a reaction Nida-Rümelin proclaims a reform, strengthening the ideals of "Humboldtsche´s Bildungsideal" (Thurau 2008). This concept argues that education is does not only serve for increasing employability, but serving to create a fully fledged personality, being aware of its identity and position within the world (Niedermeyer 2020, p.226).

It can be seen that in German universities, particularly at elite institutions such as U15 and T9[4], it is already "difficult" to graduate with a single degree, and "difficult" to graduate with a double degree, with very few people able to complete the credits of a double degree, complete the thesis of both majors, and obtain two bachelor's degrees. Few students can complete the dual degree credits, complete the thesis of two majors, and obtain two bachelor's degree certificates. In light of the university's development, most German university students opt for a single-degree system of *"double major,"* which not only ensures the integration of multidisciplinary learning, cultivates, and exercises interdisciplinary thinking, but also avoids the double academic pressure and time conflict of a double degree. The *"double major"* single-degree system provides an effective and feasible path for the integration of disciplines in German universities, which is effective and promising, and is conducive to the cultivation of composite and innovative talents, as well as accumulating momentum for the implementation of Germany's *"Industry 4.0"* technological innovation strategy. Nevertheless, still more reforms and adaptions are highly recommended.

This argumentation has revealed the practical implementation of introducing a dual degree system in German higher education. As it could be shown that the technological revolution and political demands have spurred this process, leaving an ambivalent result. On the one hand student numbers have increased coming along a higher mobility for spending a semester abroad. On the other hand, this comes along an increase of complexity by an incalculable number of new degrees leaving students disoriented. Furthermore, the reform has revealed an increased feeling of pressure and exhaustion among students. As interim conclusion it can be argued that higher education and the university system have to be adapted to the demands of changing society. Nevertheless, there are certain lessons to be learned for improving this initiated process.

3. A call for complexity: Changing demands for education

Having presented the political context for educational reforms in Germany this part will serve as a connection between the European and the Chinese context. As every educational system is embedded in a certain sociocultural context, every education is normative oriented towards instilling certain values and norms on the learners. Obviously the European and the Chinese context are built on divergent sociocultural factors. Therefore, in the following a general understanding of the paradigm shift in science is delivered, considering scientific potentials and limitations of recent disruptions, adjusting the Chinese system after the German experiences.

Starting from the scratch first of all the evolutionary origins of the institution school, latter on university have to be reminded. For generations children had learned through socialization, imitating the behaviour of their parents as role models. However, with the invention of literacy, the art of reading and writing, this kind of learning presented itself soon as not feasible anymore. *"The institution classroom evolved at the moment, that the social complexity of a society had grown to such an extent, that learning through socialization and imitation did not appear functional anymore"* (Scheunpflug, 2001, p.61). In the classroom an accelerated evolutionary path of the society can be simulated, confronting students with situations, that might happen to them in real life, without waiting for the incident to occur (ibid. p.61). Therefore, classroom settings stand as depiction of the reduced complexity of a society, where students are members of that social construction (ibid.p.66). Often students and educationist argue that the current educational system does not provide sufficient training to provide them with the necessary skills to cope with a more complex society.

---

[4] **TU9 German Universities of Technology e. V.** is the alliance of nine leading Technical Universities in Germany. For more information please consult: https://www.tu9.de/

Keeping on following this path, scientific innovation evolved according to three different stages. Shortly after the Second World War in 1948 mathematician Warren Weaver developed a model of thought depicting history as the challenge to cope with and create within an environment of ever-increasing complexity. During the first age, having its beginnings at the origins of modern science in the age of enlightenment, there were *problems of simplicity*. Due to the limited computational powers as well as limited access to scientific tools scientist focused mostly on describing and observing, searching for figure out the potential variables. Such methods were mostly writing reports on observations during scientific journeys such as Humboldt and his magnum opus *"Der Kosmos"*. Scientist could conduct simple experiments, with low technology. Here, science could detect the connection between two variables such as heat, sound, or pressure, simply physics leading to common inventions such as the telephone or the radio.

After that, with the time of accelerated industrialization, at about 1900 the age of *disorganized complexity* emerged. Those days' scientists gained access to more sophisticated technology, including more knowledge about probability theories and statistics. This came along new methods in recording and calculating. This comes along the emergence of modern social sciences, taking the evolution subjects like psychology, sociology, and political science into mind. Thanks to those innovations more precise and reliable predictions about the future could be made. Nevertheless, this period is considered disorganized as various subjects such as social science, philosophy, and natural science or mathematic were considered separate domains.

However, entering the time of tremendous scientific progress since the 1950ies now we are facing the problems of *organized complexity*. Those problems, exceed computational capacities, often not possible to be translated and described into mathematical, quantitative figures. Therefore, a new combination of quantitative and qualitative access, thinking out of the boundaries of the own epistemic community is needed to discover the interrelationships between various factors influencing each other (Weaver, 1948, pp.536–544). Especially, with the times of ever more powerful artificial intelligence and ever more sophisticated algorithms and big data that kind of thinking is recommended, as artificial intelligence faces its limitations. This becomes obvious with the Theorem of Goedel and the Church-Turing-Hypothesis, arguing, that no mathematical system can prove its ultimate legitimacy and validity out of itself. According to those concepts a Turing-Machine or better known today as a simple computer; - human calculators were called computers previously; - could calculate not more than a human being. Every computation conducted by a machine like a computer, or an artificial intelligence could be performed by a human being yet requiring different time resources often limiting human power.

Put in other words, such as mankind is impaired to prove the existence of a higher existence, no algorithm based system can prove its own validity from within (Turing, 1938, p.8). Express by Turing: *"If each man had a definite set of rules of conduct by which he regulated his life he would be no better than a machine. But there are no such rules, so men cannot be machines"* (Turing, 1950, p.452). Consequently, despite the increasing potential of artificial intelligence and computational power, educating for human thinking is still highly required, as there is no universal algorithm of truth, however human beings can find a different more empathic creative approach to complex issues.

4. Crossing scientific boundaries [3] Multi, Inter, Transdisciplinary

Traditionally the world of social science, psychology and philosophy and the world of natural science, engineering and technology seem to be separated. Here, two separate themes of thinking seem to apply building on the famous statement by German pedagogist Wilhem Dilthey: *"Nature we search to explain, the mental mind we search to understand"* (Dilthey 1924, p.144). Explanation as a scientific paradigm relies on external research objects, to be observed and described with a defined number of variables. Through method, interconnections and intersections between those variables can be revealed. Conversely, understanding as a paradigm focusses on the complex inner mental workings of a human constructivist word, requiring having glimpse about the context in which and in which between research is conducted. Meanwhile explanations require the knowledge of rules and mechanisms, understanding requires a consciousness about contexts and an empathic feeling (Beinke 2016,pp.101). Bringing both worlds together demands for high bridge-building skills, where in the next part. the case study of Northwestern Polytechnical University (NWPU) will serve as an example of such approach in a Chinese context

In classical term science at universities is structed in departments and institutions. Accordingly science can be conceived as a form of institutionalized knowledge, independently of its researchers (Böhme, 1994, p.67). Here, the findings of many generations of scientist are compiled, giving research access to experiences they have never made in their life. Organized on a basic theoretical fundament along institutions and scientific specialists, modern science stands for the *"socialized research"* (ibid.pp.72). Scientific knowledge is inclusive as everybody disposing the required skills and applied methods can prove the findings either right or wrong (Treml, 2010, p.89). Nevertheless, each department such as social sciences vs. natural science belong to a certain epistemic community, sharing an intersubjective understandings, having a shared way of knowing (Haas, 1992, p.3). In other words, they set the definition and standards what according to their membership has to be considered scientific. Due to their *epistemic practical authority* they define the selection criteria how to get from complexity to what is considered scientific knowledge (Adler, 2019, p.10). However, as no science can claim anymore, to be in possession of full explanatory power new ways of scientific corporations are needed. Nowadays, the boundaries of the disciplines, emerged in the pursuit of ordering the modern world, seem to blur. New sorts of mixed disciplines and subdisciplines are surfacing, revealing the epistemic boundaries of each perspective (Giri, 2002, p.104). New cross-disciplinary approaches, combining at least two different subjects, are required. Here, three popular approaches, multi-, inter-, and transdisciplinary access to scientific knowledge will be presented with their potentials.

Multidisciplinary: More than two subjects, such as for instance joint research between IT and psychology are involved. Research takes place within the own discipline. The research work independently on their research question. Here, the members of the team have separate but interrelated roles. At the end, the findings are put in juxtaposition, however the epistemic boundaries of each discipline are maintained, IT might be curious about the efficiency of the code, meanwhile psychology would focus on the effects of the program on the mind. Consequently, the fruitful knowledge transfer into other disciplines is rather limited.

Interdisciplinary: Likewise, at least more than two disciplines are involved. Research takes place between the disciplines. Differently, here the members work jointly on certain research questions. The members of the research team have common roles. Eventually the epistemic boundaries between the disciplines are permeable to a certain aspect, however scientist still maintain their epistemic socialization, such as taken the example improving the user interface. Consequently, working on joint questions and shared goals a transfer of knowledge and innovation is taking place. Here, an interactive, integrative, and collaborative approach is used.

Transdisciplinary: As previously more than two disciplines are involved. Research takes place across and beyond scientific boundaries. Here, many actors like scientist from relevant disciplines, stakeholders or affected non-academics are involved. Those share a conceptual framework, searching for an integration, assimilation, incorporation, and harmonization of the various disciplines. Researchers work in the mode of role release, acting out of the role, as well as role expansion, expanding the roles functions. Eventually, due to bringing so many perspectives into the research, the knowledge gain is tremendous. Nevertheless, creating a shared conceptual framework is everything apart from easy (Lawrence, 2010). An example could be found in urban development involving architects, sociologist, politicians, and citizens on an equal level.

5. The dual degree system for Chinese Higher Education

5.1 Education Reform in Chinese Higher Education

The previous part has presented several arguments for the urgency of interdisciplinary thinking. Using the keyword *"Zwei-Fächer-Studium"* in Google Scholar, 2590 articles can be found, and the number of German and foreign scholars who have researched the dual-professional single-degree system has been growing exponentially in recent years. Conversely, a search for the keyword *"double major degree"* in the China National Knowledge Infrastructure (CNKI) database yielded no relevant academic literature. This demonstrates that, despite being a hot effect in foreign teaching practice and research, the experience of the German double major single degree system has yet to capture the attention of the domestic academic circle, particularly the education circle.

Since the dawn of the knowledge economy 2.0, where economic development is highly dependent knowledge intensive activities like research, the information structure, cognitive structure, and social structure have all changed dramatically. In response to the *"great change that has not occurred in a hundred years"*, China has implemented educational reforms and encouraged the innovative development of academic discipline construction, and the characteristics of China's colleges and universities have gradually shifted to the fusion of disciplines and inter-disciplinary fusion. Xue Qikun, a representative of Chinese Academy of Sciences, stated: *"Driven by the country's major strategic needs, cross-disciplinary convergence of multiple disciplines and cross-border integration of multiple technologies will become the norm, and the development of cross-disciplines in the world's first-class universities is also a general trend* [在国家重大战略需求的驱动下，多学科交叉汇聚与多技术跨界融合将成为常态，世界一流大学发展交叉学科也是大势所趋]. *"* [5] The Ministry of Education, the Ministry of Science and Technology, and 13 other departments in 2019 announced launch the "six", "one outstanding" program together The same year the Ministry of Education, the Ministry of Science and Technology, and 13 other departments jointly launched the *"six excellence and one top* [六卓越一拔尖]*"* plan 2.0, and the construction of the *"four new"* disciplines ["四新"学科] (new engineering, new medical science, new science, and new liberal arts) has begun. During the last decade the Peoples Republic of China has developed into a hub for disruptive technologies in the field of artificial intelligence and digitization. The rapid development of the Internet, artificial intelligence, and other high-tech has gradually transformed the basic disciplines of liberal arts, such as literature, history, philosophy, and so on, into instrumental, and the shortcomings of *"separate disciplines"* have severely hampered the development of liberal arts. The construction of *"New Liberal Arts"* is a reflection and improvement of previous education, aiming to break down barriers between disciplines and move towards *"inter-disciplinary integration"*, and even some new cross-disciplinary liberal arts categories, such as Tsinghua University's establishment of a *"full-time LLM (Master of Laws) in Computational Law* [计算法学全日制法律硕士]*"* program in 2018.

According to the 2020 *"Declaration on the Construction of New Liberal Arts* [新文科建设宣言]*"*, it is necessary to achieve not only interdisciplinary and multidisciplinary development, but also recognition of the importance of interdisciplinary and multidisciplinary development, as well as cross-disciplinary education development. cross-pollination and development, but also to emphasize the nature of the liberal arts and the importance of the liberal arts themselves in the construction of the new liberal arts. Referring back to Germany a new field of digital humanities combines humanities and IT-technology. Those kinds of mixed degrees could provide an inspiration for the promotion of interdisciplinary and transdisciplinary thinking already among potential future researchers, searching to make an impact on shaping a technology intense future.

---

[5] see: 以"实"为要 推动交叉科研高质量发展 (Taking "practical" as the priority to promote high-quality development of cross-disciplinary scientific research) in: In China News 05.05.2022;
http://www.ln.chinanews.com.cn/news/2022/0505/322603.html

5.2 Construction of New Liberal Arts at Technical Universities

Northwestern Polytechnic University (NWPU) is the only first-class university in China featuring aviation, aerospace and maritime engineering education and research, and it has many national key disciplines and ace majors, which creates very convenient conditions for the introduction of the *"single degree with double majors"* path in liberal arts in NWPU. Unlike traditional pure liberal arts or pure science and technology institutions, NWPU can integrate the resources of various majors in liberal arts and promote the in-depth integration of humanities and social sciences disciplines in NWPU, and also give full play to the advantages of other majors in NWPU such as the three aviation and kinetic energy disciplines, so as to facilitate the peripheral embeddedness of the advantageous military-industrial disciplines for the construction of new liberal arts in NWPU. The peripheral embedding of the new liberal arts.

While actively responding to the construction and development of *"new engineering"* and *"new science"* as a world-class engineering university, Northwestern Polytechnical University (NWPU) has also actively promoted the construction of *"new liberal arts"*. For example, Northwestern Polytechnical University issued the *"14th Five-Year Plan of Liberal Arts Construction and Development* [文科建设发展 "十四五" 规划]*"* in December 2021, accelerating the construction and development of liberal arts in the university and giving full play to the value-led and quality-improving roles of liberal arts in talent cultivation. In 2021, the Ministry of Education approved four NWPU projects as research and practice projects in new liberal arts, and Shaanxi Province approved four projects as research and practice projects in new liberal arts. From preliminary research it can be seen on the development status of liberal arts at this university that the construction of new liberal arts at this university is still in the early transition stage, and there is still a long way to the later transformation stage, and the construction of new liberal arts in our university, if education reform blindly goes over the *"cross-discipline"* and directly enter into the *"cross-discipline"*, it is very likely that it will have a negative impact on it. The reasons are as follows:

1) Before the opening of the new liberal arts cross-disciplines, it is necessary to complete the discipline's knowledge system, accumulate and form a systematic theoretical foundation, keeping in mind that any new disciplines are based on the framework of perfect theoretical knowledge.
2) The new liberal arts cross-disciplines must be precipitated by time, and they must be gradually shifted from the discipline cross-discipline. The training program and degree system should be constantly improved, and it is critical not to swallow the whole thing and ignore time precipitation and experience accumulation.

This research is based on the characteristics of the development of liberal arts majors and real problems in Northwestern Polytechnical University (NWPU), with the goal of creating a *"single degree with double majors"* for the new liberal arts in the university's primary transition stage, in order to truly *"break the problem"* and put the construction of new liberal arts in our university into practice. NWPU 's path to new liberal arts construction can be divided into two major stages: the initial transition stage and the later transformation stage. Thus, it is believed that the construction of new liberal arts at NWPU is still in the early stages, and the direct large-scale establishment of new cross-language liberal arts is very likely to have the negative effect of *"pulling up the seedling to help the child grow up"*. In light of the current situation and actual problems of the university's liberal arts construction, specific and feasible corrective measures are proposed for the cultivation mode suitable for the primary transitional stage of the university's new liberal arts construction. This approach is visualized in figure 1 representing the various research steps.

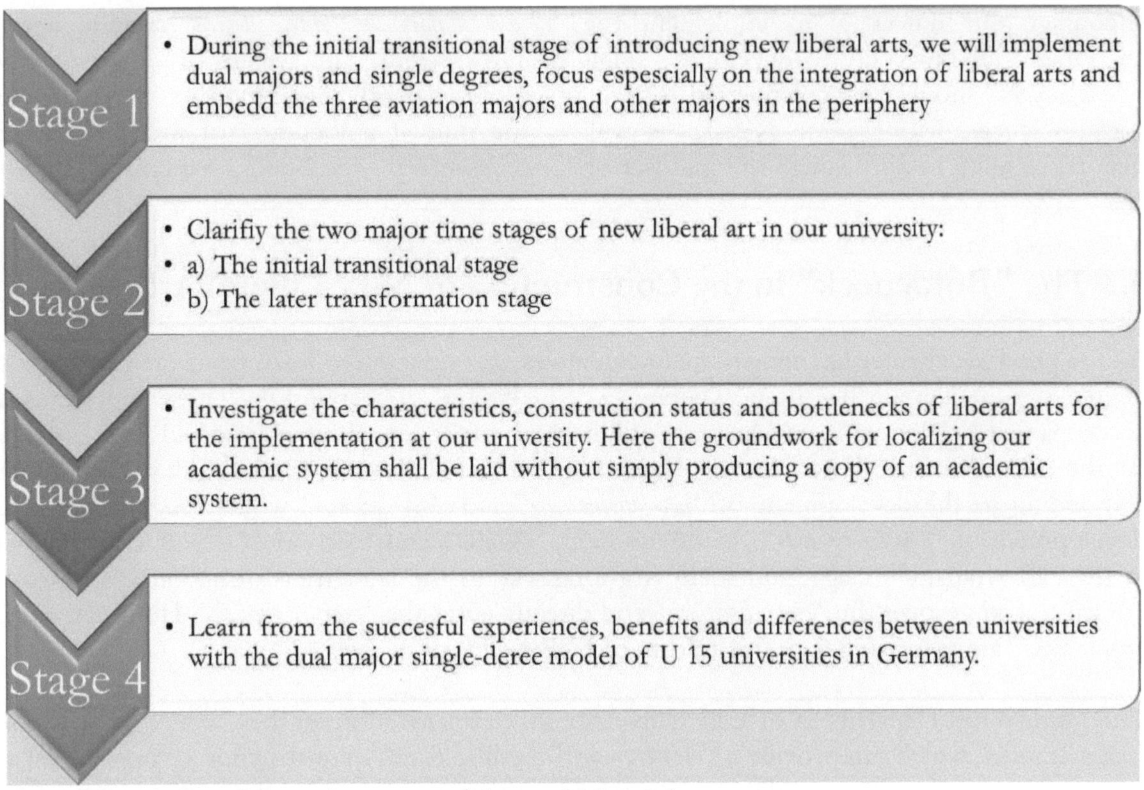

Stage 1
- During the initial transitional stage of introducing new liberal arts, we will implement dual majors and single degrees, focus especially on the integration of liberal arts and embedd the three aviation majors and other majors in the periphery

Stage 2
- Clarifiy the two major time stages of new liberal art in our university:
- a) The initial transitional stage
- b) The later transformation stage

Stage 3
- Investigate the characteristics, construction status and bottlenecks of liberal arts for the implementation at our university. Here the groundwork for localizing our academic system shall be laid without simply producing a copy of an academic system.

Stage 4
- Learn from the succesful experiences, benefits and differences between universities with the dual major single-deree model of U 15 universities in Germany.

Image 1 Description of the various steps of the research puzzle

Through the preliminary research on the development status of liberal arts at NWPU, it becomes obvious that the construction of new liberal arts there is still in the early transition stage, and there is still a distance from the later transformation stage, which needs to be shifted from *"cross-discipline"* to *"cross-discipline"* step by step in an orderly manner. The establishment of new cross-disciplinary majors is the long-term strategic goal for the construction of *"new liberal arts"*, while the dual-degree system can only be an auxiliary strategy in the initial and long-term stages because of its low coverage and greater constraints. Therefore, *"single degree with double majors"* is a feasible solution for the construction of *"new liberal arts"* at NWPU in the initial transition stage.

The aim of this research proposal is to provide a solution for the initial transition phase of the new liberal arts program at the university. Under this basic framework, the study adopts a two-step strategy: firstly, on the one hand we have to discover our source of inspiration stemming from the German reform of the higher education system, i.e., we have to explore the *"double major single degree"* model of the German U15 University Consortium in the construction of liberal arts; on the other hand, we have to *"know ourselves"*, i.e., we have to comprehensively investigate the strengths, weaknesses and characteristics of the development of liberal arts at the NWPU. A simple German Chinese transfer is not recommended as both educational systems are established on a different academic tradition and cultural fundaments. Moreover, we need to *"know ourselves"*, to accurately grasp the existing problems and bottlenecks in the construction of new liberal arts in our university, and we need to know that the construction of new liberal arts, as Mr. Zhang Bolin said, should be *"based on the academic background of Chinese history and society, and take solving the problems of China as the goal of education* [以中国历史、中国社会为学术背景，以解决中国问题为教育目标]*"*[6]. Then, two major time processes for the construction of new liberal arts in our university are put forward, and make it clear that the construction of new liberal arts in our university is still in the primary stage, and we should learn from the successful method of integration of disciplines in Germany's U15 University, integrate the advantages of liberal arts, military industry and three aviation majors of Northwestern Polytechnical University, and implement the localized *"double majors and single degree"* system suitable for our university, and

---

[6] 以中国历史、中国社会为学术背景，以解决中国问题为教育目标 (Taking Chinese history and Chinese society as the academic background and solving Chinese problems as the educational goal): in: Baidu 07.08.2018:"燃志之师"张伯苓："中国不亡吾辈在！"③ (baidu.com)

encourage our university to implement the *"double majors and single degree"* system, and to encourage our university to develop a "single degree" system. The system of *"single degree with double majors"* should be implemented to encourage the in-depth integration of humanities and social sciences disciplines in NWPU as well as the mutual embedding of military-industrial majors, so as to break through the mindset of *"small liberal arts"* and build a pattern of *"big liberal arts"*.

5.3 The "Bottleneck" in the Construction of New Liberal Arts

As the previous chapter has shown, many initiatives are surfacing to learn from the German dual degree system, employing these experiences as a source of inspiration. Those ambitions are accompanied by many efforts which are still in their infancy, searching to unfold their potential. As the case study has shown Northwestern Polytechnical University (NWPU) has been actively responding to the development of *"new engineering"* and *"new science"*, while also promoting the development of *"new liberal arts"*. At the moment, NWPU's construction of new liberal arts is still in the early transition stage, and there is a long way to the later transformation stage, so it is critical not to go over the *"cross-discipline"* and directly enter the *"cross-discipline"*. However, several *"bottlenecks"* are associated with this reform of higher education.

The Humanities Department of U15 University in Germany adopted the *"single degree with double majors"* model, which can provide a *"breakthrough"* method for the construction of new liberal arts in our university, as a good reference for solving the primary stage of the construction of new liberal arts in our university. To assist the university in promoting this academic system, a thorough understanding of the current system and the development of liberal arts at the university is required. Therefore, this research applies a focus on researching our university's current degree system, training programs, curriculum, and degree requirements for liberal arts majors, while also interviewing our liberal arts students about their acceptance of and expectations for *"single degree with double majors"* via questionnaires. A localized model of *"single degree with double majors"* will be proposed for the construction of new liberal arts in the university after fully understanding the current development of liberal arts in the university and the needs of teachers and students. What is important to keep in mind, that is foremost taking the socio-scientific background of the Chinese university context into mind.

Foremost the promotion of inter- and transdisciplinary thinking has to be translated into practical research and education of potential future researchers. Therefore, besides providing the financial and logistical resources, foremost an openness to new ways of mental models is needed. Currently, the epistemic boundaries between the disciplines are blurring. Keeping in mind, that those boundaries are the result of the scientific spirits of the age of enlightenment searching to reflect a clear ordered world in the scientific classification of subject. However, with borders blurring, becoming more permeable a different kind of thinking is required. A modern disciplinary thinking fails short to realize that their claim for universality is void, acknowledging the *"significance of other disciplines in gaining multiple perspectives about the world to which both one's as well as another's discipline contribute"* (Giri, 2002, p.106). Consequently, introducing a dual degree is foremost dependent on the willingness for dialogue and *"authentic embeddedness"*, becoming aware of one's subject in the universal complexity of the scientific world as well admitting the own epistemic limitations. This comes along the openness for including other disciplines and their epistemic access on the issue (ibid. p.108). Summarizing introducing such dual degree reform has to be conceived in collaboration with scientist, students, and educators, opening opportunities for all to shape this learning process.

5.4 Lessons learned on the way from Bologna to Xi·an

Summarizing this comparative section, it could be shown, that the Chinese educational reform find high potentials in the introduction of new liberal arts through dual degree systems. Here, the experiences made in the German context can provide a fruitful inspiration for the implementation process. Nevertheless, as this research has shown, this transition has come with several side effects, which have to be taken into consideration for a smooth educational reform. Consequently, this part will give some practical recommendations out of the lessons learned from the Bologna process.

Transition Phase: As this research has shown, reforming an established education system into a new structure often comes along a bumpy transition phase. Therefore, learning from the German example, for the Chinese context it is recommended to start thinking about interdisciplinary corporations. Those come in the form of combining subjects, like social science and natural science within the own university, but likewise widening the network. In the case of the Northwestern Polytechnical University this could be a corporation with the Northwest University of Political Science and Law, both located in Xi'an, could combine the subjects of aviation, aerospace, engineering with the lessons about political and social sciences. Moreover, a better mutual learning on the international level could be aspired, promoting corporation with universities abroad. This could come along setting up international offices as representation in the foreign country. Taking the NWPU as an example, such an office was set up in Kazakhstan most recently[7].

Comparability: A central goal of the Bologna process was to make studies more comparable. Simultaneously this has to be taken into mind for the Chinese context. Therefore, such an educational reform, creating new interdisciplinary subjects and dual degrees should be based on common indicators, taking several factors into consideration. A core factors should be the better ingraining between education and economy, jointly defining the skills needed for the future job market. Moreover, experiences from different universities and students, having graduated there, should be taken into consideration. At the same time new methods should be considered, promoting a stead exchange of lecturers. Eventually, a research on students after graduation helps to figure out, what long term career prospectives are associated with the new degree.

Workload: As shown with the statistics an increase of workload negatively affects students and their well-being during their studies. Therefore, learning from the German experience, it is advisable to firstly widen the scholarship system, that students do not face the double burden of workload pressure from university and making their living. Moreover, more mental health aspects should be integrated into the daily life at the campus, establishing offices, where students can approach with their mental issues in a confidential way. Eventually, a better integration of practical times, like doing an internship could be helpful, to acquire a real-life experience on the future job.

Orientation: As a result of the Bologna reform process the amount of degrees has been mushrooming. Therefore, students often lack a clear orientation, as to spot the differences between the degrees. Consequently, a comprehensive advising of the students is needed. This might start by giving tours for prospective students, learning about the campus and daily life at the university. Moreover, lecturers could be assigned, where students will direct to when considering changing their subject. Moreover for increasing flexibility studying according to the own interests, a smoother transition between two study programs should be enabled, where missing courses can be caught up, while considering previous academic achievements for the final degree. This comes along opening opportunities for a gap year, as well as allowing potential

---

[7] Kazakhstan Branch Campus of NPU officially opens; in: China Daily 16.10.2023; available at:
http://education.chinadaily.com.cn/2023-10/16/c_930768.htm

future employers such as tech enterprises as in the case of Xi'an to set up an career offices, where students can directly apply for internships. Moreover, career centers providing training for the application process could be a fruitful addition, helping students to gain first-hand experiences on their future aspirations.

Outlook: As it could be shown, the scientific world is changing according to the new demands of societies undergoing disruptive changes. Therefore, new ways of educating and preparing students are highly needed. Giving an short outlook, new ways of thinking out of classroom are required, overcoming the boundaries of certain subjects, creating new interdisciplinary degrees. Furthermore, it should become more easy to gain knowledge from a different field, such as an engineering students attend lectures on philosophy or a philosophy student attending courses on statistics. Eventually, universities should think comprehensively, including their lectures and students, updating their methods through regular polls. Consequently, universities are leaning hubs, that have to keep putting themselves into question for energizing a steady learning process.

6. Synthesis of German and Chinese Higher Education Reform

As shown in the introduction education always contains a certain aspect of futuristic thinking. Every type of learning is about anticipating the future, preparing, and enabling change and progress. Through this process students shall discover their full potential and develop their personality (Nolda, 2015, pp.20–32). Nevertheless, with the future having become ever harder to predict, a purely goal-oriented, teleological conception of education does not seem to fit any longer. According to Poli nobody can predict what skills will be needed (Poli, 2019, p.124). The complexity of our modern life has become as high, that simply answers are hard to be found. Therefore, a form of *"Kontextsteuerung"* is required, with classrooms setting a certain environment, trying to influence the context, corresponding to the age of organized complexity, as direct linear interventions, corresponding to gone days of simplicity, now seem to be futile (Wilke, 2020, p.20). Consequently, more than teaching facts and figures, a mindset has to be taught for students to be able for acquiring new skills or in the words of Poli: *"As far as these skills are concerned, it is necessary to develop independent personalities who stand on both feet, believe in themselves and their ideas, and are able to understand their own environment and be able to take care of themselves"* (Poli, 2019, p.124). Learning stands for acquiring as training methods for dealing with the uncertain (Scheunpflug, 2001, p.64).

Drawing a synthesis from the previous chapters, it has to be reminded that technology is never neutral. The French sociologist Bruno Latour developed a model of *"actor-network theory"* revealing, that even non-human actors like machines or algorithm can become an actor, affecting our behavior and the way we think and act (Latour 1987). A striking example is given by his Italian counterpart Massimo Airoldi. In his research *"Machine Habitus: Toward a Sociology of Algorithms"*, the author combines theoretical fundaments of sociology with the increasing cognitive power of artificial intelligence (Airoldi 2021). Consequently, any kind of technology is always embedded in the cultural context of its human users. This can be emphasized by the Chinese concept of ti-yong[体用] Established during the late period of the Qin-Dynasty, Chinese intellectuals and reformers were seeing the West through the lenses of admiration and aspiration for modernization but also with suspicion losing the Chinese identity. The concept of ti-yong[体用], which represents a balance between the essence of (Chinese) learning (ti) and (western) practical use (yong) (Kalman, 2018, p.157). Both ti-yong are interdependent on each other (Pohl, 2018, p.57). This can be summarized by Chinese architect pioneer Lin Huiyin[林徽因]:" *We must learn the fundamental principles of all art only in order to apply them to designs distinctly ours."* (Elegant, 2019, p.52). Therefore, combining the potentials of engineering and technology with creativity of liberal arts provides huge potential.

To build a new liberal arts development path, we must *"not forget the original, absorb the foreign, and face the future"*, and learn from the excellent results and theories of liberal arts construction in German U15 universities. We must also keep in mind the current situation of Chinese university development and take root in Chinese soil. Specifically, to draw on Germany's U15 University Consortium 's *"single degree with double majors"* academic system and tailor-make the university's *"single degree with double majors"* academic system for liberal arts, in order to promote academic disciplines and the development of the university's new liberal arts. It encourages preliminary cross-fertilization of disciplines, breaks down discipline and major barriers, and strives for in-depth integration of university liberal arts majors as well as embedded cross-fertilization with the university's peripheral majors of science, technology, agriculture, and medical science.

China should take the initiative to learn from the successful experiences of the world's top universities in the development of interdisciplinary and cross-disciplinary integration in the development of the *"New Liberal Arts"* path of development, but bear in mind that the differences in history, culture and the national system require that colleges and universities take full account of their own characteristics in the construction and development of disciplines, and that they should not copy blindly, and that they should endeavor to build a philosophical and social science of Chinese specialties, We should endeavor to build philosophical and social sciences with Chinese characteristics and establish a *"Chinese school of thought"*.

At present, China's *"new liberal arts"* academic research is still in the embryonic stage, and most of the related research results are empirical assumptions and designs, and the application of the research results has not been systematically planned, and there is a lack of clear goals and specific mechanisms for reforming educational practices. Most of the documents and articles promoting the construction of the new liberal arts are programmatic policies, and there is no systematic integration of the reform of the training programs and academic systems of various disciplines and sections of the university, and there is no unified operational plan for reforming the practice. Therefore, for the construction of new liberal arts, it is especially important to learn from the successful experiences of the world-class universities in interdisciplinary and cross-disciplinary integration, and to create a number of landmark achievements reflecting the development experience of liberal arts in Chinese universities, so as to promote the research of new liberal arts in a deep and practical way through the localized *"Chinese school"*, and to cultivate complex and innovative talents for our country. Cultivating Composite Innovative Talents for China.

7. Conclusion: A learning dialogue crossing socio-scientific disciplines

Concluding the message of this research can be read twofold. Firstly, the arguments brought forward serve as a plead for more interdisciplinary approaches in science and scientific education. Secondly, this research gives as a practical overview of the potentials of comparative educational research uncovering the opportunities of introducing dual degrees in Chinese higher education by learning and assessing the experiences from the German higher education system. It could be shown, that thinking science and education through the limits of epistemic boundaries of particular disciplines does not suit the demands of an ever-complex environment. Therefore, this paper has argued for a cross- and transdisciplinary approach toward higher education. As this paper pleads, universities have always served as hubs for dialogue and mutual learning. Simultaneously, like no other policy areas, education stands as the embodiment of a society and its lessons learned from their unique history, as well as their conception about the world, the role, and responsibilities within. *"National peculiarities and 'special paths' tend to be more pronounced in the field of education than elsewhere, as do national sensibilities and pride in own traditions"* (Heriard/Prutsch/Thoenes 2021, p.19).

Bringing both strings of though together, a comparative analysis of the dual degree in German higher education serves as a fruitful source of inspiration for reforms in Chinese higher education. The vast majority of liberal arts students at German U15 universities choose the *"single degree with double major"* academic system, which not only ensures the integration of multiple disciplines, cultivates, and exercises interdisciplinary thinking, but also avoids the double academic pressure and time conflicts of a double degree. The *"double major"* single degree system provides an effective and feasible path for the integration of disciplines in German colleges and universities, which is effective and promising, and is conducive to promoting the cultivation of composite and innovative talents, and accumulating momentum for Germany's *"Industry 4.0"* technological innovation strategy The urgent need for the theoretical construction of *"new liberal arts"* in the new globalization pattern is to strengthen the exchanges and mutual learning among different countries, nationalities, and cultures in the world, and to draw on all the valuable and meaningful theoretical achievements and best practices of the world's nationalities, so as to consolidate the humanistic foundation for the building of a community of common destiny for mankind. As it could be shown, those dual degrees have gained attention within the Chinese scientific community with first initiatives searching to interpret and integrate dual degree systems within the Chinese university context.

Drawing conclusion by comparative research in higher education provides a high potential for reforming the Chinese Higher Education system, uncovering the full potential of its creative young generation. Giving an outlook, more mutual learning dialogue between Germany and China can foster a better understanding of each other's´ cultural lenses as well as opening a new perspective on their respective visions for the future, contributing to a bilateral social progress.

References

Adler, E. (2019) World Ordering a Social Theory of Cognitive Evolution, Cambridge, Cambridge University Press.

Airoldi, M. (2021): Machine Habitus: Toward a Sociology of Algorithms"; Polity, Cambridge

Beinke, K. (2016): Vom Erklären zum Verstehen? Quereinsteiger/ innen im Masterstudium zum Berufsschullehramt und der Perspektivwechsel zwischen verschiedenen Wissenschaftskulturen. In: Bals, D./Eckert, A./Kaiser, M./Kaiser, F. (Hg.): Diversität im Zugang zum Lehramt an berufsbildenden Schulen. Paderborn, S. 95–110.

Böhme, G. (1994) *Weltweisheit, Lebensform, Wissenschaft,- Eine Einführung in die Philosophie*, Frankfurt am Main, Suhrkamp.

Bundesministerium für Bildung und Forschung (BMBF) (2023): Die Studierendenbefragung in Deutschland: 22. Sozialerhebung Die wirtschaftliche und soziale Lage der Studierenden in Deutschland 2021; available at: https://www.bmbf.de/SharedDocs/Publikationen/de/bmbf/4/31790_22_Sozialerhebung_2021.pdf?__blob=publicationFile&v=9

Deutscher Bundestag (2012): Vierter Bericht über die Umsetzung des Bologna-Prozesses in Deutschland; available at: https://dserver.bundestag.de/btd/17/086/1708640.pdf

Deutscher Bundestag (2016): Aktueller Begriff Industrie 4.0; available at: https://www.bundestag.de/resource/blob/474528/cae2bfac57f1bf797c8a6e13394b5e70/industrie-4-0-data.pdf

Dilthey, W. (1924): Gesammelte Schriften, Bd.5, Die geistige Welt: Einleitung in die Philosophie des Lebens. Leipzig.

Elegant, N. (2019) 'The Story of Liang and Lin', *The Pennsylvania Gazette*, vol. 118, no. 2, pp. 48–53.

European Ministers of Education (1999): Joint declaration of the European Ministers of Education - The Bologna Declaration of 19 June 1999; available at: https://www.ehea.info/page-ministerial-conference-bologna-1999

Giri, A. K. (2002) 'The calling of a creative transdisciplinarity', *Futures*, vol. 34, pp. 103–115.

Haas, P. (1992) 'Introduction: Epistemic Communities and International Policy Coordination', *Introduction: Epistemic Communities and International Policy Coordination*, vol. 46, no. 1, pp. 1–35.

Heriard, P./Prutsch, M./Thoenes, S. (2021): Making the European Education Area a reality: state of affairs, challenges, and prospects.; European Commission Publishing Brussel.

Heublein, U./Hutzsch, C./Schmelzer. R. (2022): Entwicklung der Studienabbruchquoten in Deutschland; in: DZHW-Brief 05 22; Hannover; retrieved at: https://www.dzhw.eu/pdf/pub_brief/dzhw_brief_05_2022.pdf

Hochschulrektorenkonferenz (HRK) (2021): Statistische Daten zu Studienangeboten an Hochschulen in Deutschland Studiengänge, Studierende, Absolventinnen und Absolventen Wintersemester 2021/2022; available at: https://www.hrk.de/fileadmin/redaktion/hrk/02-Dokumente/02-03-Studium/02-03-01-Studium-Studienreform/HRK_Statistik_BA_MA_UEbrige_WiSe_2021_22.pdf

Kalman, H. (2018) 'Chinese Spirit in Modern Strength': Liang Sicheng, Lin Huiyin, and Early Modernist Architecture in China', *Journal of the Royal Asiatic Society Hong Kong Branch*, vol. 58, pp. 154–188.

Lawrence, R. (2010) 'Deciphering Interdisciplinary and Transdisciplinary Contributions', *Transdisciplinary Journal of Engineering & Science*, vol. 1, no. 1, pp. 125–130.

Latour, B. (1987): Science in Action: How to Follow Scientists and Engineers Through Society; Harvard University Press.

Niedermeyer, B. (2020): Bildung und Arbeit im Kontext von Globalisierung. Überlegungen zur Aktualisierung eines uralten Verhältnisses; in: Wischmann, Anke et. al. (eds): Jahrbuch für Pädagogik 2020; p.224-234).

Nolda, S. (2015) *Einführung in die Erwachsenenbildung*, Darmstadt, Wissenschaftliche Buchgesellschaft.

Pohl, K.-H. (2018) 'Western Learning for Substance, Chinese Learning for Application' – Li Zehou's Thought on Tradition and Modernity', in Ames Roger and Hershock, P. (eds) *Li Zehou and Confucian Philosophy*, Honolulu, University of Hawai´i Press.

Poli, R. (2019) *Lavorare con il futuro-Idee e strumenti per governare l´incertezza*, Milan, Egea.

Scheunpflug, A. (2001) *Evolutionäre Didaktik- Untericht aus systemtheorethischer und evolutionärer Perspektive*, Weinheim& Basel, Beltz Verlag.

Thurau, Martin (2008): Der Bachelor-Bankrott; in: Sueddeutsche Zeitung, available at: https://web.archive.org/web/20081006013202/http://www.sueddeutsche.de/jobkarriere/643/312557/text/?page=4

Treml, A. (2010) *Philosophische Pädagogik- Die theorethischen Grundlagen der Erziehungswissenschaft*, Stuttgart, Kohlhammer.

Turing, A. (1938) *Systems of Logic Based on Ordinals* [Online]. Available at https://web.archive.org/web/20121023103503/https://webspace.princeton.edu/users/jedwards/Turing%20Centennial%202012/Mudd%20Archive%20files/12285_AC100_Turing_1938.pdf

Turing, A. (1950) 'Computing Machinery and Intelligence', *Mind*, vol. 59, no. 236, pp. 433–460.

Weaver, W. (1948) 'Science and Complexity', *American Scientist*, no. 36, pp. 536–544.

Wilke, H. (2020) 'Zum Problem der Steuerung komplexer Politikfelder Über Kosten und Nutzen hoher Komplexität am Beispiel von Gesundheit und Bildung', in Reinbacher, P., Oberneder, J. and Wesenauer, A. (eds) *Warum Komplexität nützlich ist: Auf der Suche nach Antworten mit Helmut Willke*, Wiesbaden, Springer Verlag, pp. 9–28.

Wissenschaftsrat (2012): Empfehlungen zur Akkreditierung als Instrument der Qualitätssicherung; available at: https://www.wissenschaftsrat.de/download/archiv/2259-12.html

Zhang, L. (1993) 'Cai Yuanpei', *Prospects*, vol. 23, pp. 147–155.

Zhang, L. (2020) 'Between China and West: Comparison of Liang Qichao and Cai Yuanpei's Educational Thoughts——Take "Xinmin Theory" and "Five Education Simultaneous Development" as examples', *2020 International Conference on Social Science and Education Research*, pp. 358–363.

Traversing Academic Frontiers: A Comparative Exploration of Legal Education in Germany and China

LOU Li (娄立),[1]

Abstract

Legal education serves as the bedrock upon which societies build their systems of justice and governance. This paper embarks on a concise comparative journey, briefly scrutinizing the legal education systems of Germany and China. Through a personalized lens, it explores the intricacies of these two distinct systems, shedding light mainly on pedagogical methods, institutional structures, and socio-cultural contexts. The author's expedition through doctoral studies and the ensuing research, a cross-continental voyage, offers a unique vantage point for this comparative analysis. By delving into the legal education landscapes of Germany and China, this paper not only adds to our understanding of these systems but also contributes to the broader discourse on international legal education.

Keywords: Legal education, Germany, China, comparative analysis, doctoral odyssey

Introduction

As a cornerstone of any society's pursuit of justice and the rule of law, legal education is the crucible where future lawyers and jurists are forged, and the nuances of these systems have profound implications for the practice of law and the development of legal scholarship. As the world becomes increasingly interconnected, understanding the diversity in higher educational systems becomes imperative, especially when it comes to diverse approaches and methodologies adopted by different nations in the pursuit of legal knowledge. The author's doctoral and further academic odyssey, which transcended borders and continents, uniquely positioned her to explore the profound distinctions that exist between legal educations in China and Germany.

The paper aims to navigate the contours of legal education in these two nations, dissecting their pedagogical approaches, examining their institutional frameworks, and considering the impact of their unique socio-cultural contexts. Furthermore, it provides a succinct exploration of the variations in legal education within other Germanic language-speaking jurisdictions, as well as two historically intimately related nations to Germany, illuminating their unique subtleties, informed by the author's extensive personal experiences gained through multiple exchange programs and collaborative research endeavors, both preceding and subsequent to her doctoral odyssey.

1. Legal Education in Germany: Tradition and Rigor

In the labyrinthine corridors of legal academia, where the quest for knowledge meets the demand for intellectual rigor, Germany emerges as an enduring bastion of legal education. This scholarly

[1] Faculty of Law, University of Bergen, Norway. Research interest: Nordic law, European law, and comparative law. This paper is supported by "the Fundamental Research Funds for the Central Universities" – 2023 西北工业大学发展战略研究基金项目 (No.2023FZY20, 德国 U15 大学 "双专业单学位" 学制对我校新文科建设的破局之思)

pursuit is steeped in a rich tapestry of tradition and rigor, woven together through centuries of jurisprudential evolution.[2] As the author embarks on a journey to explore the intricacies of legal education in Germany, she finds herself at the crossroads of historical legacy and contemporary pedagogical excellence. It is an exploration of a system that has evolved, adapted, and persisted, providing valuable lessons and insights for legal education systems worldwide.

1.1. Historical Context

Germany's enduring legacy in the fields of philosophy, science, and the humanities is a testament to its commitment to intellectual pursuits.[3] Yet, one facet of this intellectual heritage that is often overlooked, yet equally profound, is the realm of legal education. The German legal education system, characterized by its profound tradition and intellectual rigor, has roots that extend deep into the annals of history.[4] These foundations can be meticulously traced back to the medieval universities of Bologna, Padua, and Paris, whose influence provided the catalytic force for the emergence of legal faculties across German-speaking territories during the transformative 15th and 16th centuries.[5]

The Italian Universities, such as University of Bologna, renowned as the cradle of the modern university system, played a pivotal role in shaping the trajectory of legal education in Germany.[6] Established in the 12th century, this venerable institution became a magnet for scholars across Europe, particularly those interested in the study of Roman law. It was in Bologna that the revival of Roman law commenced, ushering in an era of legal scholarship that would reverberate across the continent.[7] The rediscovery and reinvigoration of Roman law, with its systematic and principled approach to jurisprudence, laid the intellectual groundwork for the German legal tradition.[8] This emphasis on a comprehensive legal system, governed by abstract principles and systematic interpretation, became the cornerstone upon which German legal education was built.[9]

Other eminent Italian universities, contributed significantly to the multifaceted development of legal education in Germany. Padua's unique blend of canon law and Roman law studies fostered an approach that would later characterize German legal pedagogy[10], as a case in point. The fusion of theological and legal thought created a fertile ground for the integration of jurisprudence with broader philosophical and theological debates. This synergy between different fields of knowledge would go on to shape the holistic and intellectually rigorous approach that German legal education embodies.[11]

---

[2] *See generally* Foster, Nigel G., and Satish Sule. *German legal system and laws.* Oxford University Press, 2010. *See also* Freund, Ernst. "Historical Jurisprudence in Germany." *Political Science Quarterly* 5, no. 3 (1890): 468-486.

[3] *See* Habermas, Jürgen, and John R. Blazek. "The idea of the university: Learning processes." *New German Critique* 41 (1987): 3-22.

[4] *See* Rodes Jr, Robert E. "On the historical school of jurisprudence." *Am. J. Juris.* 49 (2004): 165-184.

[5] *See* Fytsyk, Igor and Larysa Fytsyk. "Features of the implementation of the principles of academic charity on the example of the universities of medieval Europe." *Problems of Modern Teacher Training* (2023):6-14. *See also* Kelly, John Maurice. *A short history of western legal theory.* Oxford University Press, 1992.

[6] *See* Burdick, William Livesey. *The principles of Roman law and their relation to modern law.* The Lawbook Exchange, Ltd., 2004. *See also* Clark, David S. "The Medieval Origins of Modern Legal Education: Between Church and State'(1987)." *American Journal of Comparative Law* 35: 653-719. Courtenay, William James, Jürgen Miethke, and David B. Priest, eds. *Universities and schooling in medieval society.* Vol. 10. Brill, 2000.

[7] *See* Grendler, Paul F. "The University of Bologna, the city, and the papacy." *Renaissance Studies* (1999): 475-485.

[8] *See* Freund, Ernst *supra* note 1. Burdick, William Livesey *supra* notes 5. *See also* Fried, Johannes. *Die Entstehung des Juristenstandes im 12. Jahrhundert: zur sozialen Stellung und politischen Bedeutung gelehrter Juristen in Bologna und Modena.* Vol. 21. Böhlau, 1974. Toller, Fernando M. "Foundations for a revival of the case method in civil law education." *J. Civ. L. Stud.* 3 (2010): 21-66.

[9] *See* Wernsmann, Rainer. "The Structure, Purposes and Methods of German Legal Education." In *Legal Education in the Global Context*, 233-239. Routledge, 2017.

[10] *See* Freund, Ernst *supra* note 1. *See also* Kennedy, Duncan. *Legal education and the reproduction of hierarchy: a polemic against the system.* Vol. 56. NYU Press, 2007.

[11] *See* Aznar, Bernardo Bayona. "El periplo de la teoría política de Marsilio de Padua por la historiografía moderna." *Revista de estudios políticos* 137 (2007): 113-153.

The French school, with its profound influence on medieval thought, also played an indispensable role in the development of German legal education. Paris was a crucible of scholasticism, where critical inquiry and rigorous debate were prized.[12] This intellectual milieu, marked by the dialectical method of inquiry, left an indelible impression on the German legal tradition.[13] The dialectical approach, characterized by rigorous questioning and the exploration of diverse perspectives, would later become emblematic of German legal scholarship.

The 15th and 16th centuries marked a transformative period for legal education in German-speaking territories. Influenced by the intellectual ferment of these medieval universities, German institutions began to formalize their legal faculties.[14] Renowned institutions such as the University of Heidelberg, Leipzig University, and the University of Göttingen emerged as citadels of legal scholarship, drawing students and scholars from across Europe.[15] It was within these hallowed halls that the German legal tradition took root and thrived.

German legal education, through these centuries, evolved into a thriving center of jurisprudential scholarship.[16] Pioneering scholars like Friedrich Carl von Savigny and Rudolf von Jhering refined this tradition. Savigny's monumental work, "Vom Beruf unserer Zeit für Gesetzgebung und Rechtswissenschaft"(Of the Vocation of Our Age for Legislation and Jurisprudence), underscored the paramount importance of historical context in legal interpretation. This emphasis on historical consciousness and the organic development of law became foundational to the German legal tradition. Similarly, Rudolf von Jhering, another luminary of German jurisprudence, made significant contributions that enriched the German legal tradition. Jhering's jurisprudential insights, elucidated in "Der Zweck im Recht" (The Purpose in Law), advocated the idea of juristic struggle and emphasized the dynamic, evolving nature of law. His perspectives resonated deeply with the dialectical pedagogical approach of German legal education, fostering an environment where the evolution of legal principles through intellectual discourse was celebrated.

The historical context of legal education in Germany is a captivating narrative that intertwines the intellectual ferment of medieval European universities, the resurgence of Roman law, the influence of canon law, and the dialectical rigor of scholasticism.[17] These multifaceted influences converged to give birth to a distinctive legal tradition that emphasizes rigorous academic training,

---

[12] *See* Castelao-Lawless, Teresa. "Expositions and Disputations on Aristotle's Natural Philosophy at Late Medieval Universities of Paris, Oxford, and Toulouse: A Semi-Revisionist Proposal." *Faculty Scholarly Dissemination Grants* (2015): 646. *See also* Courtenay, William J., Richard Marsden, and E. Ann Matter. "The Bible in Medieval Universities." Chapter. In *The New Cambridge History of the Bible*, 2:555–78. Cambridge University Press, 2012.

[13] *See generally* Sohm, Rudolf. *The institutes of Roman law.* Clarendon Press, 1892. Moule, Gregory S. *Corporate jurisdiction, academic heresy, and fraternal correction at the University of Paris, 1200-1400.* Vol. 51. Brill, 2016. Rashdall, Hastings. *The Universities of Europe in the Middle Ages: Salerno. Bologna. Paris.* Vol. 1. Clarendon Press, 1895. *See also* Wei, Ian P. "Medieval universities and aspirations to universal significance." In *The Global University: Past, Present, and Future Perspectives*, 133-151. New York: Palgrave Macmillan US, 2012.

[14] *See* Scott, John C. "The mission of the university: Medieval to postmodern transformations." *The journal of higher education* 77, no. 1 (2006): 1-39. *See also* Ramos do Ó, Jorge, and Ana Luisa Paz. "The Invention of the Writing Subject in School: The" Studia Humanitatis" in the 15th-Century Renaissance." *Paedagogica Historica: International Journal of the History of Education* 59, no. 3 (2023): 361-379. Mamadaliev, Anvar M., Natalia V. Svechnikova, Natal'ya V. Miku, and Aude MĂŠdico. "The German System of Public Education in the Period between the 15th and Early 20th Centuries. Part 1." *European Journal of Contemporary Education* 8, no. 2 (2019): 445-453.

[15] *See generally* Paulsen, Friedrich. *The German universities and university study.* C. Scribner's sons, 1906. *See also* Holzberg, Niklas. *Antikerezeption in Deutschland von der Renaissance bis in unsere Zeit.* Rombach Wissenschaft, 2022. Rupprich, Hans. *Humanismus Und Renaissance in Den Deutschen Städten Und an Den Universitäten.* Wissenschaftliche Buchges. 1935.

[16] *See* Hammerstein, Notker. *Handbuch der deutschen Bildungsgeschichte/1 15.-17. Jahrhundert: von der Renaissance und der Reformation bis zum Ende der Glaubenskämpfe/hrsg.* von Notker Hammerstein. Beck, 1996. Hammerstein, Notker, and Christa Berg, eds. *Handbuch der deutschen Bildungsgeschichte: 18. Jahrhundert: vom späten 17. Jahrhundert bis zur Neuordnung Deutschlands um 1800/hrsg.* von Notker Hammerstein und Ulrich Herrmann. 2. Vol. 2. CH Beck, 1987. Jeismann, Karl-Ernst, and Peter Lundgreen. *Handbuch der deutschen Bildungsgeschichte: 1800-1870*, 1987. Berg, Christa, ed. *Handbuch der deutschen Bildungsgeschichte: 1870-1918.* Vol. 4. CH Beck, 1991.

[17] *See* Muther, Theodor. *Zur Geschichte der Rechtswissenschaft und der Universitäten in Deutschland.* H. Dufft, 1876.

historical consciousness, and the primacy of theoretical jurisprudence.[18] This historical foundation, meticulously established through centuries of intellectual exploration, continues to serve as the bedrock upon which German legal education rests, and it is this tradition that has made an enduring impact on the global legal landscape.

1.2. Pedagogical Approaches

German legal education is renowned for its pedagogical approaches that place a significant emphasis on cultivating a profound understanding of legal theory and doctrine.[19] Its pedagogical approach has deep historical roots and continues to define the essence of legal education in Germany.[20] The Socratic method in German legal education is a time-tested approach that encourages students to think critically, question legal principles, and engage in lively debates with their professors and peers. This method, which has its origins in the ancient philosophy of Socrates, has evolved to become an integral part of the pedagogical framework in German law schools.[21] Professors, often holding distinguished positions in the legal field, skillfully guide students through complex legal concepts by posing challenging questions and encouraging thoughtful discussions.[22] This approach not only facilitates a deep understanding of legal theory but also hones critical thinking skills, a crucial asset for future legal practitioners.

In addition to the Socratic method, German legal education recognizes the value of practical experience. Moot courts and legal clinics have gained increasing prominence in the curriculum.[23] These components provide students with opportunities to apply their theoretical knowledge to real-world legal scenarios, honing their skills in a practical setting. Moot courts simulate courtroom proceedings, allowing students to argue cases before judges and gain a comprehensive understanding of legal advocacy.[24] Legal clinics, on the other hand, enable students to work on real cases, providing legal assistance to clients under the guidance of experienced faculty. This practical exposure equips students with the skills and knowledge necessary to tackle the complex and dynamic challenges of the legal profession.[25]

The pedagogical approaches of German legal education, combining the Socratic method with practical experience, reflect a holistic commitment to preparing students for the demands of a multifaceted legal landscape. The emphasis on deep theoretical understanding, critical thinking, and practical skills aligns with the rich intellectual tradition of Germany[26]. This pedagogical framework ensures that graduates are not only well-versed in legal theory but also well-equipped

---

[18] *See* Köbler, Gerhard. *"Zur Geschichte der juristischen Ausbildung in Deutschland."* Juristenzeitung 26, no. 23/24 (1971): 768-773. *See also* Bleek, Wilhelm. *Geschichte der Politikwissenschaft in Deutschland.* CH Beck, 2001.

[19] *See* Wolff, Lutz-Christian. "Structured problem solving: German methodology from a comparative perspective." *Legal Education Review* 14, no. 1 (2004): 19-51. *See also* Hendry, Jennifer, Naomi Creutzfeldt, and Christian Boulanger. "Socio-Legal Studies in Germany and the UK: Theory and Methods." *German Law Journal* 21, no. 7 (2020): 1309-1317.

[20] *See* Klein, Eckart. "Legal education in Germany." *Or. L. Rev.* 72 (1993): 953-956.

[21] *See* Saran, Rene, and Barbara Neisser. *Enquiring minds: Socratic dialogue in education.* Stylus Publishing, LLC. 2004. *See also* Gordley, James. "Comparative law and legal education." *Tul. L. Rev.* 75 (2000): 1003-1014.

[22] *See* Rieder, Lisa, and Hanjo Hamann. "Student Participation in Legal Education in Germany and Europe." *German Law Journal* 10, no. 6-7 (2009): 1095-1112.

[23] *See* Hannemann, Jan-Gero Alexander. "Die Entwicklung der praktischen Jurisprudenz in Deutschland." In *Rechtsdidaktik zwischen Theorie und Praxis.* Nomos Verlagsgesellschaft mbH & Co. KG, 2019: 254-266. *See also* Wilson, Richard J. "Western Europe: Last Holdout in the worldwide acceptance of clinical legal Education." *German Law Journal* 10, no. 6-7 (2009): 823-846. Bücker, Andreas, and William A. Woodruff. "The Bologna process and German legal Education: Developing professional competence through clinical experiences." *German Law Journal* 9, no. 5 (2008): 575-618.

[24] *See* von Tobias Pinkel, Lisa Lüdders, and Ingeborg Zerbes. "Moot Court als didaktische Herausforderung in der juristischen Ausbildung." *Gemeinsam Lehren und Lernen:* 15-21.

[25] *See* Kilian, Matthias, and Lisa Wenzel. *Law clinics in Deutschland.* Nomos Verlagsgesellschaft mbH & Co. KG, 2022.

[26] *See* Casper, Gerhard. "Two Models of Legal Education." *Tenn. L. Rev.* 41 (1973): 13-25. *See also* Hannemann, Jan-Gero Alexander, and Jan Hendrik Lampe. "'Clinical Legal Education'—Observing, Comparing and Analyzing the Differences in Germany and China for each other's Respective Advantages." *Asian Journal of Legal Education* 2, no. 2 (2015): 157-169.

to navigate the complexities of legal practice, making German legal education a model of academic rigor and practical relevance.

1.3. Institutional Framework

Germany's legal education system is often heralded for its historical centralized framework, which served as the bedrock of uniformity and quality assurance across the nation's diverse universities. The influence of the state in shaping and overseeing this educational system is substantial, with accreditation being contingent upon meeting exacting standards.[27] A discernible trend toward decentralization has gained traction throughout history, exemplifying a shift towards greater institutional autonomy.[28]

The heart of legal education in Germany beats with the formidable Staatsexamen, a comprehensive state examination[29] that holds a revered place in the legal landscape. This examination serves as the crucible through which legal aspirants must pass, and its reputation precedes it. It rigorously assesses not only substantive legal knowledge but also the practical application of legal principles.[30] The Staatsexamen is emblematic of Germany's unwavering commitment to excellence in legal education, serving as both a rite of passage for budding lawyers and a testament to the exacting standards upheld by the nation's legal academe.
The formerly centralized nature of the German legal education system is evident in various facets. The curriculum, including the subjects covered and their sequencing, is typically prescribed by the state[31], ensuring that students from different universities receive a consistent and comprehensive legal education. Moreover, the faculty in law schools may consist of civil servants, further cementing the state's influence over the system[32].

1.4. Socio-Cultural Contexts

The socio-cultural contexts of German legal education are integral to understanding the system's evolution and functioning. Rooted in a rich history of legal traditions and academic excellence, German legal education is deeply influenced by the country's cultural, social, and historical factors. Germany boasts a rich heritage of the rule of law, underscoring the paramount significance of law and order. This enduring tradition finds its roots in the evolution of jurisprudence during the Middle Ages and the Renaissance[33], where the profound influences of Roman and natural law reshaped legal thought.[34] This tradition of the rule of law continues to

---

[27] *See* Korioth, Stefan. "Legal education in Germany today." *Wis. Int'l LJ* 24 (2006): 85-107. *See also* Jescheck, Hans-Heinrich. *Die juristische Ausbildung in Preussen und im Reich-Vergangenheit und Gegenwart.* Junker und Dünnhaupt Verlag, 1939.

[28] *See* Döring, Thomas, and Jan Schnellenbach. "A tale of two federalisms: Germany, the United States and the ubiquity of centralization." *Constitutional Political Economy* 22 (2011): 83-102. Bergmans, Bernhard. "Auf Dem Wege Zu Einem Neuen Verständnis Der Juristenberufe Und Juristenausbildungen." *Zeitschrift Für Rechtspolitik* 46, no. 4 (2013): 113–117.

[29] *See* Sattelmacher, Paul. *Die juristischen Staatsprüfungen: Prüfungseinrichtungen, Verfahren und Anforderungen, zugleich eine Anleitung zur Anfertigung von Prüfungsarbeiten.* Springer-Verlag, 2013. *See also* Geck, Wilhelm Karl. "The reform of legal education in the Federal Republic of Germany." *The American journal of comparative law* (1977): 86-119. Fang, Ye. "*Judicial Examination System of Germany and Its Significance for Reference.*" Justice of China 2 (2011): 107-109.

[30] *See* Weber, Franziska. "'Hanse Law School': A Promising Example of Transnational Legal Education? An Alumna's Perspective." *German Law Journal* 10, no. 6-7 (2009): 969-980. *See also* Morgenstern, U. Vorbereitungsdienst und zweite juristische Staatsprüfung. In: *Effizient studieren: Rechtswissenschaften.* Edition MLP. Gabler Verlag, Wiesbaden, 1999.

[31] *See* Brunnee, Jutta. "The Reform of Legal Education in Germany: The Never-Ending Story and European Integration." *J. Legal Educ.* 42 (1992): 399-426. *See also* Shartel, Burke. "Report on German Legal Education." *J. Legal Educ.* 14 (1961): 425-484.

[32] *See* Max Rheinstein, "Law Faculties and Law Schools - A Comparison of Legal Education in the United States and Germany." *Wisconsin Law Review.* 1 (1938): 5-42. *See also* Vernon, Manfred C. "Legal Education in Germany." *Ala. L. Rev.* 12 (1959): 140.

[33] *See* Sohm, Rudolf *supra* note 12.

[34] *See* Burdick, William Livesey *supra* note 5 at 19-23. *See also* Wieacker, Franz. "The importance of Roman law for western civilization and western legal thought." *BC Int'l & Comp. L. Rev.* 4 (1981): 257-282. Whitman, James Q. *The*

hold sway over contemporary German legal education[35], extolling the intrinsic role of law as a cornerstone of societal norms and order. The nexus between history and culture in Germany profoundly influences legal education. German jurists have ardently advocated for law to reflect the nation's historical and cultural tapestry,[36] a principle vividly exemplified by the historical school of jurisprudence[37]. This historical and cultural import resonates through the veins of German legal education and the legal system, permeating the development of constitutional law and regional law.[38]

The philosophical underpinnings of law and legal theory have been meticulously explored in Germany, boasting a vibrant tradition.[39] Esteemed philosophers such as Kant[40], Hegel, [41] and Heidegger[42] have delved deep into the philosophical bedrock of law, etching their influence upon the theoretical landscape of German jurisprudence.[43] Legal education consistently underscores the study of the ethical, philosophical, and political theories that underlie the edifice of law.[44] Germany's legal education is undeniably shaped by the tenets of democracy and human rights. In the wake of World War II, the nation fervently embraced the principles of democracy, liberty, and human rights, meticulously reconstructing its constitution and legal framework.[45] This ethos remains a focal point of German law and legal education, pervading the study of constitutional law and international human rights law.[46]

German legal education is also undeniably shaped by international influences. German law schools enthusiastically partake in the realm of international jurisprudence, making substantive contributions to the theoretical and practical advancement of international law and the European legal system[47].

However, it's important to consider the evolving socio-cultural dynamics. As Germany grapples with societal changes, including increasing diversity and globalization, questions arise about the

---

legacy of Roman law in the German romantic era: historical vision and legal change. Vol. 1075. Princeton University Press, 2014. Stein, Peter. *Roman law in European history.* Cambridge University Press, 1999.

[35] *See* Lobingier, Charles Sumner. "Reception of the Roman Law in Germany." *Mich. L. Rev.* 14 (1915): 562-569.

[36] *See* Zimmermann, Reinhard. *The new German Law of obligations: historical and comparative perspectives.* Oxford University Press, 2005.

[37] *See* Rodes Jr, Robert E *supra* note 3. *See also* Kantorowicz, Hermann. "Savigny and the historical school of law." *LQ Rev.* 53 (1937): 326.

[38] *See* Stolleis, Michael. *Public law in Germany, 1800-1914.* Berghahn Books, 2001. Stolleis, Michael. *A history of public law in Germany, 1914-1945.* Oxford University Press, USA, 2004.

[39] *See* Bodenheimer, Edgar. "Significant developments in German legal philosophy since 1945." *Am. J. Comp. L.* 3 (1954): 379. *See also* Herget, James E. *Contemporary German legal philosophy.* University of Pennsylvania Press, 1996.

[40] Kersting, Wolfgang. *Kant über Recht.* Paderborn Mentis 2004.

[41] *See* Radbruch, Gustav. *Rechtsphilosophie.* CF Müller GmbH, 1987, 21-33. Fulda, Hans Friedrich. *Zum Theorietypus der Hegelschen Rechtsphilosophie.* Vol. 11. Klett-Cotta, 1982. *See also* Zane, John M. "German Legal Philosophy." *Michigan Law Review* 16, no. 5 (1918): 287-375.

[42] *See* Wolin, Richard, ed. *The Heidegger controversy: A critical reader.* MIT press, 1993.

[43] *See* Thornhill, Chris. *German Political Philosophy: The Metaphysics of Law.* Routledge, 2007. Ward, Ian. *Law, Philosophy, and national socialism: Heidegger, Schmitt and Radbruch in context.* Herbert Lang Et Company, 1992.

[44] *Ibid. See also* Coing, Helmut. *Grundzüge der rechtsphilosophie.* De Gruyter, 1950.

[45] *See* Currie, David P. *The constitution of the Federal Republic of Germany.* University of Chicago Press, 1994. See also Brugger, Winfried. "Communitarianism as the social and legal theory behind the German Constitution." *International Journal of Constitutional Law* 2, no. 3 (2004): 431-460. Hartwig, Matthias. "Much ado about human rights: the Federal Constitutional Court confronts the European Court of Human Rights." *German Law Journal* 6, no. 5 (2005): 869-894. Grimm, Dieter. "Proportionality in Canadian and German constitutional jurisprudence." *U. Toronto LJ* 57 (2007): 383.

[46] *See* Eberle, Edward J. "Observations on the development of human dignity and personality in German constitutional law: An overview." *Liverpool Law Review* 33 (2012): 201-233. *See also* Michaelsen, Christopher. "'From Strasbourg, with Love': Preventive Detention before the German Federal Constitutional Court and the European Court of Human Rights." *Human Rights Law Review* 12, no. 1 (2012): 148-167.

[47] Quint, Peter E. "What Is a Twentieth-Century Constitution." *Md. L. Rev.* 67 (2007): 238-257. *See also* Hoffmeister, Frank. "Germany: status of European convention on human rights in domestic law." *International Journal of Constitutional Law* 4, no. 4 (2006): 722-731. Doehring, Karl. "Non-Discrimination and Equal Treatment under the European Human Rights Convention and the West German Constitution with Particular Reference to Discrimination against Aliens." *Am. J. Comp. L.* 18 (1970): 305-325.

adaptability and inclusiveness of its legal education system.[48] These socio-cultural dynamics raise important issues about the system's ability to meet the changing needs of a multicultural and interconnected world.[49]

At its heart, German legal education is a tribute to theoretical jurisprudence. It is an intellectual endeavor that transcends the mere memorization of statutes and case law. Instead, it is a relentless pursuit of the theoretical underpinnings that form the scaffolding of the legal system.[50] German legal scholars have long championed the belief that a profound grasp of jurisprudential theory is the bedrock upon which legal acumen is built.[51] This philosophical engagement with the law has not only shaped the way lawyers are educated in Germany but has also left an indelible imprint on legal theory worldwide.[52]

2. Legal Education in China: Modernization and Transformation
2.1. Historical Context

Unsurprisingly, akin to Germany, China's legal education system has undergone dramatic transformations in the last few centuries.[53] The historical trajectory of legal education in China stands as a testament to the nation's unwavering dedication to academic excellence and the cultivation of a resilient legal framework in recent decades, exemplified most notably in its doctoral-level legal training.[54] China's journey towards establishing a comprehensive legal education system including doctoral education can be divided into several key phases, each marked by distinctive developments.

The early 20th century witnessed the nascence of legal education in China, albeit lacking a formalized doctoral program. Legal studies were primarily offered at undergraduate levels. The era of the Republic of China brought about the inception of graduate-level legal education, with some prominent law schools and universities introducing master's programs. Nevertheless, political turbulence and conflict in the mid-20th century hindered the progress of this nascent system.[55]

Following the establishment of the People's Republic of China in 1949, the nation's legal education underwent significant reforms.[56] In the early 1950s, China reinstated doctoral-level

---

[48] *See, e.g.*, Geck, Wilhelm Karl. "The reform of legal education in the Federal Republic of Germany." *The American journal of comparative law* (1977): 86-119. Michaels, Ralf. "Welche Globalisierung Für Das Recht? Welches Recht Für Die Globalisierung?" *Rabels Zeitschrift Für Ausländisches Und Internationales Privatrecht / The Rabel Journal of Comparative and International Private Law* 69, no. 3 (2005): 525–44.

[49] *See* Schwittek, Eva. "Rechtswissenschaftlicher Kongreß: Globalisierung und Recht–Beiträge Japans und Deutschlands zu einer internationalen Rechtsordnung im 21. Jahrhundert." *Zeitschrift für Japanisches Recht* 10, no. 20 (2005): 259-272. *See also* Schultz, Ulrike. "Legal Education in Germany–an ever (never?) ending story of resistance to change." *Higher Legal Culture and Postgraduate Legal Education in Europa*, Italian Scientific Publishing, 2008.

[50] *See* "IV German Transcendental Idealism" In *Jurisprudence: The Philosophy and Method of the Law*, 60-69. Cambridge, MA and London, England: Harvard University Press, 1962.

[51] *See* Radbruch, Gustav. "II. Legal Philosophy" In *The Legal Philosophies of Lask, Radbruch, and Dabin* edited by Kurt Wilk, 43-224. Cambridge, MA and London, England: Harvard University Press, 1950.

[52] *See* Clark, David S. "Tracing the roots of American legal education–a nineteenth-century German connection." *Rabels Zeitschrift für ausländisches und internationales Privatrecht/The Rabel Journal of Comparative and International Private Law* 51, no. H. 3 (1987): 313-333.

[53] *See* Qinhua, He. "Modern Chinese Legal Education and Modern Chinese Jurisprudence." *Law* 12 (2003): 3-14. *See also* Zhenshan, Yang. "A Study of the History of Chinese Legal Education." *Politics and Law Forum* 4 (2000): 136-148.

[54] *See* Xianyi, Zeng. "Legal education in China." *S. Tex. L. Rev.* 43 (2001): 707-716. Ling, Mao. "Clinical legal education and the reform of the higher legal education system in China." *Fordham Int'l LJ* 30 (2006): 421-434.

[55] *See* Chan, Hugh. "Modern Legal Education in China." *China L. Rev.* 9 (1936): 142-148. Guifang, Qi and Xue, Yuan. "The History, Present Situation and Development Trend of Legal Education in China." *Journal of Economic Research* 21 (2009): 212-213. *See also* Chen, Zhen, and Guandong Song. "A Study of the Institutional History of Doctoral Education in the Period of the Republic of China." In *5th International Conference on Arts, Design and Contemporary Education (ICADCE 2019)*, 826-832. Atlantis Press, 2019.

[56] *See* Jieying, Dong. "1952: The Rectification and Reconstruction of Legal Education in New China." *Journal of the Party School of the Central Committee of the Communist Party of China* 11.2(2007):107-112. Ping, Jiang. "The History and Encounters of Chinese Legal Education." *Journal of China University of Political Science and Law* 1 (2008): 128-137.

legal education, placing a strong emphasis on nurturing legal research talent, thus laying the foundations for future doctoral legal education in the country. The tumultuous period of the Cultural Revolution, however, severely disrupted legal education in China. Schools and universities were systematically shuttered, and legal studies were stifled.[57]

The renaissance of China's legal education occurred in the 1980s, characterized by a resurgence of academic vigor. This period witnessed the active promotion of doctoral programs in law schools and universities, the resurgence of legal research, and the cultivation of high-caliber legal research scholars.[58] Today, China's legal education landscape is characterized by rapid expansion and diversification with challenges such as massive overexpansion.[59]

2.2. Pedagogical Approaches

The prevailing pedagogical approaches in legal education in contemporary China closely mirror those employed in Germany and other advanced Western societies.[60] China's doctoral education including that in law discipline is underpinned by a diverse array of pedagogical approaches designed to nurture legal scholars and professionals of the highest caliber.[61] The foundations of this educational system are deeply rooted in rigorous academic tradition and a commitment to blending theoretical and practical aspects of law.[62]

A hallmark of China's doctoral legal education is the emphasis on interdisciplinary scholarship. Doctoral candidates are encouraged to explore the interplay of law with economics, politics, sociology, and other related fields, fostering a holistic understanding of the complex legal landscape.[63] Furthermore, the Socratic method, introduced over time from abroad, is employed to promote critical thinking and rigorous debate.[64] Students engage in intensive discourse, honing their analytical skills, and developing a profound understanding of legal principles.[65] Clinical legal education programs[66] allow students to apply legal theories in real-world contexts. Practical internships[67] and research opportunities ensure that doctoral candidates gain hands-on experience and contribute meaningfully to legal scholarship.

[57] *See* Liheng, Zhu. "The Historical Evolution of Legal Education Work Since the Founding of New China." *Studies in the History of the Communist Party of China* 3 (2008): 39-45. *See also* Gelatt, Timothy A., and Frederick E. Snyder. "Legal Education in China: Training for a New Era." *China L. Rep.* 1 (1980): 41-60. Minzner, Carl F. "The rise and fall of Chinese legal education." *Fordham Int'l LJ* 36 (2013): 334-395.

[58] *See* Weidong, Ji. "Legal education in China: a great leap forward of professionalism." *Kobe University law review 39 (2004)*: 1-21. *See also* Depei, Han, and Stephen Kanter. "Legal education in China." *Am. J. Comp.* L. 32 (1984): 543-582. Erie, Matthew S. "Legal education reform in China through US-inspired transplants." *J. Legal Educ.* 59 (2009): 60-96.

[59] Minzner, Carl F *supra* note 56.

[60] *See* Yunsong, Ge Y. "The Ideal of Legal Education." *Chinese and Foreign Law* 26, no. 2 (2014): 548-581.

[61] *See* Guanglin, Yuan. "Target orientation of professional doctoral training: research professionals." *Degree and Graduate Education* 11(2014):5.

[62] *See* Jingchao, Deng. "Realistic Challenges and Exploratory Directions of China's Law Doctoral Cultivation." *Degree and Graduate Education* 2(2023):64-69.

[63] *See* Yannan, Chen, Zhi, Wang, and Dechun, Ba. "Resource Sharing Complementary Advantages Exploring a New Mode of Doctoral Cultivation." *Metallurgical Education in China* 2(2005):3. *See also* Li, Zheng, Wu Yuying, and Jiao, Lei. "Research on Interdisciplinary Doctoral Graduate Student Cultivation Mode under the New Knowledge Production Model." *Research on Higher Engineering Education* 1(2023):8.

[64] Pinghua, Zhang. "Case Teaching Method and the Change of China's Law Teaching Method." *Journal of Changzhou University (Social Science Edition)* 010.003(2009):98-101. Marshall, Donald, and Liu, Changqing. "The Socratic Method and the Indispensable Core of Law Teaching." *Legal Methods* 3 (2019): 11.

[65] *See* Yunsong, Ge Y *supra* note 59. *See also* Chaojun, Guo, and Quanquan, Geng. "Characteristics and Implications of Doctor of Laws Cultivation at Vanderbilt University, USA." *Coal Higher Education* 4 (2015): 4.

[66] *See* Li, Wang. "The legal mindset and legal education--thinking born from the 'legal clinic' educational means." *Journal of Law* 02(2007):90-93.

[67] *See* Gang, Yuan, He, Xin and Qing, Wan. "Exploration of the Cultivation Mode of China's Doctor of Laws Degree Candidates." *Degree and Graduate Education* 6(2021):9. Fengrui, Niu. "Realistic Challenges and Reform Path of Doctoral Cultivation Mode in the Context of 'Double First-class' Construction." *Modern Educational Science* 11(2019):5.

In summary, China's legal education system, encompassing its doctoral legal program is characterized by its incorporation of interdisciplinary, Socratic, and experiential pedagogical approaches. This comprehensive frame hopefully would equip candidates with the knowledge and skills necessary to address the multifaceted challenges of contemporary legal practice and scholarship.[68]

2.3. Institutional Framework

China's legal education system seamlessly weaves centralization and decentralization into a cohesive tapestry.[69] The central government's pivotal role in delineating curriculum standards and ensuring quality control is an indispensable aspect of this system. By maintaining consistent educational benchmarks, it upholds the integrity of legal education nationwide. Simultaneously, Chinese universities are afforded a measure of autonomy.[70] This liberty stimulates an environment ripe for innovation and adaptability, enabling institutions to swiftly respond to emergent legal paradigms.[71]

Moreover, the global outlook is paramount in China's legal education. Many institutions have thoughtfully cultivated partnerships with esteemed foreign counterparts. These international collaborations transcend borders, imbuing Chinese legal programs with diverse perspectives and insights.[72] This intercultural enrichment invigorates the educational experience, propelling it to a level of global excellence, thereby nurturing a new generation of legal scholars with a profound understanding of both domestic and international legal intricacies.[73]

2.4. Socio-Cultural Contexts

Similar to most nations, China's legal education is profoundly influenced by its intricate socio-cultural contexts. Embedded within a rich tapestry of tradition and modernity, it reflects China's historical commitment to the rule of law.[74] The Confucian heritage, emphasizing hierarchy and ethical conduct, contributes to the reverence for legal authority.[75] Moreover, China's recent economic transformation has amplified the demand for legal experts, prompting significant investment in legal education.[76] The socio-cultural landscape in China also underscores the significance of harmonizing individual and societal interests[77], an imperative echoed in the study of law. Respect for authority, strong work ethic, and the collectivist ethos further shape the learning environment.[78] Simultaneously, the recent pursuit of globalization and economic

---

[68] *See* Mei-Huan, Ho. "The Ideal Professional Legal Education." *Tsinghua Law* 3 (2006): 6-7. Mei Huan. Ho. *On Common Law Education in Contemporary China.* China University of Political Science and Law Press, 2005.

[69] *See* Baosheng, Liu, and Jing, Ma. "Discussion on the Disciplinary System of Socialist Law with Chinese Characteristics." *Regional Governance 15(2022)*:0100-0107.

[70] *See* Xiangde, Ji. "The Basic Characteristics of the Socialist Legal Education Model with Chinese Characteristics." *Hebei Law* 29.12 (2011): 9.

[71] *See* Zuoxiang, Liu. Exploration of China's legal education model. *Legal Education: Comparison and Reflection, Anthology of Modern Legal Education Forum.* 2001

[72] *See* Wenxian, Zhang. "The 'Chinese Model' and Development Path of Legal Education." *Proceedings of the Second Forum of Deans of Law Schools of 100 Leading Universities around the World in the 21st Century.* China Law Society China Law Society, 2010: 338-348.

[73] *See supra* note 67 Mei-Huan, Ho.

[74] *See* Xianming, Xu. "Carrying on from the Past and Making Progress Together to Create Brilliance - Speech at the Opening Ceremony of the 50th Anniversary Celebration of the Founding of Our University and the International Symposium on the Rule of Law and Legal Education." *Politics and Law Forum* 03 (2002): 4-7.

[75] *See* Guanlai, Liu. "Confucianism and Legal Education." *Journal of Anhui Institute of Science and Technology* 30.4 (2016): 5.

[76] *See* Fumin, Jiao. "The Positioning of Legal Education and the Optimization of Talent Cultivation Mechanism under the Perspective of 'Rule of Law China.'" *Legal Science* 36, no. 3 (2015): 42-51. *See also* Gelatt, Timothy A., and Frederick E. Snyder *supra* note 56.

[77] *See* Guanru, Liu. Confucianism, the Glory of Rule of Law after Two Thousand Years: Ruminations on Confucianism and the Rule of Law in a Harmonious Society. *Law and Society*, 14(2008):233.

[78] *See* Qilin, Ma. "Reflections on the Modernization of China's Legal Education: Cutting from Chinese Confucian Educational Thought and American Legal Education Experience." *Journal of Inner Mongolia Normal University*

liberalization has propelled China's legal education into an international realm,[79] integrating Western legal concepts and fostering cross-cultural legal scholarship[80]. This dynamic interplay of tradition, economic progress, and global engagement[81] defines the socio-cultural backdrop of China's doctoral legal education, illuminating its growth and ever-evolving character.

3. Comparative Analysis
3.1 Key Comparative Findings

A succinct comparative analysis between China and Germany's legal education systems underscores their divergent trajectories while highlighting certain converging trends. In Germany, the legal profession is rigorously regulated through the meticulous Staatsexamen, which notably includes the First and Second State Examinations and is conducted independently of academic institutions. In contrast, China mandates that aspiring legal professionals successfully navigate the formidable National Judicial Examination to attain their professional qualifications[82]. Both nations are currently witnessing the emergence of interdisciplinary scholarship, yet their approaches differ. Germany tends to maintain a clear separation between law and other academic disciplines, while China actively fosters a deeper integration of cross-disciplinary collaboration[83]. Additionally, pedagogical methodologies such as case-based learning and the Socratic method are integral to the educational landscapes of both countries. However, it is worth noting that while these refined approaches are relatively prevalent in Germany, their adoption in China remains somewhat less pronounced.

Intrinsically, China's legal education framework, rooted in Confucian principles, exhibits a pronounced centralization, with the government wielding significant influence over curriculum standards and content,[84] to ensure a degree of uniformity across institutions. A prominent emphasis is placed on civil law, reflecting the nation's burgeoning demand for legal professionals and its own unique legal tradition[85]. Germany, in stark contrast, now maintains a decentralized model that bestows universities with substantial autonomy[86] in shaping their programs. Here, the civil law tradition, although shared with China, coexists with a deep-seated historical school, where legal history and philosophy take center stage. German legal education fosters a scholarly environment emphasizing jurisprudence, critical thinking, and in-depth research, culminating in the development of keen analytical minds[87] well-versed in the intricacies of the legal sphere.

(Education Science Edition) 9 (2013): 107-111.

[79] *See* Dayuan, Han. "Challenges Facing Chinese Legal Education in the Context of Globalization." *Journal of Law* 32.3 (2011): 17-20.

[80] *See* Chunxiang, Song. "Some Issues of 'Belt and Road' Legal Talent Cultivation and Legal Chinese Textbook Development." *China Legal Education Research* 2(2018):16.

[81] *See* Renshan, Liu, and Lihong, Ding. et al. Reflections on legal education. Peking University Press, 2011.

[82] *See* Jianfeng, Pan and Hangping, Chen. "Revisiting the Relationship between Legal Education and Judicial Examinations." *Law Application* 1 (2008): 57-62.

[83] *See* Dayuan, Han, Huanfang, Du, Lei, Lu and Shixia, Gong. "Interdisciplinary Education and Research: a Path to Realize the Construction of Law Disciplines in the New Era." China University Teaching 4 (2018): 17-24. *See also* Kalivoda, Gregor. Juristische Rhetorik: Systematische, historische und interdisziplinäre Aspekte der forensischen Beredsamkeit. In Lerch, Kent D. (Hg.): Die Sprache des Rechts. *Studien der interdisziplinären Arbeitsgruppe der Berlin-Brandenburgischen Akademie der Wissenschaften*, Bd. 2, Berlin 2005, 321-342. Möslein, Florian, Gröber, Clara, Heß, Colin and Rebmann, Charlotte. "Das Recht der Digitalisierung in der rechtswissenschaftlichen Ausbildung" *JURA-Juristische Ausbildung* 43, no. 6 (2021): 651-668.

[84] *See* Chenyu, Li. "On the Current Situation of China's Higher Legal Education and Suggestions for Reform: A Comparison of Chinese and German Legal Education as a Perspective." *Contemporary Law Forum* 2(2008): 56-59. Wenyi, Huang. "Some Problems about Legal Education." *Legal Science* 5(2002): 3-11.

[85] *See* Xiantan, Huo. *The development and transformation of Chinese legal education.* Law Press, 2004.

[86] *See* Yongliu, Zheng. Academic Freedom, Professor's Rule, Professional Loyalty: A Review of German Legal Education. *Comparative Law Studies,* 4(1997):32-41.

[87] *See* Yongliu, Zheng. "Knowing and Doing through the World - German Legal Education Revisited." *Comparative Law Studies* 1 (2007): 88-101. *See also* Ji, Yang. "Some Characteristics of Higher Law Education in Germany and Their Edifications to China." *Research on Education Tsinghua University* 2(2002):37-41.

Nonetheless, both systems exhibit a shared commitment to embracing international perspectives. Chinese institutions actively seek collaborations with foreign counterparts, thereby infusing global influences into their programs.[88] Germany similarly engages in international partnerships, enriching its legal discourse through cross-cultural interactions and contributing to the global legal conversation.[89] These collaborative efforts manifest a shared recognition of the interconnected and dynamic nature of contemporary legal scholarship and practice.

3.2 Implications for Legal Education and Beyond

The comparative analysis of German and Chinese legal education systems transcends their immediate pedagogical domains, extending even beyond academia into the broader legal landscape and societal contexts.

While German legal education's tradition and rigor are celebrated, it is not devoid of challenges and complexities[90]. The historical tension between centralization and institutional autonomy, the quest for greater diversity and inclusion, and the current demands of a rapidly evolving legal landscape[91] are forces that continually shape and reshape the contours of this venerable system.

The decentralization of the German legal education model over time[92] versus the centralization in contemporary China[93] highlights the spectrum of governance structures in legal education. This contrast prompts a reflection on the balance between government oversight and institutional autonomy, raising questions about the role of the state in shaping legal curricula and the implications for legal practice and scholarship.

The intricate interplay between Confucian values, the rich tapestry of legal history, and the prevailing principles of contemporary civil law in China,[94] coupled with Germany's steadfast commitment to the civil law tradition intertwined with a deep-seated foundation in historical legal philosophy,[95] serves as a compelling demonstration of the profound fusion of culture, historical heritage, and the jurisprudential landscape. These intricate connections offer a gateway to inspiring a profound and comprehensive examination of legal pluralism within societies, allowing for a nuanced understanding of how cultural, historical, and legal elements collectively shape legal education, foster diversification, and prompt the exploration of harmonious coexistence between differing legal paradigms within complex and multifaceted societies.

---

[88] *See, e.g.,* Lancaster, Robert, and Ding Xiangshun. "Addressing the Emergence of Advocacy in the Chinese Criminal Justice System: A Collaboration between a US and a Chinese Law School." *Fordham Int'l LJ* 30 (2006): 356-373.

[89] *See* Wenzler, Hariolf, and Kasia Kwietniewska. "Educating the Global Lawyer: The German Experience." *Journal of Legal Education* 61, no. 3 (2012): 462–67.

[90] *See* Alexander, Nadja. "What's law got to do with it? mapping modern mediation movements in civil and common law jurisdictions." *Bond Law Review* 13, no. 2 (2001): 335-363.

[91] See Korioth, Stefan *supra* notes 26. *See also* Zekoll, Joachim, and Gerhard Wagner, eds. *Introduction to German law.* Kluwer Law International BV, 2018.

[92] *See* Van Amelsvoort, H. W. C. H. *Decentralization in Education in an International Perspective.* University of Twente, Faculty of Educational Science and Technology, Enschede, 1995. *See also* Ballarino, Gabriele. "Decentralization and reform of higher education. Can Germany be an example for Italy?" *Italian Journal of Sociology of Education* 3, no. Italian Journal of Sociology of Education 3/2 (2011): 46-71. Baumert, Jijrgen, and Dietrich Goldschmidt. "Centralization and decentralization as determinants of educational policy in the Federal Republic of Germany (FRG)." *Social Science Information* 19, no. 6 (1980): 1029-1070.

[93] *See* Hawkins, John N. "Centralization, decentralization, recentralization-Educational reform in China." *Journal of Educational Administration* 38, no. 5 (2000): 442-455. *See also* Liang, Bin. *The changing Chinese legal system, 1978–present: Centralization of power and rationalization of the legal system.* Routledge, 2007. Mok, Ka-Ho, ed. *Centralization and decentralization: Educational reforms and changing governance in Chinese societies.* Vol. 13. Springer Science & Business Media, 2013. Tao, Yuan. "Towards network governance: educational reforms and governance changes in China (1985–2020)." *Asia Pacific Education Review* 23, no. 3 (2022): 375-388.

[94] *See* Zhao, Jun, and Ming Hu. "A comparative study of the legal education system in the United States and China and the reform of legal education in China." *Suffolk Transnat'l L. Rev.* 35 (2012): 329. See also Rojek, Dean G. "Social control in the People's Republic of China." *Criminal Justice Review* 14, no. 2 (1989): 141-153.

[95] *See* Toller, Fernando M. *supra* note 7. *See also* Grechenig, Kristoffel, and Martin Gelter. "The transatlantic divergence in legal thought: American law and economics vs. German doctrinalism." *Hastings Int'l & Comp. L. Rev.* 31 (2008): 295-360.

China's legal system, firmly entrenched in its rich cultural and historical milieu, engages in a process of legal transplants and modernization, drawing inspiration from Germany's legal philosophy and the civil law tradition.[96] China's legal education has likewise borne witness to and exemplified this transformative evolution. Concurrently, Germany diligently engages in a process of introspection, proactively drawing from cognate paradigms,[97] notably exemplified by its discerning study of the western legal education system.[98] This ongoing endeavor embodies an erudite commitment to continuous improvement and an unwavering pursuit of excellence in legal pedagogy.

Comparative legal education plays an indispensable role in illuminating the intricacies of these transplantations, offering profound insights into the challenges, adaptations, and the far-reaching implications for both nations involved in the legal exchange. The contrasting paradigms of legal education in Germany and China eloquently accentuate the inherent importance of embracing diversity in educational methodologies. This underscores the pivotal notion that a uniform, one-size-fits-all solution is rarely applicable, for the spectrum of educational approaches at our disposal serves as a versatile means to intricately address the unique needs and aspirations of varied societies, epitomizing the intricate tapestry of global learning.

4. Doctoral Journeys: Individual Narratives and Insights

The author's doctoral study in Germany was a profound exploration of law, culture, and personal growth. Marked by intellectual growth and cultural immersion, the author believes an exhilarating and enlightening law doctorate pursuit in Germany would be an exceptional chapter in any international student's academic life. The training the author received on German soil fortified the bedrock of her scholarly journey, instilling in her a deep-seated appreciation for the meticulous nature of German legal scholarship. The pursuit of rigor and excellence became not just a pedagogical aspiration but a way of life.

4.1 Lessons from the Doctoral Lens

Embarking on the path of pursuing distinct legal degrees in both China and Germany offers a remarkable vantage point for conducting a comparative analysis of these two diverse legal educational systems. This educational journey unfolds as a rich tapestry of experiences, providing invaluable insights and lessons that underscore the intricate and multifaceted dynamics within the realm of legal scholarship and pedagogy. Through her unique academic odyssey, the author has had the privilege of delving into the nuances, strengths, and idiosyncrasies of both legal systems.

The Chinese legal education system, firmly rooted in tradition, ardently fosters a comprehensive grasp of legal codes and doctrines, employing a predominantly lecture-based approach. This approach bestows students with an intimate knowledge of statutory law but often at the expense of critical thinking and practical legal skills. Consequently, the Chinese doctoral programs underscore the primacy of possessing a solid legal foundation, yet it urges the necessity of accentuating the cultivation of critical analysis and pragmatic legal competencies. This lesson is not exclusive to China but resonates universally[99], highlighting the importance of equipping legal scholars with both intellectual prowess and pragmatic skills.

---

[96] *See* Chen, Jianfu. "Modernization, westernization, and globalization: legal transplant in China." In *One Country, Two Systems, Three Legal Orders-Perspectives of Evolution*, 91-114. Berlin, Heidelberg: Springer Berlin Heidelberg, 2009.
[97] *See* Ostertag, Juergen R. "Legal Education in Germany and the United States--A Structural Comparison." *Vand. J. Transnat'l L.* 26 (1993): 301-340.
[98] *See* Miller, Russell A., and Peer Zumbansen, eds. *Comparative law as transnational law: a decade of the German law journal.* Oxford University Press, USA, 2012. *See also* Max Rheinstein *supra* note 31.
[99] *See, e.g.*, James R. Maxeiner; Keiichi Yamanaka, "The New Japanese Law Schools: Putting the Professional into Legal Education," *Pacific Rim Law & Policy Journal* 13, no. 2 (2004): 303-328. Matthew J. Wilson, "U.S. Legal

In Germany, the author's doctoral studies prioritized the development of deep research competencies, nurturing scholarly independence. Her experience of pursuing a German doctorate in law underscored the profound value of academic autonomy. This autonomy, however, carries with it the responsibility to steer the scholarly journey towards relevance and practical significance. The dissertation process, marked by extensive academic inquiry, allows the author to delve deep into niche areas of law, thereby contributing to the expansion of legal knowledge.

A prevailing narrative within German law schools reveals a consistent pattern where, amidst the academic journey, profound and extraordinary friendships unfailingly blossomed between devoted doctoral candidates and their esteemed German doctoral supervisors. This connection was nothing short of an epitome of mutual and equitable respect, transcending the traditional roles of mentor and mentee. Encouraging doctoral students to chart their own academic course by the supervisors empowers them to explore their unique interests and contribute to the expansion of legal knowledge in their chosen fields. This seamless integration of personal and academic bonds further reinforces the ethos of academic autonomy within the German doctoral system.

In the realm of doctoral training in law, another profound dichotomy emerges when the author delved into the pedagogical paradigms of Germany and China, specifically within the domain of academic seminars and colloquia. In Germany, these intellectual congregations assume a pivotal role in the pursuit of erudition. Doctoral aspirants are not sequestered within the solitary chambers of their research; instead, they are fervently urged to actively partake in academic symposia and colloquia. Within these sanctums, doctoral candidates seize the opportunity to disseminate their research, articulate their discoveries, and engage in erudite dialogues. This dynamic exchange with seasoned faculty members and fellow scholars serves as a crucible for intellectual advancement, while the invaluable insights gleaned from these interactions serve as a touchstone for the refinement and augmentation of their scholarly undertakings. Through such cerebral discourse, the author's doctoral cohorts are nurtured within an academic ecosystem that flourishes on the tenets of intellectual candor and rigorous dialectic, thereby molding them into adept academicians skilled in critical ratiocination and proficient in the robust defense of their academic tenets.

Though the study of jurisprudence is by no means bereft of research and scholarly discourse, based on the author's firsthand experiences, the Chinese pedagogical system frequently endows greater weight to structured coursework and examinations, manifesting an orientation that leans toward examination-centricity and somewhat diminishes the focus on the consistent exchange and debate of research discoveries. The integral role of academic symposia and colloquia in the educational journey may not claim the same eminence. While Chinese candidates are indeed engaged in research endeavors, they may not experience the same regular and systematic orchestration of scholarly congregations witnessed in Germany.

Germany's commitment to multilingual research is unmistakably evident. In German law schools, doctoral colleagues of the author immerse themselves in the intricate tapestry of multilingualism, showcasing proficiency not only in English but also in a spectrum of Germanic and Romance languages. This comprehensive linguistic repertoire equips them to navigate, dissect, and reference legal literature spanning multiple languages. The acquisition of such multilingual competence not only serves to enhance the depth of their research endeavors but also positions them for a future career in the global legal arena, be it in academia or the practice of law. There has also been a discernible surge in the recognition of the significance of multilingual research within the framework of doctoral legal training in China, with a special emphasis on English. As per the author's astute observations, Chinese institutions are progressively honing their doctoral programs to better synchronize with the requirements of the globalized legal landscape, thus emphatically highlighting the perpetually evolving nature of legal education within the country.

4.2 Embracing the European Scholarly Panorama

As the author immersed herself in the intellectually abundant academic milieu, her experiences transcended the mere walls of lecture halls and seminar rooms, stretching far beyond the territorial confines of Germany. Professional training and academic exploration have been not only a scholar's continental sojourn, but also an odyssey through Germanic realms for her. The expedition extended across borders, allowing the author to witness the rich tapestry of legal traditions in Germanic-speaking areas and beyond.

The author's scholarly explorations during research visits to the Netherlands, Switzerland, and Norway illuminated distinct facets of legal training in these European nations, offering valuable academic observations. The Netherlands, with its pragmatic approach to law, gave the author a glimpse into the Dutch legal mindset. With a legal culture deeply rooted in pragmatism and efficiency, the author perceived the Dutch approach to law emphasized a remarkable balance between theory and practice.

In German-speaking region of Switzerland, the author encountered a unique blend of interactivity, multilingualism, and global focus that defines the Swiss legal educational landscape. The Swiss legal education system distinguishes itself through a highly interactive, student-centered pedagogy, in contrast to China's lecture-based system and Germany's emphasis on academic rigor. Given Switzerland's diversity, students there cultivate multilingual competence, a distinctive attribute that sets Switzerland apart from China and Germany, both of which have traditionally favored a predominantly monolingual approach in legal education before the doctoral level. Impressively, Swiss legal education epitomizes a profound international orientation that infuses students with a global outlook from the outset. In contrast, Chinese legal education tends to be more inwardly focused on domestic matters, while German legal education, though esteemed, typically adheres to a European perspective. Swiss legal training encompasses comprehensive modules on international law and comparative legal systems, meticulously equipping students for distinguished careers within the worldwide legal landscape. This inherent global perspective underscores the cosmopolitan essence of Swiss legal education, providing the author with a unique and holistic understanding of the interconnected nature of contemporary law.

Across multiple academic sojourns in Norway, the author unearthed three salient facets meriting close scrutiny through her own immersive experiences. The diminutive country is remarkable for its unwavering commitment to gender equality and diversity within legal education. This stands in contrast to China, where traditional gender norms still exert significant influence, and Germany, which is making progress but may not have reached the same level of diversity awareness as Norway. At universities, Norway's legal education system incorporates the study of Indigenous law with a dedication to recognizing and preserving the rights and traditions of its Indigenous communities, which is not commonly seen in China and Germany. Norway's legal training resonated deeply with its focus on human rights and inclusivity. Its commitment to social justice and the development of an inclusive legal framework left the author an enduring impression.

In addition to the Germanic-speaking regions, the author's research sojourns encompassed the academic pilgrimage in the culturally resplendent landscapes of Italy and France. The public universities opened their venerable doors, ushering her into their hallowed halls. In Italy, the fusion of history, culture, and legal scholarship was nothing short of captivating. As the author delved into her research, the resonances of Roman law and the Italian ardor for legal heritage left an indelible imprint on her intellectual pursuits. The enriching cultural palette of exquisite cuisine, timeless art, and profound history further heightened her daily life.

France, with its profound academic elegance and unwavering commitment to precision, revealed new horizons within the author's academic odyssey. It was not solely an exploration of legal systems but a profound encounter with the quintessential French way of life. The harmonious symphony of language, art, and intellectualism in France deepened the author's comprehension of European legal culture and added a layer of finesse to her academic pursuits.

This odyssey in Europe wasn't just about academics; it was a transformational passage. It cemented the author's conviction that legal knowledge transcends borders, and it is the tapestry of diverse experiences that enriches the scholarly journey.

Conclusion

Traversing academic frontiers in the realm of legal education through the lens of the author's doctoral journey has unveiled the rich tapestry of pedagogical methodologies, institutional structures, and historical contexts that distinguish Germany and China. This comparative discussion not only enhances a comprehension of the specific legal education systems but also underscores broader implications for legal scholarship and international collaboration. As legal education continues to evolve in response to global challenges, this exploration emphasizes the significance of cross-cultural dialogue and the exchange of ideas in shaping the future of legal practice and scholarship.

The German legal education system is continuously renowned for its academic excellence and the emphasis it places on the development of critical thinking and analytical skills. Exemplary young legal researchers, particularly those pursuing doctoral degrees, are tasked with delving into exhaustive research, showcasing a profound mastery of legal theories and concepts. This approach not only deepens their knowledge but also nurtures their ability to think independently and critically, an invaluable asset in the ever-evolving field of law. This emphasis on rigorous research and critical thinking has also become more pronounced in Chinese legal education, mirroring the German approach.

A pursuit of a doctorate in law from Germany is a testament to the enduring appeal of the German legal education system. The author who has undertaken this arduous journey is drawn to the rich intellectual tradition, rigorous methodology, and profound insights that German legal doctoral programs offer.

As a legal education powerhouse from the author's lens, Germany has not only imbibed valuable insights from its counterparts in Germanic-speaking regions but has, in turn, enriched these traditions. Its emphasis on academic rigor and research-driven scholarship has been acknowledged and emulated. Its commitment to critical thinking and problem-solving, which is integral to German legal education, has seeped into the pedagogical approaches of other nations in the Europe.

Prior to, during, and subsequent to the author's doctoral odyssey in Germany, she was sponsored to pursue studies, engage in pedagogy, and immerse herself in legal trainings at prestigious institutions and research havens spanning diverse geographical domains. These invaluable opportunities and profound experiences were made attainable through Germany's steadfast dedication and magnanimous investment in cultivating a global perspective among doctoral researchers. They were also shaped by the equal treatment and intensive nurturing of international scholars, by the remarkably frequent and intimate academic interchange, as well as the expansive tapestry of research collaborations that spanned the European Union, the European Economic Area, and the vast expanse of the broader pan-European landscape. Ultimately, at its core, this academic odyssey for the author was fundamentally catalyzed by

China's resolute stride toward internationalization, fueled by China's burgeoning appetite for individuals with a cosmopolitan mindset.

The author's doctoral compatriots, much like herself, hold in high regard the rigorous and meticulously orchestrated doctoral tutelage they received in Germany—a lifelong treasure, irrespective of whether their destinies unfolded within the ivory towers of academia or amid the ever-evolving landscapes of various industries and legal practice. Whether they chose to continue their professional sojourn in the embrace of Germany or ventured across borders for career advancement post-graduation, this formative experience endured as a steadfast companion on their journeys. Amidst her academic expedition in Germany and the broader European expanse, the author harbors deep gratitude for the diverse and upwardly mobile doctoral community that warmly enveloped her, a fellowship to which she is proud to belong. In earnest, the author extends a sincere invitation to aspiring legal scholars, beckoning them to embark on this transcultural odyssey, to savor its intricacies, and to harvest its many fruits. She firmly asserts that those who heed this call will undoubtedly experience substantial growth, akin to her own and her esteemed German doctoral contemporaries of law, in multiple dimensions.

Carolina Maria de Jesus -
researching a black brazilian author in Leipzig

Dr. Raquel Alves dos Santos Nascimento[1]

Abstract

My hands, cradled to the sound of John and Alice Coltrane, write and rewrite, record and then de-record what goes on inside the reflections… all very inconstant. What is, may soon not be anymore... the world out there is changing, will people too? Between high and low notes, played more or less slowly in the constant frenetic blowing, I come across the high pitch of my thoughts and the gravity of not being able to touch them, gather them and record them. They hover and fall incomplete on my sheets of paper, not even the most perfect cutting is able to complete them and they remain like that, a sample of an idea, a reflection, a greater thought.
(Nascimento, Raquel: excerpt from a personal diary of a research stay in Leipzig (30.04.2020)

First Words

I could feel the cool autumn wind when I left Frankfurt airport that October 2019. A mild welcome for someone who had left the 35-degree heat of the city of Fortaleza in Brazil. The beach days leading up to my departure would be days to remember during the research (and pandemic) year in the city of Leipzig.

Curious eyes looked at me when, upon arriving by train, I entered the tram that would take me to the house of a great friend. Perhaps they would wonder where I would have come from with my long braids, my black skin and my almost fluent German if it weren't for my pauses and accent. Laughed loudly and happily with the friend who hadn't seen her for years and who would shelter me in the first few days. Everything was even more curious when we mixed German with Portuguese. The eyes tried to avoid us, but they couldn't.

I began to imagine how intriguing it would have been for Germans to read the work of Carolina Maria de Jesus, also dark black like me and with a deep voice bringing harsh messages of poverty that swept away all those who were proof that the development of the "country of the future" " was not being so fair. Would they have had eyes as wide as those looking at me on that train? I don't know, but I knew that my research stay had already started there. I was experiencing what perhaps the work of Carolina Maria de Jesus would have experienced at first: the eyes of curiosity.

I began to imagine how intriguing it would have been for Germans to read the work of Carolina Maria de Jesus, also dark black like me and with a deep voice bringing harsh messages of poverty that swept away all those who were proof that the development of the "country of the future" " was not being so fair. Would they have had eyes as wide as those looking at me on that train? I don't know, but I knew that my research stay had already started there. I was experiencing what

---

[1] *Raquel Alves dos Santos Nascimento* is a researcher for German and Romance Studies at the Universidade d São Paulo (Brazil) and the University Leipzig (Germany). Besides that she has a profound experience as translator and interpreter.

perhaps the work of Carolina Maria de Jesus would have experienced at first: the eyes of curiosity.

Carolina Maria de Jesus was a black brazilian author that for several years since 1970 was forgotten but was a literature phenomenon in 1960. Her first published book *Quarto de Despejo* was published in 1960 and almost instantly became a bestseller in Brazil subsequently being translated into 15 languages and published in 40 countries. The book was groundbreaking in that it described daily life in the favela from the first-hand experience of Carolina Maria de Jesus who had lived in the community. Her depiction was a unique voice from the inside, inciting curiosity and intrigue around the world about this little known reality told by a black Brazilian woman author, and would be the focus of my research for the subsequent months ahead.

Bringing all this information and a little more in my luggage, we arrived at my friend's house, who received me with a dish made with one of the many varieties of pumpkin, and I was the one who widened my eyes with curiosity. It was interesting to see how the seasons have a whole way of eating, dressing, exercising, socializing and living. In Brazil, these nuances are so small that we almost don't notice them and, therefore, we don't value them. I realized that it was the various ways of seeing and experiencing Carolina that led me there.

Known as "escritora favelada" [writer from the favela], Carolina Maria de Jesus, would go on to publish three other books during her lifetime: Casa de Alvenaria, Provérbios e Pedaços da Fome and another six after her death other three posthumously: Diário de Bitita (1986), Meu estranho diário (1996), Antologia Pessoal (1996), Onde estás Felicidade (2014), Meu Sonho é escrever (2018), Cliris (2019).

A romanticist in spirit, Carolina did not restrict herself only to writing prose, she was a poet, playwright and a screenwriter; she wrote short stories, composed sambas, and was a performing circus artist. She was an ardent creative of many talents and rebelled against the attempts to be pigeonholed into a parochial understanding of her. This reminded me of Audre Lord who wrote in her poem "Self definition and my poetry" a warning to black women about the need for the mainstream to choose only one of its many selves. Exactly what happened to Carolina.

Under the framework of the "favelada that writes", it seemed to make it possible to glimpse and soften the author's boldness to write an autobiographical diary when writing was restricted to the elite. In texts about her written in Brazil and abroad, accessed in the German context, there seemed to be an echo in the background: how dare you put in jeopardy an entire economic development of the city as an example of the miracle economy of the country of the future? How dare you? A mixture of attraction and repulsion. In consonance with the lines of Spivak (2010), the subaltern Carolina Maria de Jesus dared to write, print in literature her own spelling, her own look, her humanity so despised and made invisible.

Giving priority to the documental and sociological character seems to have been the way to absorb all that boldness and sell the book. In this context, the images of author in her surroundings of misery have the fundamental role of sharpening the curiosity of the elite and print "veracity to the document". Thus, the photos of the shack, the ragged residents, dirty clothes, scarves on their heads, children with languid looks and down-to-earth make up the perfect illustration for the caption of the slum dweller who writes only about and from that place. In addition, there was a great opportunity to create a discourse consonant with social and civil movements prevailing at the time. and it is in this moment that Carolina becomes a celebrity: she grants interviews, is invited for important elite dinners, she is awarded the title of "São Paulo citizen" and a member of the Academy of Letters at the Faculty of Law, makes important trips in Latin America and leave the favela. Leaving the favela diminishes the elite's interest in it. The place you were framed began to be outdated and, instead of continuing to talk about a context not experienced by the elite, the author now speaks from within the context of the middle class in Casa de Alvenaria and, daring to go beyond publishing some of her fictional writings. That was not gut accepted and the interest in her diminished. However, his successful book continued to be translated around the world and reached the highest number of editions in Germany that has been noted and ultimately, just as his work travels there, I also traveled to the country to study the contrasts of how it was appreciated through foreign eyes.

Into my research, settled in a routine, reflecting on my research, becoming familiar with the library and my colleagues I need to remember that I am from a postgraduate system full of bureaucracy and, above all, with a limited term of a maximum of 4 years, all these experiences and associations were always filled with a lot of anxiety. Everything needed to be turned into text, methodology or part of the thesis soon, as I had only two years of research left. The days followed and with them passed the period of accommodation and transition. Soon I was introduced to the doctoral students of the Leipzig Department of Translation and managed to draw up, together with the help of my advisor in the department, an action plan to give direction to the stay. I started by looking for the translated editions of the book "Quarto de Despejo" by Carolina Maria de Jesus and for that there was no better place than the German National Library in Leipzig.

The German National Library in Leipzig is one of the most complete and rich in German history. The other is in Frankfurt and is more recent, created to ensure that no more books were lost as they were lost during the war period when the city of Leipzig was bombed. It was there where I found the 10 editions of the translated book by Carolina Maria de Jesus. Recovered editions, since 1962, from 5 different publishers and some don't even exist anymore. It was there that I got emotional, looking at all those very tall bookcases, because I realized how far this author's work could reach. I felt part of that story.

Of course, that whole sense of grandeur didn't last long. All that belonging had already fallen to the ground at least 40 years ago and it was already clear to me that I would not find anything about the book, or the author, or the translation of her book at the University of Leipzig.

However, about Translation itself, it was possible to learn, understand and experience a lot and that was the great asset of going through that University and that institute. However, participating in colloquia at the Institute for Applied Linguistics and Translation Studies in the winter semester of 2019 broadened my research perspectives by helping to discuss research projects and strategies of my fellow students and also accepting the suggestions and tips of the supervisors. The discussions inspired me to try out strategies for improving my methods.

The conversations with my supervisor made me think more and better about the structure of my work: from the table of contents to the content of the individual chapters. The fellow students in the doctoral room also helped me with formatting questions.I was compelled to think about how Carolina's book was presented to the German public and what would have caught their attention in the early 1960s. Would it be a photo of the author stamped on the cover? Could it be the German title "Diary of Poverty"? Would they also, at this first moment, be interested in my cover and title? I don´t know. What I do know is that the contact with publishing archives in Leipzig and Marbach made it possible to collect important data, correspondence and documents. They gave me a bigger picture of the making of the book and the translated version of the Brazilian book despite the difficulties imposed by the pandemic that begins in *March and hits and everything closes, all research stops and everyone self isolates.*

These moments of seclusion made me spend nights wondering why I was spending these moments of crisis and global pandemic in a room alone. I thought about how providential it was for my younger sister and her husband to come to my parents' house in December 2019, when we still had no idea what was to come. Knowing that everyone is together at home reassures me, but yesterday also made me think: Why am I not there too? I could not be with my parents and sisters, but with my husband in our house, rediscovering with him a way to make routine, anxieties and fears not paralyze us. I kept thinking about the purpose of it all, the purpose of spending these times with certain people or alone. I got a little sad, I'm not going to lie. I kept thinking: why me alone? And that question kept echoing in my head all night. In the morning, I attended a panel debate on Carolina Maria de Jesus and something answered me, deep down, no. I was not alone, because besides God, I had her company and I had a mission. I asked that little voice from the back what that mission would be. I was so tired, not even knowing if a doctoral thesis would constitute a mission. I remembered the opportunities and challenges that were thrown at me this month and they all had to do with getting to know Carolina and her work better. I think that amid the clouded thoughts of those moments, I understood. I thanked and asked in prayer: May I have the strength to fulfill this mission, may my family be there waiting for me when I return and may my marriage become more and more intense and alive from this hard experience of the hiatus. I asked God for strength, perseverance and wisdom. I asked Carolina for company and enlightenment. May my mission be to compose, with several other sisters and brothers, the circle that will put her in the literate place that she has always been and that my text be clear, engaging and put one more brick in the reconstruction of her legacy.

That was a rather emotional description, I know. It's just that never before has it been so everyday to think about death and hear about deaths, and doing research has become small in the face of questioning life. But at the same time that this distance made me doubt my possibility of continuing my research stay there and even questioning whether this research was really important to me, it also intensified the need for exchange and mutual help within the scope of my research stay.

As soon as work at the institute and visiting libraries was possible again, I was able to finish a first version of the analysis chapters for the paratexts in relation to translation and make a survey on the reading of the paratexts of each edition with some sections of the translated text and to the subjects of the institute so that I could still collect data on site in Germany.

In general terms, my research work aimed to present a critical analysis of the German translation of *Quarto de Despejo* (engl. titel Child of the Dark), by Brazilian writer Carolina Maria de Jesus. The focus centering on the translation from the perspective of the paratextual elements inside the book, translated in 1962 by Johannes Gerold and reedited nine times between 1962 and 1989. Quarto de Despejo was published in Brazil in 1960 and quickly occupied first place on the list of best-sellers in the country. The book, written in the first person, marks the inception of the autobiographical genre, with a voice outside the canon narrating a condition of housing and survival in a favela that at the time was still new in the São Paulo imagination. The German translation of *Quarto de Despejo* accepts Brazil's estimations of the work, but also finds fertile soil in a political-ideological moment in the former West and East Germany of the 1960s that revealed an opening to other cultures and literature. The analysis of the paratextual elements that constitute the book, such as cover, flap text, back cover, preface, and afterword, revealed an importance given to the political social aspects of *Quarto de Despejo* and aimed to guide the understanding and reading of this translation. This can be seen in the responses of test-readers of both the book and the paratexts revealing to what extent they were influenced by these translations. Additionally, these paratexts present features of the Übersetzungsauftrag [order/translation project]. We employed Corpus Linguistics as a methodology to expand textual analysis basing our research primarily on Descriptive Translation Studies and the paratext theory of Genette (2009).

Of all the facets of this work, I would like to bring here a little of the experience with the test-readers that were my pleasant surprise during the course of this research in Leipzig. After days and days of isolation alone in the dorm room, looking at the walls and learning to live with myself, my fears, the distance from the family and affections due to the COVID-19 pandemic, I was able to count on the willingness and contribution of 6 post-graduate test-readers in Translation or German Studies at the University of Leipzig, between 25 and 30 years old, three males and three females.

Thus, getting in touch with the volunteers in my research, in addition to putting me back in touch with people and new friendships, allowed me to talk about Carolina and her work to an audience that had never heard of her and introduce her to a new generation. , writings that moved so much with readers in the 1960s, 1970s and 1980s. This was of paramount importance in the construction of translation analyses, for example, since only this temporal distance could reveal relevant translation issues to argue, for example , a retranslation of the work.

In this sense, the analysis of the test readers' questionnaires went from being a pleasant surprise to being the icing on the cake, as they added new elements to the hall of analyzes and perceptions about Carolina and her book translation. If we cross data from the different perspectives of understanding the answers to the questionnaires, either by summarizing the data by questions or by questionnaire specifically, we will realize that in the prism of the questions we will see the recurrence of the presentation of a different social context, the documental value of the work, discomfort in reading such miserable situations, derogatory terms, poetic quality, abstraction, voyeurism, unusual constructions and lexical choices and the importance of paratextual elements to contextualize and guide the reading.
An example of this was the recurrence of the recurring term 'Neger', today a taboo, and described as disparaging from the mid-1970s, was one of the annoyances mentioned by test readers. One of the test readers commented: "expressions like 'Neger, Negerin, Negerkind' startled me in a way. But this can be explained perhaps by the time".

However, it is a fact that in 1962, the term was still used in German society without any evidence of an injury. But both the civil movements that echoed at the time in the United States of America and the presence of a somewhat expressive minority of German blacks, should already point to the discomfort generated by the use of the term, even if it were to determine no longer belonging to German society. Furthermore, effective and official changes in the use of a term rarely occur without a movement in society leading to them. As a black-skinned visiting researcher, these reflections on the term also helped me to reflect on my presence in that society.

As it turns out, Carolina did not visit Germany at the height of her recognition, but her work did have to pass through the scrutiny of the German literary system which, in a way, imposes, as in Brazil, limits on her literary reach, classifying -o as a record or report without literary pretensions. But unlike Brazil, this classification found, paradoxically, in that system a niche destined to the literatures of reports, being therefore, in the end, considered, in a certain way, as part of the literatures.

In this sense, many times, going through the sieve of other systems, can reveal nuances of the work that the original system had not been capable of, or was prepared to identify. Which also ends up revealing characteristics and limits of the original system itself. By being able to experience both the postgraduate system in Brazil and Germany, - remembering that even within Brazil there are peculiarities in the system depending on the state and the university and it is possible that this happens in Germany as well - I was able to perceive, in general lines, starting with the researcher status in both countries that in Germany the researcher has a vacancy similar to a job vacancy and the researcher seems to be more valued. In Brazil, what you see a lot are researchers who need to undertake to bear the costs of living when they do not occupy a vacancy at the university that needs to be obtained through a public competition, therefore restricted.

In addition, if we are to think about tranquility for carrying out the research and resources, we have that the Brazilian researcher finds himself much more crowded and overloaded with the deadlines he has to meet, even though he often needs to do odd jobs to complement the value of the scholarship . In Germany the deadline is not an issue. It was possible to feel lighter in the researchers of the German system that I met. There I realized that it is indeed possible to carry out research concentrating the focus only on each research process with the calm, lightness and pleasure necessary for a healthy process. In this sense, the postgraduate system in Brazil has a lot to evolve to achieve the balance of extracting the best in creativity and research development from its researchers without them having to suffer so much and often get sick.

The writing of a thesis is intense and the illness caused by the demand for a certain perfection is latent. In the days when in Leipzig university activities were prohibited by the worldwide sanitary conditions already mentioned here. Some reflections about this writing occurred to me and they are a brief example of the size of the insecurity that this whole process can generate:

Oh if my lyrics flowed like the air coming out of the trumpet of John Coltrane or Miles Davis! Ah, what a beautiful song it would be, huh... what a pretension of mine too, huh??? This swirling air that dances in my ears wildly and softly. Music! Music without lyrics but that says so much... music without a voice and yet it makes my vocal chords vibrate in a breath of comfort and calm. But it's not like that. I can't see a hand in front of me. I'm not sure where I'm going and it scares me... What will I find? I don't know what will come out of my writing or when it will come out. Do I need to know? Or is it one more procrastinating boycott, this wanting to see what one cannot?

(NASCIMENTO, Raquel. excerpt from a personal diary of a research stay in Leipzig)

Still, with so many insecurities in writing and in the face of a pandemic that has turned everything that was so close and accessible, distant, it is a reality to say that the technical knowledge acquired in Leipzig with the professors and fellow researchers took my research to another level, since understanding the effects of a translation in the German literary system while in Germany turned on lights for me that would never have been turned on being in Brazil. From visiting the book publishers that still exist, to interviewing translators of Brazilian literature into German, Afro-German writers and discovering unpublished documents. The lights were turned on and illuminated many research paths, such as the semiotics of the covers of editions of the translation, questionnaires with test readers who were unaware of the work and the author, bibliographical research of researchers who focus on Latin literature -American and/or Brazilian in Germany and on the translation of works of Brazilian literature into German.

Therefore, I was thankful to be able to return to Brazil with a luggage full of new, intriguing and complementary information about Carolina Maria de Jesus and with the thesis that paratextual elements, such as covers and prefaces, can determine the understanding and reading of a translation, allowing it to identify and notice more or less its literary intensity. Above all, I was able to experience and identify some of the various ways of seeing and experiencing Carolina in Germany.

II. New ways for Linguistics

"The significance of discerning differing motivations of mutual language learners in China and Europe – A comparison between the Standard Chinese language (普通话) and selected European languages"

Alix Mercedes Natascha Neumeier [1]

Abstract

These abstract aims to explore and compare the motivations for mutual language acquisition of European languages and the Chinese language (Putonghua 普通话 , Standard Chinese). Understanding why individuals choose to learn a particular language is vital for language educators and policymakers to develop effective language learning strategies and improve their programs as well as to increase the number of language learners. Various motivations drive individuals to learn European languages. Not only for professional advancement and job opportunities that would otherwise not be available to the learner, but also for academic purposes, personal travels, and cultural exchanges:

While motivations for acquiring European languages often revolve around professional, academic, or cultural purposes, learning Chinese is commonly driven by economic opportunities stemming from China's prominence in global trade and commerce. Consequently, different pedagogical approaches and strategies may be required to effectively cater to learners of diverse motivations and goals. Motivators in language learning might differ in terms of individual or collective motivations for Western or Asian, e.g., Chinese learners.

Understanding these motivations for learning specific languages equips language educators and policymakers with the ability to design relevant curricula, to implement effective teaching methodologies, and provide suitable resources. By recognizing and highlighting the motivations behind language acquisition, learners can be encouraged and supported, fostering a deeper appreciation for different languages and cultures. This might also affect improvement of the relationships between the concerned countries on a lower or higher level. Furthermore, comparing the motivations between European languages and the Chinese language allows for a comprehensive understanding of the diverse factors influencing language learning decisions and paves the way for further research and exploration in this field.

Keywords: Motivations, Language acquisition, European languages, Chinese language, Effective language learning strategies

1. Significance of the Chinese language and European languages

This essay is going to examine differing motivations for mutual language acquirement of the Chinese language (Standard Chinese, Putonghua 普通话) as well as of other European languages, specifically the Indo-European languages – the Germanic and Romance languages – English, German, French, Spanish and Portuguese. Following a history of conquering and subsequently subjugating other countries under the yoke of colonialism, the prevalence for the English, the French and the Spanish language has been developed so thoroughly that these

[1] Alix Mercedes Natascha Neumeier is a Master Student of Chinese Studies at the University of Trier. Her submission was advised by Dr. LIU Huiru (刘慧儒)

languages have managed to persist until today. Aside from the Anglocentrism in the world community not only limited to but also including politics and economics, not only the English language, but also the French language, both as wide-spread languages have historically been important tools in communicating and bartering around the world. These languages, as well as Spanish and Portuguese, have played a major role in connecting countries and increasing world trade and economic relations.

The significance of the Chinese language, *Putonghua* 普通话, which is internationally known as Standard Chinese (*Xiandai biaozhun Hanyu* 现代标准汉语) or Mandarin[2] , the official language of the People´s Republic of China, has grown significantly in the last few decades. With the emergence of the new Belt-and-Road Initiative, the New Silk Road, China has positioned itself as the pioneer of a new globalization[3].

Language acquisition has become more accessible to people through the emergence of a new digital age and the increasing availability of the internet and its resources to a larger amount of the world population. Comparing the different motivations of language learners living in different countries while learning different languages is essential for further development of language programs and improved language proficiency worldwide. Understanding the motivations and the connected success rates in subsequent studying is another important factor in improving language acquisition and mutual recognition and appreciation. It will prove useful for a deeper understanding of one another, including mutual learning strategies and more efficient study methods.

2.   The importance of differing motivations in acquiring a foreign language

Motivations in language learning play a significant part in the rate of success the learner will have in acquiring the language. In language teaching and learning not only the language itself is taught, but also the culture, as it is an equally important part of the learning process. In the intercultural orientational process of learning a new language and the course of understanding the differences and similarities between the foreign and native language, students may obtain their individual perspectives. They are learning to switch between various perspectives of the native and target language in both a linguistic and cultural context. Throughout this process, the students learn about culture by understanding it as more than just facts about different people and their customs. More importantly, culture is now seen as the context through which people exchange meaning and understanding in communication with others, and how they understand their own social world[4]. For this reason, knowing and understanding language learners´ motivations is crucial to their development and further involvement with the language and culture of their choice.

2.1. The influences of Standard Chinese in Europe

The Standard Chinese language in Europe

Chinese is one of the United Nations´ official languages next to Arabic, English, French, Russian and Spanish. As of 2023 the most spoken languages worldwide are as follows: English with its status as the most spoken language in the world (1,456 billion), closely followed by (Standard) Chinese (1,138 billion), and Hindi (609.5 million), Spanish (559.1 mil) and French (309.8 mil).[5]

---

[2] The term "Mandarin" describes a group of Sinitic dialects, belonging to the Sino-Tibetan language family.

[3] Wolfram Elsner, *Das chinesische Jahrhundert: Die Nummer eins ist anders* (Frankfurt am Main: Westend-Verlag, 2020), chap. 10, 316

[4] Angela Scarino, "Assessing Intercultural Capability in Learning Languages: A Renewed Understanding of Language, Culture, Learning, and the Nature of Assessment" *The Modern Language Journal* 94, no. 2 (2010): 324–29. http://www.jstor.org/stable/40856136: 324.

[5] The most spoken languages worldwide 2023", Statista, Statista Research Department, last modified June 16, 2023, https://www.statista.com/statistics/266808/the-most-spoken-languages-worldwide/.

English and French are the working languages of the United Nations Secretariat as they have a significant historical background. Chinese is not only spoken in Mainland China, Hong Kong (China S.A.R.), Macau (China S.A.R.) and Taiwan, but also in Singapore, Malaysia, and Tibet. There is also a high concentration of Chinese populations living in other countries, as the United States, Canada, or the United Kingdom.[6]

The "Law on the Standard Spoken and Written Chinese Language of the People´s Republic of China" mandates the promotion of Standard Chinese by the Chinese government, though it also permits the use of ethnic minorities´ languages. Around 70% of people in Mainland China can speak Standard Chinese with only 10% having acquired fluency. Over one-fifth of the global population uses Standard Chinese as their native language, approximating to over one billion Chinese speakers. The Chinese language has also greatly influenced other Asian languages and characters like the Japanese, Korean or Vietnamese language.[7]

Knowledge of the Chinese language in Europe is not as widespread as it is in Asia. The highest percentage of people who speak Chinese as a native language or as a foreign language in Europe belongs to the UK with 0.52%. The UK is followed by Malta (0.52%), Austria (0.36%), Belgium (0.35%), Germany (0.32%), France (0.26%), Ireland (0.22%) and Portugal (0.2%). The other European countries reach only 0.14% or less, including Spain with 0.1%.[8]

2.2.   The influences of European languages in the People´s Republic of China

Over the last few years, Europe has become an immensely popular destination for student exchanges, holiday trips, and work opportunities for Chinese people, especially university students. The most favored European countries for student exchanges include Germany, Italy, France, the UK, Spain, and Portugal.[9]

The most studied European language in China is English. It is a mandatory school subject and continues to be in high demand in both academic and professional settings like the workplace. French is second in popularity which stems mostly from its cultural influence as a language of culture, concerning art and fashion, and its status in international diplomacy. As it is an optional language subject in many Chinese schools and universities, the interest in French as a secondary language continuously grows. Germany´s reputation as a country of higher education and job opportunities is attractive to Chinese students and has subsequently gained popularity in recent years. As a result, plenty of Chinese education institutions offer German language programs catering to this increasing demand. Another European language which is becoming progressively popular, is Spanish. Multiple Spanish-speaking countries are growing in the business and tourism sectors which heightens the interest rate of Chinese people interested in learning the Spanish language. Because of this, Chinese universities and language institutes offer Spanish language courses and exchange programs with universities from Spanish speaking countries.

---

[6] "Chinese Speaking Countries 2023", World Population Review, accessed August 30, 2023, https://worldpopulationreview.com/country-rankings/chinese-speaking-countries.

[7] Law on the Standard Spoken and Written Chinese Language of the People´s Republic of China," Ministry of Education of the People´s Republic of China, moe.gov.cn, last modified July 21, 2009, http://en.moe.gov.cn/Resources/Laws_and_Policies/201506/t20150626_191388.html.

[8] "Chinese language knowledge in Europe," Language Knowledge, accessed August 30, 2023, https://www.languageknowledge.eu/languages/chinese.

[9] "2023 年欧洲最受欢迎的九大留学城市" (The nine most popular cities for studying abroad in Europe in 2023), Baidu, Admissions Agency Network, Official Xinyuyuan Information Technology Account, Wuhan, Hubei, last modified December 08, 2022, https://baijiahao.baidu.com/s?id=1751635079134835334.

2.2.1. Germanic languages: English and German

The umbrella term of Indo-European languages includes the Germanic and Romance languages: English, as an Anglo-Frisian language as well as German are both considered as Germanic languages with a wide reach in terms of history and region.

English, being the lingua franca of global communication, is often acquired for professional advancement, academic purposes, personal travel, and cultural exchange. Before Brexit, the United Kingdom (UK) was an essential part of the European Union (EU) and the cultural sphere of the European community. The process of Brexit began officially with the United Kingdom European Union membership referendum in 2016 and ended with the withdrawal of the UK from the EU in 2020. With the official parting of the UK from the European Union and the European Single Market, the cultural atmosphere in Europe has changed. Yet, it still is as of 2022 with 96% by far the most studied foreign language at the upper general education level in the European Union. Spanish (27%), French (22%), and German (21%) are ranked as other popular languages.[10]

As Germany is one of the largest economies in the European Union and has strong trade relations with China, the German language is sought after for its job opportunities in multinational companies and academic pursuits. Learning German can provide Chinese learners with these opportunities and make it possible for them to explore Germany´s rich cultural heritage. The similar sentence and grammar structure compared to Chinese, opposed to other languages as French or English, makes the language especially attractive to Chinese learners.

2.2.2. Romance languages: French, Spanish, and Portuguese

Other lingua francas include Chinese, Arabic, French, Spanish and Russian. French and Spanish, as the two languages belonging to the Indo-European language family, have managed to retain their relevance as a lingua franca not only on the European continent but also on other continents due to a history of conquests and colonization. French and Spanish are two of the most common and well-known Romance languages, as well as Portuguese, which has also played an important role in the historic context of colonization. As already mentioned, these countries and therefore their languages have a certain appeal to the Chinese population because of their vastly different landscapes and cultural peculiarities. French attracts learners due to its cultural prestige, global influence, and potential career prospects. Spanish provides a gateway to diverse cultures in Latin America and is valuable for travel, business, and cultural appreciation. Portuguese offers a similar appeal, especially for individuals interested in Brazil and its emerging economic market.

2.2.3. Motivations for Chinese language acquirement

Contrastingly, the motivations underlying the acquisition of the Chinese language are distinct. Chinese is the most widely spoken language in the world, with China's rapidly growing global influence creating numerous economic opportunities. Individuals seeking to participate in international trade, business ventures, or to cooperate with Chinese companies are motivated to learn the language. Additionally, academic and research purposes, as well as cultural curiosity, attract learners to explore the Chinese language, culture, and history.

---

[10] What languages are studied the most in the EU?" Eurostat, ec.europa.eu/Eurostat, last modified September 23, 2022, https://ec.europa.eu/eurostat/web/products-eurostat-news/-/ddn-20220923-1.

2.3. Motivations for language acquisition in Asian and European countries

2.3.1. Comparison of motivations in language learners – differences and similarities Comparisons in motivations concerning the Chinese language and European languages, as English or German are important in distinguishing commonalities in the learner´s progress and eventual success.

2.3.2. English speakers studying Chinese

Native English speakers studying Chinese on an advanced level who had taken a Modern Language Aptitude Test and a phonological working memory test have been questioned on their motivation and strategy uses. Their learning had proven to be impacted most by aptitude, strategy use, and motivation, though these methods were different in how well they were able to predict their individual listening, reading, and speaking skills in the language.[11] Naturally, achieving advanced proficiency in a foreign language as an adult learner requires the convergence of multiple factors. These include receiving quality instruction, having frequent chances for various forms of output, and maintaining high levels of motivation. Additionally, exposure to cultural insights that elucidate the language's pragmatics, adopting effective language learning strategies, and experiencing tangible rewards are essential for successful language acquisition.[12]

2.3.3. Chinese speakers studying English

Focusing on language learning motivation in a Chinese cultural setting, where English study is mandatory for many students, a survey was conducted in Taiwan, assessing motivation orientation, expectancy, and self-evaluated skill. These findings revealed that expectancy served as an intervening construct between motivation orientations and self-evaluated skill. Required motivation was the strongest predictor of expectancy, while integrative motivation did not play a significant role.[12] [13]The cultural norm of the learning process in China is heavily focused on exams, emphasizing standardized requirements while de-emphasizing the individual.[14] The Chinese Imperative motivator plays a big role in the students´ motivation. Motivation constructs might need to be reconsidered in non-Western cultural settings for effective teaching practices. To uncover the unique motivators in different cultures, researchers must consider their own subjective perspectives and internalized cultural values. This can be achieved through a localized, scientific, research-based approach that is open to new potential motivators. Validity should be measured regardless of its validity in other cultural settings[15].

3. Value of understanding differing motivations in language learning

In general, the motivators of learners in Western and Asian countries differ, as they are based on their respective individual and collective societies. For future language learning opportunities and cooperation on an intercultural and global basis, it is essential to strive for a mutual understanding of motivators which might influence the process of learning. Here, especially the reputation of countries or the cultural associations with a certain language are of high importance. Eventually the economic potential of multilingualism should be taken into account.

---

[11] Paula Winke, "An Investigation Into Second Language Aptitude for Advanced Chinese Language Learning.," *The Modern Language Journal* 97, no. 1 (2013): 109–30, http://www.jstor.org/stable/23361741, 109.

[12] Winke, "An Investigation Into Second Language Aptitude for Advanced Chinese Language Learning, 122-123

[13] Chen, Judy F., Clyde A. Warden, and Huo-Tsan Chang, "Motivators That Do Not Motivate: The Case of Chinese EFL Learners and the Influence of Culture on Motivation." *TESOL Quarterly* 39, no. 4 (2005): 609–33, https://doi.org/10.2307/3588524, 609.

[14] Chen, Judy F., Clyde A. Warden, and Huo-Tsan Chang, "Motivators That Do Not Motivate: The Case of Chinese EFL Learners and the Influence of Culture on Motivation." *TESOL Quarterly* 39, no. 4 (2005): 609–33, https://doi.org/10.2307/3588524, 612.

[15] Chen, et al. "Motivators That Do Not Motivate: The Case of Chinese EFL Learners and the Influence of Culture on Motivation.," 626

References

Baidu. "2023 年欧洲最受欢迎的九大留学城市 " (The nine most popular cities for studying abroad in Europe in 2023), Admissions Agency Network, Official Xinyuyuan Information Technology Account, Wuhan, Hubei. Last modified December 08, 2022. https://baijiahao.baidu.com/s?id=1751635079134835334.

Chen, Judy F., Clyde A. Warden, and Huo-Tsan Chang. "Motivators That Do Not Motivate: The Case of Chinese EFL Learners and the Influence of Culture on Motivation." *TESOL Quarterly* 39, no. 4 (2005): 609–33. https://doi.org/10.2307/3588524.

Elsner, Wolfram. *Das chinesische Jahrhundert: Die Nummer eins ist anders*. Frankfurt am

Main: Westend-Verlag, 2020. Kindle.

Eurostat. "What languages are studied the most in the EU?" Last modified September 23, 2022. ec.europa.eu/eurostat, https://ec.europa.eu/eurostat/web/products-eurostat-news/-/ddn-20220923-1.

Language Knowledge. "Chinese language knowledge in Europe." Accessed August 30,

2023. https://www.languageknowledge.eu/languages/chinese.

Ministry of Education of the People´s Republic of China. "Law on the Standard Spoken and Written Chinese Language of the People´s Republic of China." moe.gov.cn. Last modified July 21, 2009. http://en.moe.gov.cn/Resources/Laws_and_Policies/201506/t20150626_191388.html.

Scarino, Angela. "Assessing Intercultural Capability in Learning Languages: A Renewed

Understanding of Language, Culture, Learning, and the Nature of Assessment." *The Modern Language Journal* 94, no. 2 (2010): 324–29. http://www.jstor.org/stable/40856136.

Statista. "The most spoken languages worldwide 2023", Statista Research Department. Last modified June 16, 2023. https://www.statista.com/statistics/266808/the-most-spoken-languages-worldwide/.

Winke, Paula. "An Investigation Into Second Language Aptitude for Advanced Chinese

Language Learning." *The Modern Language Journal* 97, no. 1 (2013): 109–30. http://www.jstor.org/stable/23361741.

World Population Review. (An interactive visualisation of language knowledge in Europe, based on the latest Europe-wide survey of languages in Europe by the European Commission.) "Chinese Speaking Countries 2023". Accessed August 30, 2023. https://worldpopulationreview.com/country-rankings/chinese-speaking-countries.

Phase Research of a Comparative Study on Motivation in Foreign-Language Learning of Chinese and International College Students

LIANG Pei-yu (梁沛愉)[1]

Abstract

Motivation in foreign language learning is closely related to language achievement and enhancement of language acquisition. Analyzing motivation in foreign-language learning of college students with distinct cultural backgrounds will help understand the different expectations of language learning and provide the correct learning strategies. This research explores the motivation in foreign-language learning of Chinese and international college students based on Gardner's socio-educational model, Dörnyei's ought to L2 self and learning experience theory and a questionnaire adapted from Gardner's Attitude/Motivation Test Battery (AMTB), in which 32 Chinese students and 6 international students participated. Three main conclusions can be drawn from the result: Both Chinese and international students have combined motivation; international students have a stronger ought to L2 self motivation; and the dimension of instrumental motivation of the two groups differ from each other.

Keyword: Motivation; Language learning; Chinese and international college students

Introduction

Comparative studies on motivation in foreign or second language learning arose in 1990s and are still a conspicuous topic. Motivation is the one most important factor involved in a person's learning of a foreign language (Nida. 1956), and it has been proved that geographical settings might affect motivation (Kormos & Csizer, 2008). Therefore, it is deserving and feasible to compare the motivation in foreign-language learning of different groups with distinct cultural backgrounds. Comparing and analyzing motivation in foreign-language learning of Chinese and international college students contributes to the investigating general motivation in foreign-language learning and enhancing of teaching and learning methods. However, comparative studies on motivation in foreign-language learning of Chinese and international college students still have to be conducted.

This research phase tests 32 Chinese college students and 6 international students with a questionnaire based on Gardner's socio-educational model and AMTB, which also combined with Dornyei's ought to L2 self and learning experience. The paper's research is guided by the question: *What are the similarities and differences between the two groups' motivation in foreign-language learning?*

---

[1] Liang Peiyu (梁沛愉) is a student for German Studies at the Northwestern Polytechnical University Xi'an(PRC) (西北工业大学).
This submission was advised by Dr. Li Jie (李洁) Associate Professor at the Northwestern Polytechnical University Xi'an(PRC)

RESEARCH PROCESS

Method

The research adopts two theories in motivation in foreign-language learning, Gardner's socio-educational model, which often employs Attitude/Motivation Test Battery to test the components, and Dörnyei's Motivational Self System. Some components of the two theories are excluded basically because these components are not object and clear enough to be tested and are not suitable for research on comparing motivation in foreign-language learning of two groups with different cultural backgrounds.

The socio-educational model was raised by Gardner in 1974. The model includes integrative motivation, which refers to learners' interests in target languages and their culture and desire to communicate with target languages and instrumental motivation, which refers to utilitarian benefits such as higher salaries. The socio-educational model has been an essential motivation model and have been proved to be reliable and valid (Masgoret & Gardner, 2003).

Gardner and Lambert (1972) raised the Attitude/Motivation Test Battery (AMTB) to detect each component of motivation in the socio-educational model. AMTB, which has already proven its validity (Gardner, 1985), includes four main components, integrativeness, attitudes toward the learning situation, motivation, and situational anxiety. Integrativeness is assessed by three scales, attitudes toward the language group, interest in foreign language, and an integrative orientation of language study. Attitudes toward the learning situation mainly refer to the attitudes toward the teacher and the attitudes toward the course. Motivation combines the learner's attitudes, aspirations, and effort with respect to concerning learning the language (Gardner, 1985). The component is excluded because it might have a different definition and is too subject and vague to be measured.

While Gardner's socio-educational model mainly focuses on motivation among learner-groups with remarkably different cultural backgrounds, Dörnyei's Motivational Self System (2009) defines an individual's motivation in foreign language learning. The Motivational Self System has three categories, the ideal L2 self, which refers to learner's imagination and expects of proficiency and characteristics in language acquisition, ought to L2 self and L2 learning experience, that is, learner's relationship or previous experience with the target language. Ought to L2 focuses on preventing potential external pressures and risks and the obligation to learn foreign languages. In this research, "ideal L2 self" is excluded, considering that this category is too subject and often used to measure individual's motivation in foreign-language learning.

Notably, some authors in mainland China advocate "certificate motivation," considering that for many Chinese college students' certificate in English levels is strongly associated with the future job-hunting process and even graduation from college (Gao, 2013). Certificate motivation has some similarities with Dönryei's ought to L2 self. Thus, the questionnaire includes the category "ought to L2 self". Furthermore, since all the participants have acquired at least one foreign language and have taken language courses, learning experience is also included. Motivational Self System has significantly enhanced understanding of the components and dynamics of language learning motivation, especially concerning intended effort (Nagle, 2020).

Based on the above, this research questionnaire contains components and motivations of both Gardner's socio-educational model and Dornyei's Motivational Self System. The evaluation adapts the Likert Scale, ranging from strongly agree, slightly agree, neutral, slightly disagree, to strongly disagree.

Subject

During this phase, 32 Chinese college students and 6 international college students were investigated. All of them have acquired at least one foreign language and are undergraduates. Among the 32 Chinese participants, 17 are first-year students, 8 are sophomore-year, and 7 are junior-year. The international sample consists of 1 first-year student, 2 sophomores, and 3 seniors.

RESULT AND DISCUSSION

The corresponding results are reported in Table 1. The results demonstrate that Chinese college students have combined motivations involving all categories. Meanwhile, the result highlights a relative favor in language learning. Although, according to the result, fewer Chinese college students claim they have culture-integrative motivation, they consider it when learning foreign languages. Indeed, the results show that five out of the seven questions reported 0.00% "strongly disagree." Moreover, most Chinese college students believe that learning a foreign language is useful in job-hunting and future careers, revealing a tendency for instrumental motivation.

Table 1   **Results of Chinese Sample of Motivation in foreign language learning**

Chinese Sample						
Category	Question	Strongly agree	Slightly agree	Neutral	Slightly disagree	Strongly disagree
Culture Integrative Motivation	meet and converse with more and varied people	28.12%	46.88%	15.62%	9.38%	0.00%
	have many foreign language native-speaking friends	25.00%	46.88%	25.00%	3.12%	0.00%
	understand and appreciate the lifestyles in other countries	28.12%	43.75%	21.88%	3.12%	3.12%
	try to learn the language when staying abroad	59.38%	40.62%	0.00%	0.00%	0.00%
	communicate with people who speak a foreign language	28.12%	28.12%	28.12%	0.00%	0.00%
	have a good impression of target language speakers	3.12%	40.62%	40.62%	9.38%	6.25%
	be interested in the culture of the target language	28.12%	28.12%	28.12%	0.00%	0.00%
Interest in language learning	be willing to work hard to learn foreign languages well	28.12%	56.25%	9.38%	6.25%	0.00%
	be willing to learn many foreign languages	28.12%	37.50%	31.25%	0.00%	3.12%
	be willing to understand more complex aspects of languages	21.88%	50.00%	18.75%	6.25%	3.12%
	have a desire to study foreign languages	12.50%	53.12%	15.62%	12.50%	6.25%
	like the target language	25.00%	53.12%	3.12%	12.50%	6.25%
Learning experience	like the foreign language teachers	18.75%	40.62%	25.00%	6.25%	9.38%
	find the language course	12.50%	34.38%	31.38%	9.38%	9.38%

Category	Question					
Learning experience	like the foreign language teachers	18.75%	40.62%	25.00%	6.25%	9.38%
	find the language course interesting	12.50%	34.38%	34.38%	9.38%	9.38%
	like the learning materials	25.00%	53.12%	3.12%	12.50%	6.25%
Instrumental Motivation	need foreign language for career	25.00%	62.50%	6.25%	3.12%	3.12%
	to be more educated	15.62%	21.88%	43.75%	9.38%	9.38%
	believe foreign language is useful in job hunting	21.88%	56.25%	6.25%	3.12%	3.12%
	believe learning a language could win respect	6.25%	31.25%	40.62%	9.38%	12.50%
Ought to L2 self	to pass the exam	15.62%	28.12%	25.00%	21.88%	9.38%
	to obtain a graduation certificate.	15.62%	34.38%	28.12%	15.62%	6.25%
	Learn a foreign language because of parents' request	3.12%	9.38%	21.88%	40.62%	25.00%
	Learn a foreign language because of the college's requirement	9.38%	15.62%	50.00%	21.88%	3.12%

The results of the international students, reported in Table 2, also indicate a combined motivation and a strong tendency of culture integrative motivation. It must be underlined that very few international college students claim they "strongly agree" with interest in language learning. Additionally, international students have stronger ought to L2 self-motivation, and all samples agree that they learn a foreign language to pass the exam or obtain a graduation certificate.

Table 2   Results of Foreign Sample of Motivation in foreign language learning

Foreign Sample						
Category	Question	Strongly agree	Slightly agree	Neutral	Slightly disagree	Strongly disagree
Culture Integrative Motivation	meet and converse with more and varied people	33.33%	66.67%	0.00%	0.00%	0.00%
	have many foreign language native-speaking friends	33.33%	50.00%	16.67%	0.00%	0.00%
	understand and appreciate the lifestyles in other countries	33.33%	33.33%	16.67%	16.67%	0.00%
	try to learn the language when staying abroad	50.00%	50.00%	0.00%	0.00%	0.00%
	communicate with people who speak a foreign language	33.33%	50.00%	16.67%	0.00%	0.00%
	have a good impression of target language speakers	16.67%	50.00%	16.67%	16.67%	0.00%
	be interested in the culture of the target language	0.00%	50.00%	50.00%	0.00%	0.00%
Interest in language learning	be willing to work hard to learn foreign languages well	16.67%	66.67%	16.67%	0.00%	0.00%
	be willing to learn many foreign languages	0.00%	83.33%	16.67%	0.00%	0.00%
	be willing to understand more complex aspects of languages	0.00%	50.00%	16.67%	16.67%	16.67%

	have a desire to study foreign languages	0.00%	83.33%	16.67%	0.00%	0.00%
	like the target language	0.00%	83.33%	0.00%	16.67%	0.00%
Learning experience	like the foreign language teachers	0.00%	66.67%	16.67%	16.67%	0.00%
	find the language course interesting	16.67%	50.00%	16.67%	16.67%	0.00%
	like the learning materials	16.67%	50.00%	16.67%	16.67%	0.00%
Instrumental Motivation	need foreign language for career	33.33%	50.00%	16.67%	0.00%	0.00%
	to be more educated	16.67%	83.33%	0.00%	0.00%	0.00%
	believe foreign language is useful in job hunting	50.00%	50.00%	0.00%	0.00%	0.00%
	believe learning a language could win respect	16.67%	50.00%	16.67%	16.67%	0.00%
Ought to L2 self	to pass the exam	33.33%	66.67%	0.00%	0.00%	0.00%
	to obtain a graduation certificate.	16.67%	83.33%	0.00%	0.00%	0.00%
	learn a foreign language because of parents' request	0.00%	66.67%	0.00%	0.00%	33.33%
	Learn a foreign language because of the college's requirement	16.67%	50.00%	0.00%	33.33%	0.00%

Based on the above results it can be concluded that it has both similarities and differences between the two groups' motivation in foreign-language learning. Both Chinese and international college students have combined motivation. International college students have however stronger ought to L2 motivation and are eager to be more educated and obtain graduation certificate.

CONCLUSION

This paper studies the motivation in foreign-language learning of Chinese and international college students. The corresponding results lead to three major conclusions. First, Chinese, and international college students demonstrate a combined motivation, although each portion might vary. Second, international college students have stronger ought to L2 self. Finally, although Chinese and international college students have relatively apparent instrumental motivation, Chinese students are more declined to job hunting and future career, while international students tend to learn foreign languages because they wish to be more educated.

This research reveals similarities and differences between the motivation of Chinese and international college students in foreign-language learning. However, the motivation in these two student groups remains to be tested. The limitation of this research is that the data size is relatively small and deficient, particularly the foreign data samples. Due to this limitation, the conclusions must be further verified, posing a future research direction.

References

An Q., Zhang X. (2022). Exploring Motivation Difference in Foreign Language Learning among Chinese, American and British University Students, *Journal of PLA University of Foreign Languages, 45(5)*, pp. 68-76

Dörnyei Z. (1990). Conceptualizing Motivation in Foreign-Language Learning, *Language Learning, 40(1)*, pp. 45-78 Gao Y. *et al.* (2003). Motivation Types of Chinese College Undergraduates, *Modern Foreign Languages (Quarterly),*

26(1), pp. 28-38

Gardner R.C., Smythe P. C., Clément R. (1979). Intensive Second Language Study of Attitudes, Motivation and Language Proficiency, *Language Learning, 29(2)*, pp. 305-320

Gardner R. C., Lalonde R. N., Moorcroft R. (1985). The Roles of Attitude and Motivation in Second Language Learning: Correlations and Experimental Considerations, *Language Learning, 35(2)*, pp. 207-227

Gardner R. C., MacIntyre P. D. (1993). On the Measurement of Affective Variables in Second Language Learning, *Language Learning, 43(2)*, pp. 157-194

Gu F. (2013). *Research on Adjustment Strategies of English Certificate Motivation of College Students.* Master's thesis, Sichuan International Studies University, Chongqing, P. R. China

Kormos J., Csizér K. (2008). Age-Related Differences in the Motivation of Learning English as a Foreign Language:

Attitudes, Selves, and Motivated Learning Behavior, *Language Learning, 58(2)*, pp. 327-355

Masgoret A.-M., Gardner R. C. (2003). Attitudes, Motivation and Second Language Learning: A Meta-Analysis of Studies Conducted by Gardner and Associates, *Language Learning, 53(1)*, pp. 123-163

Nagle C. (2020). Using Expectancy Value Theory to understand motivation, persistence, and achievement in university - level foreign language learning, *Foreign Language Annals, 54(4)*, pp. 1238-1256. doi:10.1111/flan.12569

Nida E. (1956). Motivation in Second Language Learning, *Language Learning, 7(3-4)*, pp. 11-16

III. Mutual Learning between Europe and China

A Comparative Research between German and Chinese preschool Education

ZHANG Shurui (张淑蕊)[1]

Abstract

German preschool education (PE) differs from Chinese PE in many facets. Comparing PE between Germany and China in history development process, aims and curriculum, and organization and form helps gain some experiences from the perspectives of aims, organization, and the cooperation between family and kindergarten in the process of the transformation of Chinese PE.

Keywords: preschool education; Germany; China; aims and curriculum; organization and form

INTRODUCTION

The experiences of children in early childhood play a crucial role in their whole process of growing up. Therefore, the development of PE is not supposed to be overlooked. Until now, Chinese PE has made great progress in many aspects. Especially for the recent years the popularization of related institutions, higher quality of teaching staff and more reasonable curricula have to be mentioned. However, there are still many unsolved issues and defects which to some degree hamper the further advance of the preschool education system in China. In comparison Germany has a long history of PE and up to now, it has formed a relatively perfect system. This study consists of two sections. In the first section, this study compares the German and Chinese PE in three facets, namely, the historical development process, aims and curriculum, organization, and form. In the second section, based on the first one, the experiences of German PE will be analyzed, that are worthy learning for China. In this way, more possibilities of the development can be explored, that Chinese PE advances progressively.

ANALYSIS

The historical development process of PE

1. Germany

Before Renaissance, the pattern of PE in Germany mainly presented itself as family education. At the beginning of 19th century, the first of daycare centers appeared in Germany, which aimed to solve the issue of children in workers families, which were not equipped with the ability of education (Li, 2011). In 1837, Friedrich Froebel established an educational institution toward preschool children in Germany and he named it "Kindergarten" creating the first of its kind in history (Ma F. & Ma X., 2012).

---

[1] ZHANG Shurui (张淑蕊) is a Bachelor Student of German Studies at the Northwestern Polytechnical University (西北工业大学), Xi'an (PRC)

2. China

Likewise, in the Chinese ancient society, the family education predominated in the PE. 1903, behind the background of learning western countries' techniques and educational system, the first kindergarten of China was set up in Wuchang. In the 1920s, with the spread of more advanced educational theories in China, more preschool educational institutions reflecting these theories appeared. In 1951, PE was officially incorporated into the new evolving education system (Gu & Zhang, 2021). By contrast, specialized preschool educational institutions of Germany emerged earlier than China and the former formed a relatively mature theoretical structure, which has been studied by Chinese pedagogists for many times.

Aims and curriculum of PE

1. Germany

In Germany, the aims of PE are presented as the following six aspects: first, helping children form their points; second, encouraging children bravely express their views; third, making children be familiar with their surroundings; forth, cultivating children's ability of hand labor; fifth, doing some musical training, for example, singing and dance, to foster their rhythm; sixth, making children be acquainted with various rules of life, for example, the traffic rules. In line with these educational aims, the curriculum of German kindergarten comprised from games, life education, language, movement, rhythm and music education, image and labor education, truth and environment education, real life, and housekeeping education (Ma F. & Ma X., 2012).

2. China

In China, *Kindergarten Regulations* released in 1996 stipulated aims of Chinese PE: first, promoting the development of children's normal physical growth and coordinated body function; second, shaping favorable life and health habits, and the interest of participating in the sport exercises; thirdly, developing intelligence of children, enhancing the ability to rightly apply sensations and communicate through language, fostering the cognition of environment, salutary interests and preliminary handmade ability; fourth, making children form merits and cheerful character; fifth, cultivating children's preliminary ability to sense and display beauty. The curriculum of Chinese kindergarten aligns with these five aims: health, language, science, society, and art.

Taken together, German PE inclines to nurture children's ability of cognition, expression and adjusting to surroundings. Meanwhile, its curriculum presents the features of diversity, emphasizing practice, covering larger span, and behaving more specific. Contrary to Germany, Chinese PE tends to cultivate values and enhance intelligence of children. Therefore, associated curriculum is more theoretical and linked tightly to the knowledge of textbooks.

Organization and form of PE

1. The types of organization

(1) Germany

The preschool institutions features a wide diversity. On the whole, the preschool education system can be divided into four forms:

Kindergarten. This form is the most general in Germany as the main organization which provides children aged from 3 to 6 with education. According to different sponsors and educational methods, kindergartens can also be divided into three parts: public kindergarten, independent kindergarten, and private kindergarten (Zhou, 2017). According to the kinds of recruited children, kindergartens can be sorted into normal kindergarten, special kindergarten, accompanying kindergarten of school, which targets at some children, who meet the entrance age and whose physical and psychological development relatively lagging behind other children.

Children club or children store. Children clubs are mainly set up by churches or charity agencies; children stores were products of Students' Campaign in the 1960s in Germany, which paid more attention to the development of children's collective and social spirits (Zhou, 2017).

Preschool. Preschools fit in some children who do not reach the entrance age and whose psychological development has already met the demands of entrance.

Nursery. Nurseries are responsible for the children aged from 0 to 3, whose parents are occupied by their employment and do not have time to care for them.

(2) China

The preschool institutions consist of three parts: nurseries, kindergartens, and preschools. The object of nurseries is children younger than 3 and it takes educational method of the combination of health care and education. Kindergartens face to kids aged from 3 to 6, which is the most widespread form in China (Yang, 2019). Preschools of China differ from Germany, which recruit the children who age 5-6 and don't enter kindergartens.

2. The class's scale and the form of PE

(1) Germany

One of the characteristics of German PE is mixed-age classes. These classes are sorted according to children's difference in the capacity of cognition and behaviour, instead of age. Every class accommodates about 20 children. The activities of kindergarten are mostly carried out in the form of groups or individuals, and children have rights to decide the content and form of these activities (Ma F. & Ma X., 2012).

(2) China

In China, age is the most considered factor when kindergartens arrange the classes, which exceed generally 30 children. These activities are basically decided by teachers and in the collective form. Due to having more children in a single class, teachers face difficulties to focus on the growth and learning situation of every kid individually. Children have also less freedom in the selection of their activities
.

3. The cooperation between family and kindergarten

(1) Germany

Germany puts emphasis on the cooperation between family and kindergarten. The majority of kindergartens set up related institutions for the collaboration, which invite parents to take part in various activities and discuss the teaching plans at the start of every semester with them, so that parents are clear with the arrangements and activities of kindergartens. Furthermore, parents are encouraged to contribute by voluntary work in the kindergarten.

(2) China

In China, the cooperation between family and kindergarten barely stays formal or superficial and parents behave negatively during this process. Parents can also participate in some activities of kindergarten, in which teachers just introduce them their children's conditions, instead of discussing the teaching plans (Ma F. & Ma X., 2012).

Taken together, in the organization and form of PE, Germany provides a more diverse forms of preschool institutions and the scale of classes is smaller, which is more beneficial to pay attention to every child and to that children nurture their independence. Moreover, the cooperation between family and kindergarten is viewed as closer.

CONCLUSION

Concluding this essay, a comparison between the German and the Chinese preschool education system was conducted. By contrast, German PE has many aspects worthy to be affirmed and learned. In short, these experiences can be summarized to the following three points:

Make the aims of PE comprehensive

Through the discussion of differences of the aims of PE between Germany and China, it has been found that Germany attaches more importance to children's comprehensive development of the abilities of cognition, expression, adjusting to the environment and practice. Contrasting with Germany, China appears to stress more the increase of knowledge and intelligence. Therefore, properly enriching the aims of PE is an important action to promote the transformation of PE in China. Relevant departments should formulate and release new aims of PE, which promote the all-round development of children.

Make the organization and form of PE more flexible

German preschool institutions present the feature of diversity, which aim at different groups of children. China is also supposed to set up more kinds of institutions to meet diverse demands of children and parents, for example, establishing special kindergartens for disabled kids. Moreover, the scale of German kindergarten classes is relatively smaller, which to some degree does not apply in China because of Chinese larger population. Whereas Chinese kindergartens can focus more on the cultivation of the independence of every kid when they arrange curriculum for children.

Enrich the closeness between family and kindergarten

Kindergartens don not just belong to children and teachers, and parents, as the first teachers in the process of the growth of their children, should also deeper engage in the work of kindergartens. Enriching the closeness between family kindergarten makes parents more acquainted with the performance of kids in the kindergarten, so that they can adjust their educational methods for the time at home. It is also more convenient for parents to offer their suggestions on the teaching plans of kindergarten and can set more their mind at rest. Chinese kindergarten should also provide more opportunities and approaches with parents to take part in the work of them, which effectively facilitates the collaboration between the family and kindergarten.

In conclusion, the German preschool system provides China some valued experiences, which need to be put further into practice. The first thing that should be done is to enrich mutual communication of Chinese and German kindergartens and other preschool institutions. Nowadays, in China, there aren't so many projects or activities about it. Promoting official and civil communication of Chinese and German preschool educators will make it clearer for Chinese educators what they should notice, when they learn from those experiences and merge them into the Chinese preschool system. Although there is still a long way to go, Chinese kindergartens featured with diverse nurturing aims, flexible organization and form, and harmonious interactions between family and kindergarten are worthy being expected.

REFERENCE

Li, G. (2011):Deguo Xueqianjiaoyu Jiankuang [Overview of German Preschool Education] Basic Education Review, 2011(15), 27-28.

Ma, F.& Ma, X. (2012):Zhongguo Deguo Xueqianjiaoyu Bijiao Ji Qishi [Comparison and Enlightenment of Preschool Education in China and Germany] Journal of Kaili University, 30(01), 151-154.

Zhou, X. (2017):Deguo Xueqianjiaoyu Tese Jidui Woguo De Qishi [Characteristics of German Preschool Education and its Enlightenments to China] Modern Communication, 2017(08), 168-169.

Yang, M. (2019):Zhongguo He Deguo Xueqianjiaoyu Zhidu Bijiao [Comparison of Preschool Education System between China and Germany] Modern Communication, 2019(18), 149-150.

Gu, G.& Zhang, M. (2021):Zhongguogongchandang Fazhan Xueqianjiaoyu De Bainian Licheng, Chengjiu Ji Jingyan [The History, Achievements and Experience of the Communist Party of China in Developing Preschool Education] Theory and Practice of Education, 2021(31), 29-35.

Comparative Study of German Undergraduate German Language Programs in China and Germany

ZHOU Yuchen (周禹辰)[1]

Abstract

In this article, the author takes the perspective of a scholar during her study in Germany to provide a brief comparative study of German and Chinese universities in the undergraduate German language programs. Drawing from a thorough review of prior research by various experts and combining it with personal experiences, the article contrasts the characteristics of German and Chinese universities in terms of the education system, course selection progress and study content. The aim of this research is to offer practical and feasible suggestions as well as insights to Chinese students studying in Germany and German students studying in China.

Keywords: Education System, Comparative Study in China and Germany, German Language Programs

Introduction

1.1 The globalized world and its impact on ID education

This article will use a combination of literature review and practical research to discuss the similarities and differences between Chinese and German universities in their undergraduate programs for German language majors. Subsequently, it will probe deeply into the distinctive features of the respective higher education systems, curriculum structures, and study contents in China and Germany. Furthermore, the article aims to explore developmental trends in this field, with the intention of providing insights and suggestions for both Chinese students studying in Germany and German students studying in China. The motivation of this essay to facilitate a deeper and more meaningful cultural exchange between the two countries, enhancing a more profound mutual learning process.

1) <u>Review of Domestic and International Literature</u>

Although there is a preference among scholars for comparative topics concerning the development of higher education in China and Germany, there is a scarcity of literature closely related to the subject matter of this paper. In this research topic, there is a lack of Chinese-language literature. Firstly, there is a tendency to opt for a comparison of science, technology, engineering disciplines such as mathematics, physics, chemistry, and biology, rather than German language studies (Jiang&Liu, 2015), when it comes to professional selection. Secondly, discussions around higher education often contrast with secondary vocational education research

---

[1] *ZHOU Yuchen (周禹辰)* is a Master student at the Albert-Ludwigs-University Freiburg Germany. Besides that, she has supported the preparation and implementation of this project as a scientific assistant. This submission was advised by Dr. LI Jie (李洁) Associate Professor at the Northwestern Polytechnical University Xi'an (PRC)

or focus on applied universities in Germany (Hu, 2016), or even studies related to early childhood education (He et al., 2012). Direct comparisons solely within the realm of higher education institutions are relatively rare. Lastly, aspiring students who wish to study abroad lack official channels to succinctly and comprehensively understand the current status of universities in China and Germany.

German-language literature, in contrast, tends to focus more on the development of intercultural German as a foreign language in China. While there are scholars who have researched the current situation and future prospects of German language majors in China (Szurawitzki, 2019), as well as the teaching qualifications of German language instructors in Chinese universities (Liu et al., 2019), a greater proportion still consists of Chinese scholars using German to introduce German language programs in China. For instance, the expansion of German language majors across various universities in China has been discussed (Wang, 2013). The next chapters will elaborate on that with insights into German as Chinese academic systems.

2)   A Comparative Analysis of Undergraduate German Language Programs in China and Germany: A Case Study of the University of Freiburg and Beijing International Studies University

In this chapter, the author will conduct a comparative analysis based on subjective experience, objective data, and existing literature. Drawing from the author's academic journey – studying at Beijing International Studies University from 2015 to 2017 in China, and subsequently attending the University of Freiburg in Germany from 2017 to 2021 – this chapter aims to provide a comprehensive comparison. It will primarily focus on three aspects: program duration and specialization options, curriculum structure and organization, and study content.

2.1 Program Duration and Specialization Options

In general, undergraduate studies in China typically span four years, while in Germany, the theoretically shortest duration is three years, though the essence is largely similar. During the author's attendance at a certain university in Beijing, the specific study time was also three years, with the fourth year predominantly dedicated to internships and thesis writing, and fewer specialized courses. The three-year duration in Germany is a recommended timeframe, and many students extend it to four years. Conversely, in China, most students graduate within the stipulated time. China's study duration is primarily calculated in years, whereas Germany employs a semester-based system.

In terms of specialization, both Chinese and German undergraduate programs do not initially distinguish specific directions. The first and second years of university are considered foundational learning stages, during which all students study core subjects regardless of their intended specialization. In China, the first two years primarily emphasize language learning, whereas in Germany, for the Bachelor's degree in German Language and Literature, students are generally expected to possess a solid language foundation, leading to an immediate focus on specialized directions from the start.

With the emerging trend of broad-based education, there is a current emphasis on blended learning in China, aiming to provide students with a well-rounded education that not only excels in language proficiency but also enhances their awareness of culture, economy, and politics. This holistic approach is intended to prepare students to play pivotal roles in national development.

In contrast, German undergraduate programs in German language studies continue to maintain early specialization. During the first semester, students are required to take exams in three distinct directions. Successfully passing anyone of these exams confirms that a student meets the standards for the chosen specialization. This examination is known as the "Orientierungsprüfung" or orientation exam. A general overview is given in figure 1.

Program duration and specialization options	Regular duration	Actual duration	Specialization	Major Content
Chinese Universities	4 years	3 years	Undifferentiated at the beginning	Blended learning (with translation between German and Chinese)
German Universities	3 years	Indefinite	Differentiated at the beginning	Initial specialization into directions

Figure 1 Overview of program structures

2.2 Curriculum Structure and Process

Once students have selected their major of study, they follow their courses. However, among the top fifteen comprehensive universities in Germany, the German language major, considered as the primary field of study (in German: Hauptfach), comes with mandatory requirements for a minor field of study (Nebenfach). Additionally, there is a "complementary area" (in German: Ergänzungsbereich) where students can freely choose courses outside of their major to supplement their credits. As a result, the curriculum distribution in Germany offers high flexibility, but credit requirements necessitate careful calculation.

During course selection, students must strictly adhere to their corresponding examination guidelines (in German: Prüfungsorientierung, abbreviated as PO). Examinations align with course outlines organized into modules (Modul). Within the same module, there might be several components. Furthermore, a recommended course progression plan (Studienverlaufsplan) is provided. Nevertheless, this plan serves as a reference, and it is essential to ascertain whether a course will be graded (in German: Prüfungsleistung/Studienleistung, abbreviated as PL and SL; the former is graded according to Germany's five-point scale, while the latter requires only a passing grade).

From this, it is evident that the curriculum arrangement for German language majors in Germany is exceedingly intricate. In the later years of study, it is highly possible for students to experience delays in their academic progress due to limited availability and constrained class sizes for discussion courses. For German language majors, courses can be chosen from any term, offering flexibility across all semesters.

In the early stages of the undergraduate program, there is a possibility of direct closed-book exams (in German: Klausur) for German language majors. The examination format for introductory courses in the first semester is exclusively closed-book exams, but this approach gradually decreases in frequency for larger courses and discussion classes in the subsequent three semesters. By the fifth semester, it is largely eliminated.

From the outset of undergraduate studies in Germany, emphasis is placed on cultivating the ability to draft academic papers. In courses where discussion classes culminate in a written assignment, the final exam often involves authoring a substantial paper. As the writing styles differ between German linguistics, medieval studies, and modern literature, instructors guide students through the relevant techniques during classes.

Bachelor's theses in German language majors typically range from 30 to 40 pages in length and do not require an oral defense. Once completed, they are submitted, and a total of 180 credits is the requirement for graduation. If an exam is not passed, there are usually opportunities for re-examination or resubmission of assignments within a specified timeframe. In certain cases, students can opt to withdraw altogether. German universities allow students to enroll in classes without registering for exams. If the result is not graded, a failure does not affect the exam transcript.

Minor field of study scores and major field of study scores are proportionally factored into the overall graduation average. For the major, the Bachelor's thesis holds significant weight, while other exam scores (PL) hold a lesser proportion.

In Chinese universities, the course arrangement largely aligns with the study process in secondary education. At the beginning of each semester, German language majors can access their class schedules online, and exam enrollment is automatic. With the exception of oral language classes taught by foreign instructors, most major-specific exams are closed-book. Public course exams may involve open-book exams or the submission of essays at the end of the term. Exam formats and schedules are communicated by instructors, and students directly participate in the exams. If a student fails an exam, they need to retake it the following year. If there are too many failed exams, the student may be required to repeat the year. As all exams in China are graded, all exam results are included in the transcript. For interpretation courses, assessments are oral, while for translation courses, daily assignments contribute to the grade, and other exams remain in closed-book format.

In summary, Chinese universities have a straightforward and accessible course selection and examination process, which is relatively simple to understand. However, the exam format tends to be uniform, and there is limited practice in daily writing, leading to challenges when students, especially in their final year, encounter difficulties while writing their graduation thesis. In China, universities typically arrange for thesis defense after the completion of the undergraduate thesis. Those different course arrangements and focus of education are visualized in figure 2.

Course Arrangement and Process	Course Distribution	Major Course Arrangement	Examination Format	Examination Score Calculation	Undergraduate Thesis
Chinese Universities	Low flexibility	Automatic enrollment, no registration required	Closed book exams	All exams are graded	Oral exam required
German Universities	High flexibility	Complex	Closed-book exams at the beginning + Papers	Partial grading + Partial pass	No oral exam required

Figure 2 Overview of course arrangements

2.3 Study Content

The initial four semesters after enrollment in a German university are dedicated to foundational coursework. At the University of Freiburg, the German language major commences with introductory courses in linguistics, medieval history, and medieval German grammar, as well as literary analysis and theory. Starting in the second semester, students select introductory discussion seminars (in German: Proseminar) based on various modules aligned with their interests. Course offerings for these seminars are randomized.

During the early stages, the author studied modern literary novels, analyzed courtly medieval lyric poetry, translated from Middle High German to modern German, delved into the intricacies of German grammar structures, and examined the classification of historical German dialects. Around the fifth semester, students begin to choose their specialized direction and corresponding discussion seminars. Advanced seminars (in German: Hauptseminar), also open to master's students, are introduced at this stage. The specialization of the author was German linguistics, which led to courses in psycholinguistics, pragmatics, text linguistics, and interactional linguistics. The author also explored language change phenomena such as alterations in German syntax.

During the preparation of my undergraduate thesis, the author participated in a discussion group (in German: Kolloquium) where graduating undergraduates and master's students shared their selected topics under the guidance of a professor. This setting allowed for the exchange of ideas, advice, and enhancements. For more details, please refer to the attached Appendix 2 to 4.

In the early three years of the German Department at Beijing International Studies University, there is no specialization, and all students are required to study a comprehensive curriculum. The initial two years primarily focus on German language learning courses, including German speaking, listening, and writing. To enhance understanding of the target country, courses such as Overview of German-Speaking Countries and Introduction to German Literature are offered, along with an introduction to German linguistics (please refer to the attached Appendix 1). By the third year, courses begin to emphasize practical and professional aspects. Students gain insights into translation studies, practice written and oral translation, delve into intercultural content, explore how foreigners perceive Chinese culture, and engage within in-depth linguistic research. There's even a course on professional communication, where students simulate job interviews and product marketing in German. In the fourth year, students are not engaged in specialized courses; the focus shifts to authoring their undergraduate thesis under the guidance of instructors, often accompanied by internships.

From this, it's clear that the emphasis and intensity of the undergraduate curriculum differ between China and Germany. In Germany, the German language major focuses on cultivating students' academic understanding and directing their academic interests, aiming to educate future research scholars. In contrast, the Chinese German language major aims to not only ensure students achieve fluency in a foreign language within a short period but also emphasizes practical application, employment readiness, and talent development, as shown in figure 3.

Study Content	Foundational Learning in First Four Semesters	Practicality in terms of employment	Research Specialization	Purpose
Chinese Universities	Language Acquisition +Overview of German-speaking countries + Limited Linguistic and Literary Knowledge	High	Low	Application-focused
German Universities	Linguistics+ Medieval Studies + German Literature	Low	High	Research Scholar Cultivation

Figure 3 Aims and Visions of Study Programs

4.   Conclusion and Outlook

This paper has summarized the similarities and differences in undergraduate German language programs between China and Germany using specific examples. The differences are as follows:

1)   The education system:

In Germany, the education system is more flexible, with clear and specialized program directions. In contrast, the Chinese education system is more regimented, and undergraduate program directions are not as finely delineated.

2)   Course selection process:

In German universities it is intricate, and there is autonomy in exam formats and grading criteria. Examination methods are diverse, with a later focus on paper-based assessments. In Chinese universities, course selection is not required, but exam formats are relatively uniform, with automatic registration and inclusion of all exam results.

3)   Study content:

German universities emphasize theoretical foundations, with distinctive focus on reading Middle High German and medieval literature. In later stages, the aim is to nurture specialized research scholars. Chinese universities dedicate the initial two years to language acquisition, followed by a shift towards practical content, including translation-related courses, aiming to achieve applicability.

In conclusion, this study has highlighted the distinctive characteristics of German and Chinese undergraduate German language programs. The differences encompass the education system's structure and flexibility, the approach to course selection and examination, and the emphasis on theoretical versus practical content. This understanding serves to illuminate the varied academic pathways available to students in these two countries.

Some similarities can also be observed: regardless of the university, the undergraduate thesis stage requires students to find mentors specializing in specific fields to assist with the writing process. Additionally, foundational courses in literature and linguistics are incorporated in both cases. The educational arrangements in German and Chinese universities are fundamentally aligned with their respective national contexts and cultures: Germany emphasizes individualized needs and academic exploration, while China is more inclined towards collective learning and nurturing versatile talents. However, whether in China or Germany, specialized courses in the German language major only constitute a portion of the overall curriculum. Chinese universities provide a range of general education courses, while German universities supplement their curriculum with additional minor programs. This illustrates that both countries consider the diversity of content in specialized learning.

The aim of this paper is to foster closer and more amicable exchanges between the two countries, and even between China and European universities. It is hoped that related resources will become more abundant. This paper, exemplified by Beijing International Studies University and the University of Freiburg, seeks to provide an objective and authentic comparison, laying the foundation for broader and more in-depth research in the future.

As a potential outlook for the further corporation, both Chinese and German Universities should complement each other's strengths and weaknesses: On the one hand German Universities should place more emphasis on vocationally relevant training, providing scholars with additional career paths. On the other hand Chinese Universities should acquire more professional knowledge, enabling students to benefit when pursuing scholarly pursuits or studying abroad. In summary, theory and practice should be effectively integrated for the optimal development of the discipline and the success of academic exchange between both educational systems. Concluding those systems should never be considered as static, however focus on promoting a spirit of innovation, mutual learning from external stimuli and experience.

References

He, N., Yu, Y.& Xiong, G. (2012): 21 Shiji De Zhongde Jiaoyu Bijiao. [Comparison between Chinese and German Education in 21st Century]. Kejiao Wenhui, 2012.03, 1-2.

Hu, F. (2016):Guoji Shuangshuoshi Peiyang Moshi De Yanjiu Ji Jiejian – Yi Tianjin Waiguoyu Daxue He Xisakesen Ciweikao Yingyong Keji Daxue Weili.[Research and Reference on the International Dual Master's Degree Training Model — A Case Study of Tianjin Foreign Studies University and University of Applied Sciences Zwickau in Saxony, Germany] Kejiao Daokan: Dianziban, 2016(3), 21-22.

Jiang, S.& Liu, X. (2015):Deyu Zhuanye Shuoshi Yanjiusheng Shengtai Wenming Lilunlei Kecheng Jianshe Chuangxin Yanjiu ——Yi Nanchang Hangkong Daxue Weili [Studies on Innovation of Construction of Courses of Eco-Civilization Theories for Postgraduates of German: Taking the NCHU as Case Studies.] Tongling Xueyuan Xuebao, 2015 (4), 125-129.

Liu, Q., Liu, X.& Deschka, D.R. (2019): Deutschlehrerqualifizierung in China am Beispiel der Kooperationsprogramme der Fremdsprachenuniversität Guangdong und der zweiten Fremdsprachenuniversität Peking. [On Professional training for Chinese teachers of German - An example from the cooperation project of Guangdong University of Foreign Studies and Beijing International Studies University with the Goethe-Institute] Informationen Deutsch als Fremdsprache, 46, 1, 79-89.

Szurawitzki, M. (2019): Zukunftsvisionen für die chinesische Germanistik. [German Studies in China – Future Perspectives] Informationen Deutsch als Fremdsprache, 46, 1, 70-78.

Wang, W. (2013): Das Germanistikstudium in China in der Expansion. Eine Problembetrachtung. [The Expansion of German Studies in China. Examination of a problem] From: https://www.vr-elibrary.de/doi/10.7788/bue.2013.66.1.29.

6. Appendix

Appendix 1: Transcript from Beijing International Studies University

北京第二外国语学院学生成绩单
BEIJING INTERNATIONAL STUDIES UNIVERSITY

姓名: / NAME:
专业: 德语 / SPECIALTY: GERMAN LANGUAGE AND LITERATURE
学习期限: 2015-2019 / STUDY PERIOD: 2015-2019
学制: 4年 / SCHOOL SYSTEM: 4 YEARS

学年学期 ACADEMIC YEAR	课程名称 COURSE	学时/学分 HOURS/ CREDITS	成绩 SCORES
2015-2016 1ST TERM	计算机基础与应用 FUNDAMENTALS AND APPLICATIONS OF COMPUTERS	4.00	
	体育 PHYSICAL EDUCATION	1.00	
	现代汉语 MODERN CHINESE	2.00	
	心理健康 PSYCHOLOGICAL HEALTH EDUCATION	1.00	
	德语 I GERMAN I	14.00	
	学习方法和学习管理 LEARNING METHOD AND MANAGEMENT	1.00	
2ND TERM	古代文学 ANCIENT CHINESE LITERATURE	2.00	
	思想道德修养与法律基础 IDEOLOGICAL AND MORAL CULTIVATION AND FUNDAMENTALS OF LAW	3.00	
	体育 PHYSICAL EDUCATION	1.00	
	中国近代史纲要 OUTLINE OF MODERN CHINESE HISTORY	2.00	
	古希腊文化概论 AN INTRODUCTION TO ANCIENT GREEK CULTURE	2.00	
	影视艺术赏析 APPRECIATION OF MOVIE AND TELEVISION ART	2.00	
	德语 II GERMAN II	14.00	
	德语国家国情 I FOLK CUSTOMS OF GERMAN-SPEAKING COUNTRIES I	2.00	
2016-2017 1ST TERM	第二外语 (英语) SECOND FOREIGN LANGUAGE(ENGLISH)	4.00	
	马克思主义基本原理 BASIC PRINCIPLE OF MARXISM	3.00	
	体育 PHYSICAL EDUCATION	1.00	
	西方古典文学选讲 SELECTED WESTERN CLASSICAL LITERATURE	2.00	
	心理健康与心理咨询 MENTAL HEALTH AND MENTAL CONSULTATION	2.00	
	德语国家国情 II FOLK CUSTOMS OF GERMAN-SPEAKING COUNTRIES II	2.00	
	德语 III GERMAN III	8.00	
	德语口语 I ORAL GERMAN I	2.00	
	德语视听 I GERMAN LISTENING AND VIDEO I	2.00	
	德语写作 I GERMAN WRITING I	2.00	
	德语语言学导论 INTRODUCTION TO GERMAN LINGUISTICS	1.00	
2ND TERM	第二外语 (英语) SECOND FOREIGN LANGUAGE(ENGLISH)	4.00	
	毛泽东思想与中国特色社会主义理论体系概论 INTRODUCTION TO MAO ZEDONG'S THOUGHT AND THE THEORETICAL SYSTEM OF SOCIALISM WITH CHINESE CHARACTERISTICS	3.00	
	体育 PHYSICAL EDUCATION	1.00	
	形势与政策 SITUATION AND POLICY	1.00	
	江南城市与文化传统/中华水文化 SOUTHERN CITIES AND CULTURAL TRADITIONS / CHINA WATER CULTURE	2.00	
	中国近代文化史 CULTURAL HISTORY OF MODERN CHINESE	2.00	
	德语 IV GERMAN IV	8.00	
	德语口语 II ORAL GERMAN II	2.00	
	德语视听 II GERMAN LISTENING AND VIDEO II	2.00	
	德语文学概论 CONSPECTUS OF GERMAN LITERATURE	1.00	
	德语写作 II GERMAN WRITING II	2.00	
	历年平均成绩 AVERAGE RECORD		

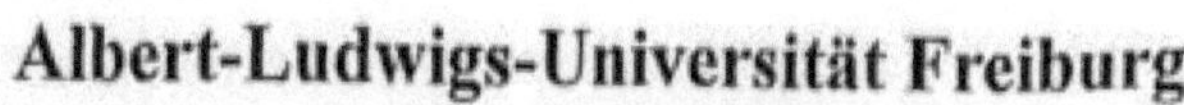

Albert-Ludwigs-Universität Freiburg

Gemeinsame Kommission
der Philologischen und
der Philosophischen Fakultät

Transcript of Records/Leistungsübersicht

für

geb. am

Studiengang: Bachelor of Arts (B.A.)

Hauptfach: Deutsche Sprach- und Literaturwissenschaft

	Note/Status	ECTS-Punkte	Bemerkung
I. Studienbegleitende Leistungen			
M 1 - Grundlagen der Germanistischen Linguistik			
Einführung in die Linguistik		5	
Vorlesung aus dem Bereich Deskriptive Grammatik: Struktur des Deutschen		5	
M 2 - Grundlagen der Neueren deutschen Literaturwissenschaft			
Grundzüge der Gattungspoetik		5	
Techniken und Methoden der Literaturwissenschaft		3	
M 3 - Grundlagen der Germanistischen Mediävistik			
Einführung in die Sprachgeschichte und mittelalterliche Literatur		5	
Seminar Sprachlich orientierte Lektüre: Minnelyrik - Weltlich/geistlich		5	
M 4 - Vertiefung Germanistische Linguistik I - Deskriptive Grammatik			
Proseminar aus dem Bereich Deskriptive Grammatik: Einführung in die Orthographie		6	
M 5 Vertiefung Neuere deutsche Literaturwissenschaft I Historischer Überblick			
Epochenvorlesung: Vom Humanismus bis zur Frühaufklärung		2	
Epochenvorlesung: Von der Aufklärung bis zur Klassik		2	
M 6 Vertiefung Germanistische Mediävistik I Ältere deutsche Literatur			
Vorlesung aus dem Bereich Gattung/Autor: Angst - Zur Literarisierung einer Emotion im Mittelalter		2	
Proseminar aus dem Bereich der älteren deutschen Literatur: Lexikalische Überschneidungen, semantische Umbesetzungen - Geistlich-weltliche Interferenzen in der Minnelyrik und darüber hinaus		6	

ID: 4052394

Albert-Ludwigs-Universität Freiburg

Gemeinsame Kommission
der Philologischen und
der Philosophischen Fakultät

Transcript of Records/Leistungsübersicht

für

geb. am

Studiengang: Bachelor of Arts (B.A.)
Hauptfach: Deutsche Sprach- und Literaturwissenschaft

	Note/ Status	ECTS- Punkte	Bemerkung
M 7 - Vertiefung Germanistische Linguistik II - Text/Sprachliche Interaktion			
Vorlesung aus dem Bereich Text/Sprachliche Interaktion: Pragmatik und Interaktion		2	
Proseminar aus dem Bereich Text/Sprachliche Interaktion: Einführung in die Textlinguistik		6	
M 8 - Vertiefung Neuere deutsche Literaturwissenschaft II - Literaturwissenschaftliche Fallanalysen			
Proseminar aus dem Bereich der deutschen Literatur von 1500 bis 1850: Märchen		6	
Proseminar aus dem Bereich der deutschen Literatur von 1850 bis zur Gegenwart: 1968 und die Folgen - Enzensberger und Uwe Timm		6	
M 9 - Vertiefung Germanistische Mediävistik II - Sprachgeschichte älterer Epochen			
Proseminar aus dem Bereich Sprachentwicklung vor 1800: 'Deutsche' Schreibsprachen des Mittelalters? Varietät und Ausgleich vor 1800		6	
M 10 - Ergänzung			
Hauptseminar aus dem Bereich der Germanistischen Linguistik: Gender, Sprache, Kommunikation		5	
M 11 - Spezialisierung Germanistische Linguistik I			
Proseminar aus dem Bereich Sprachstruktur/Sprachwandel: Einführung in die historische Syntax des Deutschen		6	
Proseminar aus dem Bereich Sprachliches Handeln: Multimodale Ansätze in der Interaktionsanalyse		6	
Proseminar aus dem Bereich Sprache und Kognition: Einführung in die Psycholinguistik		6	

ID: 4032194

Albert-Ludwigs-Universität Freiburg

Gemeinsame Kommission
der Philologischen und
der Philosophischen Fakultät

Transcript of Records/Leistungsübersicht

für

geb. am

Studiengang: Bachelor of Arts (B.A.)
Hauptfach: Deutsche Sprach- und Literaturwissenschaft

	Note/ Status	ECTS- Punkte	Bemerkung
M 12 - Spezialisierung Germanistische Linguistik II		8	
Hauptseminar aus dem Bereich Sprachliches Handeln: Multiethnolekt und Deutschrap		5	
Hauptseminar aus dem Bereich Sprache und Kognition: Soziolinguistik und Kognition		2	
Kolloquium zu ausgewählten Themen linguistischer Forschung			

Gesamtnote der studienbegleitenden Prüfungen

II. B.A.-Arbeit   10

Werbekommunikation und Gender –
Ein Vergleich zwischen dem Chinesischen und Deutschen.

III. Fachnote

IV. ECTS-Punkte   120

Designing for a Globalized World: Lifelong Learning and Interdisciplinary Collaboration in Industrial Design Education

WANG DanPing (王丹萍)[1]

Abstract

In an era marked by globalization, cultural diversity, and sustainability, the field of Industrial Design (ID) stands at the nexus of innovation and responsibility. This paper proposes a comprehensive framework that incorporates two key components: lifelong learning and interdisciplinary collaboration. It explores the profound impact of globalization on design practice, industry, and education, highlighting the vital role of lifelong learning in maintaining expertise in the evolving design landscape. Complementing this, the concept of interdisciplinary collaboration is examined, emphasizing the value of multifunctional skills and holistic approaches to solving design problems. Examples of successful implementation in Europe and China regarding lifelong learning and interdisciplinary collaboration illustrate the outcomes they have achieved in education amidst globalization.

Multi-party collaboration among government, industry, and educational institutions has also accelerated the exploration and practice of innovative educational models. This paper summarizes obstacles and proposes recommendations that China must overcome in its future education for the globalization of industrial design. Looking to the future trajectory of design education, it underscores how lifelong learning and interdisciplinary collaboration can cultivate adaptable designers who shape the globalized design world. Ultimately, the paper highlights the crucial synergies between these attributes in producing designers who drive innovation across borders and disciplines.

Keywords: Globalization, Industrial Design Education, Lifelong Learning, Interdisciplinary Collaboration

Introduction

1.1 The globalized world and its impact on ID education

"Global education is education that opens people's eyes and minds to the realities of the globalized world and awakens them to bring about a world of greater justice, equity and Human Rights for all," as defined by the Maastricht Declaration on global education in 2002. (Maastricht Global Education Declaration 2002). The transition from national to global education is often presented as not only a logical next step, but also a necessary one because 'The forces of globalization affect the lives of everybody on the planet' (Butt, 2011, p. 423). In the current climate, engineers must be flexible, creative, and solution-focused with a strong understanding of human-centered design and an ability to work in multidisciplinary contexts (Grasso and Martinelli 2007).

The globalized world, characterized by rapid technological advancements, heightened international connectivity, and diverse cultural interactions, has profoundly reshaped the realm of Industrial Design (ID) education. As geographic boundaries blur, markets interconnect, and

---

[1] *WANG DanPing (王丹萍)* is a student for Industrial Design at College of Humanities and Design· Industrial Design at the Chengdu Technological University (成都工业学院) (PRC)

supply chains span continents, industrial designers face the imperative of crafting products that resonate universally and fulfill global needs. Consequently, the priorities of design education have evolved, necessitating the development of competencies beyond technical adeptness. Designers must now possess a profound comprehension of cross-cultural aesthetics, user preferences, and sustainability considerations to address the multifaceted demands of a global audience. Furthermore, the interconnected fabric of industries underscores the call for collaborative and interdisciplinary approaches. In this context, designers collaborate with experts from diverse fields to innovate solutions that transcend conventional disciplinary confines. As a result, ID education has evolved to emphasize not only technical skills but also intercultural competence, adaptability, and the ability to navigate complex, globalized design challenges.

1.2 Importance of lifelong learning and Interdisciplinary collaboration for design education in response to globalization

The ability to learn and adapt to new skills and training is an increasingly important basic skill in today's ever-changing technological universe. (Laal, M., & Salamati, P., 2011) .The paramount significance of lifelong learning and interdisciplinary collaboration emerges as fundamental constructs to effectively prepare designers for the multifaceted challenges posed by a globalized milieu. Lifelong learning, characterized by the perpetual acquisition of skills and knowledge, assumes a pivotal role in ensuring designers' sustained relevance amidst dynamic industry evolution and technological progress.

Moreover, the contemporary design landscape demands heightened emphasis on interdisciplinary collaboration. Design challenges frequently transcend traditional boundaries, necessitating cooperative efforts with specialists spanning various domains, including engineering, sustainability, and social sciences. The notion of interdisciplinary collaboration wherein designers adeptly harness diverse knowledge realms, becomes an indispensable facet for generating innovative and comprehensive solutions that surpass conventional compartmentalization.

In synthesis, the confluence of lifelong learning and interdisciplinary collaboration constitutes a synergistic framework indispensable to the evolving sphere of ID education. Globalization significantly impacts ID education by expanding its scope and incorporating cross-cultural dimensions. Both large enterprises and higher education are developing towards internationalization, which raises new requirements for design students (Xuefei Huang, Roger Ball, Wei Wang. 2021).

2. Strategies for Lifelong Learning and Interdisciplinary Collaborative Practice in ID Education: Europe and China

2.1 Europe: Lifelong learning in ID education

Lifelong learning plays a pivotal role in our life. The 21st century context requires a new set of competences beyond the obvious ICT literacy: communication, collaboration, social and cultural skills, creativity, critical thinking, problem-solving, productivity in a globalized world, learning to learn skills, self-direction, planning, flexibility, risk taking, conflict management and a sense of initiative and entrepreneurship (Voogt & Pareja Roblin, 2012). Literature cases like Jonassen and Carr's work on "Mindtools" underscore the role of technology in supporting lifelong learning. Lifelong learning creates the challenge to understand, explore, and support new essential dimensions of learning such as self-directed learning, learning on demand, collaborative learning, and organizational learning.(Fischer, G. 2000).

Several European countries, educational institutions, and universities have developed policies and strategies to promote lifelong learning for designers. These initiatives are aimed at enhancing the skills and knowledge of designers throughout their careers. European Union: Erasmus+

Programmer.[2] The Erasmus+ Programmer, funded by the European Union, supports education, training, youth, and sport initiatives. Within the realm of design education, Erasmus+ offers opportunities for students, teachers, and professionals to participate in exchanges, training, and collaborative projects across European countries. This promotes cross-cultural exposure and lifelong learning through international experiences.

The Design Council's Design Academy in the UK offers training and workshops for design professionals at various career stages. These programs focus on skills development, innovation, and applying design thinking to real-world challenges. The Design Academy supports designers in continuously updating their skills and approaches. Lifelong Learning in Dutch higher education institutions, including universities and universities of applied sciences, prioritize lifelong learning through flexible programs and part-time study options. The Netherlands Organization for Scientific Research (NWO) funds projects that promote lifelong learning in higher education and encourage collaboration between institutions and businesses. As a connector, they fulfill an important bridging function between researchers, governments, politics, knowledge institutions, industry and other knowledge users[3]. Finland Aalto University's Professional Development Studies Aalto University in Finland offers professional development studies targeted at design professionals and individuals interested in design. These courses cover topics such as sustainable design, user-centered design, and design management, enabling designers to stay relevant and advance their careers.

2.2 Europe: Interdisciplinary Collaboration in ID education

In the current climate, engineers must be flexible, creative, and solution-focused with a strong understanding of human-centered design and an ability to work in multidisciplinary contexts (Grasso and Martinelli 2007). Collaborative projects and research sources need to be integrated into design courses, and design schools need to enhance the partnerships with companies (Boyarski 1998). Publications such as "Design for the Real World" by Victor Papanek emphasize the significance of interdisciplinary thinking in design. Additionally. The "Transdisciplinary Design" framework proposed by Dorst and Cross advocates for embracing multiple disciplines to tackle design challenges. European educational institutions and universities have demonstrated a heightened recognition of the pivotal role of interdisciplinary collaboration in ID education. They have executed well-crafted policies and initiatives to cultivate such synergies. For instance, Aalto University's School of Arts, Design and Architecture in Finland fosters interdisciplinary collaboration through its dedicated platform "Aalto Studios," facilitating cross-disciplinary cooperation for innovative projects. Moreover, their "Creative Sustainability" program stands as an embodiment of interdisciplinary methodologies, addressing sustainability challenges via design-oriented solutions. Similarly, Politecnico di Milano champions interdisciplinary collaboration through the "Design and Innovation for Sustainability" program, uniting students from diverse realms like design, engineering, and business to craft sustainable innovations.

In this vein, the Royal College of Art asserts its commitment to interdisciplinary collaboration with the "Innovation Design Engineering" program. This initiative engages students of varied backgrounds, encouraging collaborative exploration at the confluence of design, engineering, and entrepreneurship. Germany, renowned for its emphasis on education and practical training, extends its reach to the realm of design. For instance, the collaboration between Pforzheim University's School of Design and Mercedes-Benz Design accentuates the integration of real-world challenges into education. Meanwhile, TU Delft's Faculty of ID Engineering orchestrates

---

[2] European Commission. "Erasmus-plus." Last modified Agu11,2023. available at https://erasmus-plus.ec.europa.eu/
[3] Chinese government website. "nwo." available at https://www.nwo.nl/en/nwo-strategy-2023-2026

interdisciplinary harmony through initiatives like "Integrated Product Design," where students craft holistic solutions integrating technical, social, and cultural facets.

2.3 China: Lifelong learning in ID education

China has been actively working on various policies and initiatives to promote lifelong learning for designers. China's 13th Five-Year Plan for Education (2016-2020):The government's education plan emphasized the need to develop lifelong learning systems and promote continuous professional development for various fields, including design[4]. The plan aimed to strengthen vocational education and training, encouraging designers to acquire new skills throughout their careers. Design Education Reform and Innovation Plan (2015-2020): Initiated by the Ministry of Education, this plan aimed to enhance the quality of design education across China. It emphasized interdisciplinary education, international collaboration, and industry integration, encouraging designers to develop skills that align with global trends.

Continuing Education in Universities: Many Chinese universities offer continuing education programs, short courses, and workshops for professionals, including designers. Renowned institutions like Tsinghua University and Tongji University provide opportunities for designers to enhance their skills and knowledge through part-time and non-degree programs.

Government Initiatives for Creative Industries: The Chinese government has been supportive of the creative industries, including design. Policies and initiatives aimed at fostering innovation and entrepreneurship provide opportunities for designers to engage in lifelong learning to stay competitive and innovative. A large number of government or business organization design competitions and activities have emerged, which has enhanced the industry and people's understanding of ID. (Xuefei Huang, Roger Ball, Wei Wang 2021).

National Art Education Platform: The "National Art Education Platform" was developed to enhance art and design education at all levels. This platform supports both formal education and lifelong learning in various artistic disciplines. Online Learning Platforms and MOOCs:China has seen the rise of online learning platforms and Massive Open Online Courses (MOOCs) that offer design-related courses. Platforms like XuetangX and Coursera provide opportunities for designers to engage in self-paced learning.

2.4 China: Interdisciplinary Collaboration in ID education

The cultivation of Chinese ID talents should include creativity, operational skills, understanding, a global vision, and international experience (Yuan and Zhang, 2018). China has been increasingly recognizing the value of interdisciplinary collaboration in ID education and has initiated several policies and projects to encourage such collaborations.

China's Ministry of Education issued the "Action Plan for Artificial Intelligence Innovation in Colleges and Universities" in 2020, which calls for promoting the construction of China's "new engineering disciplines". This includes paying attention to the cross-fertilization of AI with multidisciplinary professional education in computer science, ID, mathematics, statistics, law, and other disciplines. The aim is to form a new model of "Artificial Intelligence + X" composite professional training. The Chinese government has also launched initiatives to promote innovation and entrepreneurship, including the implementation of the innovation-driven development strategy and further promotion of mass entrepreneurship and innovation. These policies encourage interdisciplinary collaborations among students and professionals.

---

[4] Chinese government website. "zhengce." available at https://www.gov.cn/zhengce/zhengceku/2017-01/19/ content_5161341.htm

Collaboration with Industry: Many Chinese educational institutions collaborate with industries to provide students with real-world projects that require interdisciplinary collaboration. These projects encourage students from different disciplines to work together on design challenges. In China's automotive industry, collaborations with design schools have been prominent. For instance, SAIC Motor Corporation and Geely Auto have partnered with universities like Tongji University and Hunan University for design projects related to automotive aesthetics, user experience, and sustainability. Additionally, Xiaomi, a leading tech company, organized the "Mi Ecosystem Design Contest" in collaboration with design schools such as Tsinghua University and Jiangnan University. This contest challenges students to create innovative designs for Xiaomi's ecosystem products, such as smart devices and accessories.

Furthermore, certain universities, like Tongji University, have established design incubators and innovation centers. For instance, Tongji University's College of Design and Innovation (D&I) promotes interdisciplinary collaboration through programs like "Transdisciplinary Design Innovation." This initiative encourages collaboration among design students, engineers, business students, and other disciplines to address complex challenges.

3. Conclusion and Suggestions

3.1 Common Strengths

Both Europe and China recognize the significance of lifelong learning and interdisciplinary collaboration in ID education. The importance of nurturing a diverse skill set to meet the demands of a globalized world is acknowledged in both regions. Moreover, both Europe and China underscore the imperative of fostering collaboration among designers, engineers, and industry stakeholders to engender inventive and enhanced solutions. Consequently, the formulation of pertinent governmental and educational policies assumes a pivotal stance in advancing the cause of lifelong learning and interdisciplinary synergy. Concurrently, the establishment of expanded conduits for continuous education tailored to designers and allied professionals stands as a collective endeavor pursued jointly by China and Europe. This concerted effort facilitates broader access to lifelong learning and interdisciplinary education, rendering it more accessible and user-friendly for a wider spectrum of individuals.

3.2 Suggestions

China has made significant progress in promoting lifelong learning and interdisciplinary collaboration in ID education. However, there are areas for improvement. One of the challenges is that institutions offering ID majors need to further enhance the flexibility of their curriculum. Some of the current issues arise from the fact that the professional training program is structured as a four-year undergraduate setup, established prior to admitting first-year students to the university. However, design is a field that evolves rapidly, and the dynamic changes in the market concurrently impact the demand for higher-level talent training. Therefore, universities should adopt a more flexible mechanism to cope with the influence of globalization on education. Additionally, while Chinese design schools and enterprises have already engaged in various interdisciplinary industry collaborations, it is evident that these resources and opportunities are more inclined towards larger enterprises and higher-ranked universities, leading to unequal distribution of educational resources.

Furthermore, despite the prevalence of online learning platforms, ensuring the credibility and effectiveness of these platforms remains crucial. China could concentrate on developing certification or accreditation mechanisms for online courses, encouraging broader participation in learning beyond the campus and facilitating the attainment of socially recognized certificates. Governments at all levels can establish more design research centers and innovation hubs where students and professionals from diverse fields can collaborate on cutting-edge projects. These centers could function as incubators for interdisciplinary ideas and solutions.

References

Anonymous. 2010. "Outline of the National Medium- and Long-Term Education Reform and Development Plan (2010-2020)". *China Ethnic Education* 8, no.3, 1-17.(in Chinese)

Butt, G. 2011. "Globalisation, geography education and the curriculum: what are the challenges for curriculum makers in geography?" *The Curriculum Journal*22. no.3, 423–438.

Boyarski, D. 1998. "Education: Designing design education." SIGCHI30. no.3, 7–10.

Central People's Government of the People's Republic of China. Last modified Agu30,2023

https://www.gov.cn/zhengce/zhengceku/2017-01/19/content_5161341.htm

Council of Europe. 2002. The "Maastricht Global Education Declaration", available at https://rm.coe.int/168070e540

Durling, David, and Andrew J. Johnson. 2003. "Product design engineering: a new interdisciplinary programme." *European Journal of Engineering Education*28, no. 3, 353-362.

David H. Jonassen,- Chad Carr. 1998. "Computers as Mindtools for Engaging Learners in Critical Thinking". *TechTrends*43. no.2, (March):24-32.

Design, Manufacturing and Engineering Management, University of Strathclyde, United Kingdom(pp. 1-6). The Design Society.

European Commission. "Erasmus-plus." Last modified Agu11,2023. available at https:// erasmus-plus.ec.europa.eu/

Fischer, G.,2000). Lifelong Learning—More Than Training. Journal of Interactive Learning Research, 11(3), 265-294.

Grasso, D. and Martinelli, D., 2007. "Holistic engineering." *Chronicle of Higher Education.* 53, B8–B9.

Huang, Xuefei, Roger Ball, and Wei Wang. 2021. "Comparative study of industrial design undergraduate education in China and USA." *International Journal of Technology and Design Education*31, no. 3, 565-586. https://doi.org/10.1007/s10798-020-09563-4.

Kees Dorst and Nigel Cross, 2001. "Transdisciplinary Design." Cambridge, Massachusetts: MIT Press, ISBN 978-0262041893.

Laal, M., & Salamati, P. 2011. "Lifelong learning: why do we need it?" *Procedia-Social and Behavioral Sciences.* doi:10.1016/j.sbspro.2011.12.0

Experience of Internationalization of German Higher Education for China

LIU Yuetong (刘玥彤) [1]

Abstract

The internationalization of German higher education looks upon a deep history and rich experience, but it is also facing new problems in the early 21st century, such as the difficulty of international students to graduate, the influx of refugee students, policy tightening, and the development of digitalization. To vigorously enhance the international influence of higher education, the Merkel government has promoted the deep development of internationalization of German higher education through innovative paths of policy, personnel, project, education provider mobility, and mobility of program works and services. These new measures reflect the four-way cooperation among the government, universities, third-party educational institutions and enterprises, the dual innovation of concept and technology, and the experience of educational reform in line with the trend, which is an important inspiration for the current internationalization of higher education in China.

Keywords: Germany; higher education; internationalization

Introduction

In the development process of modern higher education, internationalization has gradually become an important strategy for the development of higher education in various countries. As a developed country in higher education, Germany disposes a profound history and rich experience in internationalization of higher education. The roots of the German internationalization process can be traced back to the Humboldt period. Latter on the university concept of "unity of research and teaching" promoted Germany to become the world's academic kingdom at that time, especially during the republic of Weimar.. After World War II, Germany focused on Europe, eagerly promoting integration, to deepen educational cooperation and academic exchanges among member states of the European Community.

In contrast to the past nowadays the circumstances for international education have changed. In the post epidemic era, anti-globalization, populism, and other thoughts are rising in different regions of the world, which makes it more difficult for China to promote foreign exchange and cooperation of higher education. Studying the innovative measures of internationalization of German higher education in the 21st century is of great significance for promoting the internationalization process of China's higher education, cultivating talents with a global vision for the construction of a "community of human destiny", and promoting exchanges and cooperation of higher education between China and Germany.

---

[1] *LIU Yuetong (刘玥彤))* is a Bachelor student for German Studies at the Northwestern Polytechnical University Xi'an (PRC) (西北工业大学). Besides that, she has supported the preparation and implementation of this project as a scientific assistant.

The innovative path of internationalization of German higher education covers various aspects such as education subjects, education concepts and education reforms. By virtue of its own educational advantages, based on its own characteristics, and by promoting the flow of factors in the process of internationalization, Germany has finally formed an internationalization experience that meets its own reality. The following analysis will look upon this process.

This essay envisages to the present the evolution of German international higher education, providing several inspiration for innovating the Chinese counterpart. Therefore, this essay is structured as following. In the first part, the construction of the German Higher Education system will be described. After that, the second part will look upon the interconnectedness of German university focusing on building networks. Moreover, the third part will have a look upon the importance of education as a tool for improving international relations. Eventually, the concluding part will provide three valuable lessons, that will serve as inspiration for the innovation of Chinese higher education. Concluding, this essay argues, that education is a dynamic process, requiring openness to innovation as curiosity for attracting foreign students. As it will be shown, China provides the potential to become a hub for creative foreign talents.

Construction of Higher Education System

The internationalization of education is essentially a fierce competition for global education resources, which requires close cooperation among the government, higher education institutions, third-party education institutions and enterprises. The rapid development of internationalization of higher education in Germany is attributed to the four-party cooperation among the federal government, higher education institutions, third-party educational institutions, and enterprises, which constitutes an internationalization cooperation system for higher education. The government provides policy guarantee for the internationalization of higher education, promulgating internationalization policies with continuity and comprehensiveness, covering student mobility, teaching promotion, financial support, scientific research cooperation, etc., and giving full attention and strong support to the foreign cultural service departments and cultural diplomacy forces of all parties, which guarantees the implementation of the internationalization policy of higher education with rich content, thorough consideration and stable timeliness.

As the main body of internationalization of higher education, institutions of higher education have expanded their autonomy in terms of appointment of professors, curriculum, teaching activities, etc., which inadvertently increases their freedom in the process of internationalization of higher education, enabling them to cross various fields of internationalization and seek diversified development through active participation in national higher education programs, cross-border cooperation in running schools, and cooperation between schools and enterprises. Third-party internationalization agencies are the hub of quadrilateral cooperation and, as specialized organizations serving higher education, are professional, systematic, and standardized. They are also the initial initiator of organized foreign cultural exchanges in Germany, and maintain long-term good interaction with universities, government and enterprises, which are not only recognized by German universities, but also cooperate with the government tacitly, and can reflect the government's intention as a non-governmental organization, so as to facilitate the formation of the power of politics and academia to merge. In addition, they have their own alumni network to stay connected with the sponsored students, which lays the foundation for subsequent exchanges and cooperation, and plays a leading role in the internationalization of higher education in a well-organized manner.

In 2019, some 150,000 students, graduates and scholars received funding from the German Academic Exchange Service (DAAD), and 33,000 students took part in German transnational education programs worldwide.[2] As the new blood of internationalization of higher education, enterprises are an indispensable part of the multi-level governance structure of internationalization of higher education, as they build extensive research networks for organizations, universities and other partners, broaden the channels of funding, and establish a pathway for the transfer and exchange of talents on an international scale.

Multiple networks across educational boundaries

The trend of "anti-globalization" has increased the barriers to education in countries around the world. Along with the changes in the direction of international students and the tightening of student visas and visas for related staff, the internationalization of higher education requires new conceptual guidance and technological innovation to break the mobility dilemma. Conceptual innovations are most significant when they drive the overall development of the sector and change the way people think. As the world becomes an increasingly interconnected whole, competition for education between different countries intensifies.

How to maintain the most important traditional values while accepting the new changes under the wave of globalization has become a problem that German higher education must face. "It is also obvious that educational institutions have to be more adaptable and resilient to serve this changing world. Universities have to change themselves if they want to preserve the most basic traditions and value standards." Therefore, Germany, on the basis of constantly exploring an education system that is both adapted to its own national conditions and in line with international standards, has insisted on focusing on the skills of the future and learning without borders, and has launched a series of education initiatives, including the "dual system" of vocational education and the "Excellence in Universities Program", to promote the reform and development of higher education. It has launched a series of educational initiatives, including the "dual system" of vocational education and the "university excellence programme", to promote the reform and development of higher education in response to the challenges and opportunities brought about by globalization.

Take the initiative to plan and promote cooperation and exchanges among colleges and universities, so as to realize in the future the use of cyberspace as the basic environment for education and teaching, the normalization of cyber teaching applications, teaching management and education governance, and cyber-enabled higher education across national boundaries and multicultural integration.[3]

Seizing the opportunity to expand international influence

Germany has a tradition of seizing the opportunities of global change to promote the internationalization of higher education. After World War II, in the face of the reorganization of the world pattern, Germany took advantage of the process of European integration, took the "European Community dimension" as the focus point, increased the strength of higher education exchanges and cooperation with member states of the European Community, and jointly implemented the "Erasmus Program", which led to the expansion of international students in Germany. The Erasmus program has increased the number of international students and accelerated Germany's return to the world's leading higher education country.[4]This experience was also continued during Merkel's administration. During Merkel's administration, she led Germany to cope with five crises: the global financial crisis in 2007, the subsequent

---

[2] DAAD.Jahresbericht 2019[EB/OL].(2020-06-30)[2021-04-18].https://static.daad.de/media/daad_de/pdfs_nicht_barrierefrei/derdaad/daad_jahresbericht_2019.pdf.
[3] Jennifer Dusdal. Higher education in Germany-recent developments in an international perspective[J].Routledge,2019,55(2):292-294.
[4] Hendrik Berghaeuser,Michael Hoelscher.Reinventing the third mission of higher education in Germany:political frameworks and universities' reactions[J].Tertiary Education and Management,2020,26(6):57-76.

European debt crisis, the refugee crisis in 2015, climate change and the new coronary pneumonia epidemic, during which the internationalization of German higher education experienced several twists and turns, but eventually resolved the crises one by one with rapid response and precise countermeasures.

In the face of the controversy over university tuition fees in the states after the economic crisis, the federal government and third-party educational institutions launched a series of scholarships and grants targeting different countries of origin and covering various groups of students, which skillfully solved the financial problems of students without destroying the freedom of legislation of the states and successfully combined the concepts of "high quality" and "high cost-effectiveness". The "high quality" and "high cost-effectiveness" of German universities have been successfully built into the gold standard of German universities. In the context of the UK's departure from the European Union, the raging epidemic of C.P.D. and the challenges of European integration, Germany has taken a more proactive role as a European leader, assuming the presidency of the Council of the European Union from July to December 2020 and giving the European Research Area (ERZ) a new foothold by providing excellent initiatives in education, research and innovation, coordinating relations between EU countries, and promoting exchanges and cooperation in higher education.

Lessons for China to become a hub for international education

Germany's experience in the internationalization of higher education has provided many useful lessons for China. Especially three lessons shall be discussed as a concluding outlook.

First, adhere to the strategy of "open education" and carry out "local internationalization". In the face of the wave of anti-globalization and the crisis of China-US relations, it is urgent to learn from foreign experience, based on local culture, encourage the participation of multiple subjects, develop a suitable path for China's internationalization development: focusing on student-centeredness, providing stable policy support and institutional safeguards for the internationalization of higher education; focusing on the construction of faculty, through the recruitment and training of qualified teachers; and focusing on the development of the internationalization of higher education in China, we will improve the overall level; focusing on the reform of education and teaching, we will innovate the mode of educating people, and promote the concepts of internationalization and the operation mechanism to enter into the curriculum and teaching; focusing on the education of humanities, we will integrate the internationalization elements into the education of humanities through the construction of humanities curriculum system, the establishment of Chinese culture exchange centers on the campuses and the dissemination of Chinese stories.

Secondly, we will follow the trend of virtual internationalization and promote open practice and innovation. We will make full use of the existing online distance learning platforms, make efforts to develop new online teaching platforms, promote internationalization by using "Internet+Education" and "Intelligence+Education" educational technologies in teaching methods, and build and share online educational resources; use information technology to break through the physical limitations of academic exchanges and cooperation, and explore new forms of international academic exchanges and cooperation; explore global remote internships with the help of computer technology, and obtain cross-border work opportunities, helping students to improve their professional skills, digital application skills, and international literacy, and become better global citizens.

Thirdly, we are seizing the opportunity of the return of talents to promote the convergence of internationalized talents. China's successful response to the new coronavirus epidemic has demonstrated excellent governance strength and a responsible great power style, which will make China an important destination country for students and will bring about a trend of international students and foreign talents returning to China.

We will seize the opportunity to attract students from friendly countries and countries along the "Belt and Road" to study in China and build the "Study in China" brand; optimize the Chinese-foreign cooperative education system to make it easy for students to access international high-quality education resources; and formulate a more proactive policy to attract international students and foreign experts to accelerate the construction of talents. It will also formulate more proactive policies to attract foreign students and experts and accelerate the construction of a talent convergence zone and a talent return highland.

References

[1]DAAD.Jahresbericht2019[EB/OL].(2020-06-30)[2021-04-18].
https://static.daad.de/media/daad_de/pdfs_nicht_barrierefrei/derdaad/daad_jahresbericht_20
19.pdf.
[2]Hendrik Berghaeuser,Michael Hoelscher.Reinventing the third mission of higher education in Germany:political frameworks and universities' reactions[J].Tertiary Education and Management,2020,26(6):57-76.
[3]Jennifer Dusdal. Higher education in Germany-recent developments in an international perspective[J].Routledge,2019,55(2):292-294.

How to build an engineering alliance between China and Europe under the influence of educational diplomacy

SHI Yue (石玥)[1]

Abstract

Educational diplomacy provides an important complementary form of civil diplomacy. The construction of the China-Germany engineering alliance is in line with the interests and needs of the two countries as well as the common expectation of both sides. Through a case study of The University of the Greater Region and TU9, the article has sorted out the theoretical framework for the construction of a China-Germany engineering alliance. Through SWOT analysis, the internal and external factors affecting the cooperation of Sino-German engineering alliance are explained, eventually forming the construction path including the basis, organization form, influence obstacles and other aspects.

Keywords: educational diplomacy, China-Germany diplomacy, engineering education, educational alliance

Research Background

As globalization proceeds, cooperation between countries in the field of education is also receiving wider attention. The number of international students in OECD countries - reaching nearly 4.4 million international students in 2020 - has increased by 70 percent in the last decade. The number of international students in OECD countries - reaching nearly 4.4 million international students in 2020 - had increased by 70 percent in the last decade. The volume of official development assistance flows for scholarships in 2020 stood at USD 1020 million (OECD, 2022b)[2]. Educational diplomacy, on the other hand, takes a more macro view of international students, and inter-country educational activities. Many interregional or global "university consortia" have emerged. Examples include the European "Big Regions" University Consortium, the New Silk Road University Consortium, and several others. In addition, the combined effects of industrialization and globalization have led to a growing demand for globally literate engineering professionals. At present, there are inter-university and inter-consortium joint training, credit recognition, and other basic forms of cooperation. In 2010, the Sino-European Engineering Education Union (SEEEP) was established. Moreover, Germany, as a world-renowned country for engineering, has also established the German Nine-University Union (TU9) and actively participates in the European inter-regional higher education alliance. On the occasion of the 50th year of diplomatic relationship with Germany, the two countries also provide room for potential cooperation in higher education. Building a China-Germany "engineering alliance" from the perspective of educational diplomacy is not only in line with the development trend but also solves the talent gap. Therefore, a SWOT analysis will be applied to

---

[1] SHI Yue(石玥) is a Bachelor student of German Language and Literature at the Northwestern Polytechnical University (西北工业大学), Xi'an (PRC). This submission was advised by Dr. GUO Yi (国懿) Professor at the Northwestern Polytechnical University Xi'an (PRC)

[2] Department of Economic and Social Affairs Statistics SDG Indicators Database

German cross-border university consortia, proving inspiration for Chinese higher education in a global context

This essay is structured as following. Firstly, a theoretical definition of educational diplomacy will be provided, putting this concept into the wider context of diplomacy. Building on that the next section will present the University of the Greater Region and Germany TU9 engineering alliance in relation to China. After that, a SWOT analysis will present the potentials and challenges of this alliance. Eventually the conclusion will provide valuable lessons for the future development of global university alliances in the European-Chinese context as a way of educational diplomacy.

2. Theoretical Background and Research Questions

Educational diplomacy refers to a form of diplomacy in which a sovereign state, with the purpose of safeguarding national interests, uses educational and teaching activities as a carrier to improve the knowledge, skills, and comprehensive quality of the educated people in other countries and to influence their emotional attitudes[3].As a kind of interstate diplomatic behaviour, it is usually closely related to the concepts of cultural diplomacy, public diplomacy and soft power building in terms of theoretical research. On the eruption of the Cold War, cultural diplomacy was valued by countries as an important national strategy[4].The U.S. Department of State defines public diplomacy as "government-led activities designed to inform and influence public opinion in other countries"[5]. Education diplomacy and public diplomacy are both government-led diplomatic acts to "influence the sentiments of other countries towards their own countries," but the coverage of public diplomacy is wider, including not only the international exchange of talents, but also the news media and daily exchanges[6].Therefore, some scholars believe that educational diplomacy is an important way to achieve public diplomacy. In addition, Joseph Nye defined the concept of "soft power" (soft power) from the perspective of the state in 1990, arguing that "soft power" is a kind of relying on attraction, rather than by means of coercion or enticement to 'soft power is a means of achieving objectives by attraction rather than by coercion or inducement"[7]. The concept of "soft power" has attracted widespread attention since its introduction. Countries have taken the shaping of national image and the transmission of values as an important tool from the level of national strategy. In this process, inter-country educational cooperation naturally plays an important role. Admittedly, educational diplomacy can be used as a sub-proposition of cultural diplomacy, public diplomacy, and soft power building, but education, with its qualities such as longevity and potential of influence, profoundly affects international policy and national image, as well as emotions towards a certain country, and deserves to be discussed separately[8]. It can be seen that educational diplomacy is of great strategic importance for national development. To sum up, educational diplomacy, as a far-reaching diplomatic practice, deserves extensive attention and strategic layout at the macro level.

This study will focus on comparing the current situation of educational diplomacy between China and Germany, as well as the construction of engineering alliances between China and Germany, analyze in depth the role and influence of educational diplomacy in their construction, and propose a path for China to construct engineering alliances from the perspective of educational diplomacy.

---

[3] Zhou, Guping; Liang, Han (2008): "Belt and Road Initiative and Educational Diplomacy." Comparative Education Research, no. 4(04), p.3-9.

[4] Cong, Xia (2017): "Research on British Council Education Association under the Perspective of Cultural Diplomacy." Shanghai International Studies University, no. 1;p.230.

[5] Liu, Zehao (2022): "Analysis of German public diplomacy's revelation to China." International Public Relations, no.150(18),p.:22-24.

[6] Su, Shumin (2008): "Public Diplomacy and the Shaping of China's National Image." Teaching and Research:73-77.

[7] Nye, Joseph (2005). "Soft Power: The Means To Success In World Politics"Public Affairs. 20.

[8] Powell Colin.(20019: "Statement on International Education Week"(2001): p.34-35
https://2001-2009.state.gov/secretary/former/powell/remarks/ 2001/4462.html.

3. Methodology

3.1 Research Subjects

In order to explore the path of the China-Germany engineering alliance construction, the author takes The University of the Greater Region and Germany TU9 engineering alliance as case study, specifically analyzing the factors affecting the construction of the path and forms the construction path according to the analysis results.

3.2 Data Analysis and Research Process

3.2. 1 The University of the Greater Region

One of the primary cooperation bases of the University of the Greater Region is geography. The University of the Greater Region is located in a region consisting of the Rhineland in Germany, the Walloon Region in Belgium, and the Lorraine Region in France, with the Grand Duchy of Luxembourg. This region has historically been strategically important. Despite the historical controversy, the establishment of the Grand Region is a logical step as globalization has become an important trend and cooperation is needed by all countries and can benefit them.

The co-operation in the Greater Region is based on a top-down linkage. Several major universities in the Grand Alliance region first spontaneously formed a partnership, and as it developed smoothly and as the national strategy required, the government stepped in to manage it, fueling its legitimacy and policy preferences. From this perspective, the alliance is a typical example of the extension of civil diplomacy to the field of education.

In terms of organizational structure, the Alliance stands as a " three-dimensional organizational and management structure based on the alliance contract, with upward and downward mobility and full participation"[9]. The alliance contract ensures that the alliance operates according to rules and regulations. The three-dimensional organization, on the other hand, is reflected in the three main divisions of leadership, coordination and service formed in a combination of both top-down and bottom-up situations. In addition, an advisory board was introduced with representatives from students, administration, and public institutions.

3.2.2 TU9

In contrast to The University of the Greater Region, the main goal of the TU9 is to secure Germany's leading position in the field of engineering, and therefore the experience of the TU9 is more applicable to the development of the respective engineering alliances than to the construction of international or interregional alliances[10]. Importantly, the basis for the TU9's co-operation lies in a common mission and vision - to increase Germany's international competitiveness. The organizational structure of the TU9 introduces a monitoring approach in addition to functional departments similar to those of the Grand Union, which are monitored by the TU9 mainly through the Union Assembly (Mitgliederversammlung) and the annual report to ensure effective operation.

In addition, the TU9 is actively aligning itself with international standards. Firstly, the issue of degree recognition has been resolved by changing to a three-tier system, which will help to align with internationally recognized degree systems and enhance international recognition. TU9 also offers English Master's programs to minimize the obstacles caused by language barriers.

---

[9] Li, Chen; Zhu, Ling (2018): "Exploration of Regional Economy-oriented University Union--Thinking Based on the Experience of European 'Big Region 'University Union." Research on Higher Engineering Education,no. 1;p.125- 127.

[10] Zheng, Lina (2021): "The practice and revelation of strategic management of German Polytechnic University Union." Modern Education Management, no. 1; p.121- 122.

Meanwhile, TU9 has also established a special Mooc platform, which is taught by professors from the Union, to ensure the specialization and increase the influence, and has also actively established short-term international exchange programs such as summer schools and the "Engineering Experience Week" (TU9-ING-Woche). After having presented the TU 9 and its international network, the next section will look upon the strength and weakness of this alliance.

4. Findings and Discussions

Having conducted a SWOT analysis several aspects for future corporation could be elaborated. To sum up, the main factors affecting the construction of the China-German Engineering Alliance are cooperation basis, organizational structure, obstacles, and possible solutions.

4. 1 Cooperation Basis

The establishment of engineering alliance between China and Germany does not have geographic advantages, but the establishment of good diplomatic relations between China and Germany offers an important part of maintaining a stable global situation. Educational diplomacy, as a supplement to civil diplomacy, is of great significance to the friendly exchanges between countries as well as to the cooperation in the field of education. According to SWOT analysis, a current as potential status of China-Germany engineering alliance is shown in Fig 1:

	Strengths	Weaknesses
Internal environment	➢ All share a common vision for the development of engineering; ➢ All need globally literate engineering talent	➢ Geographically distant ➢ Lack of intellectual property rights and protection
	Opportunities	Threats
External environment	➢ Both Germany and China have a broad market in the field of engineering; ➢ Specialised fields of study can be mutually reinforcing and upgrading.	➢ Unilateralism and trade protectionism are on the rise, affecting co-operation.

Fig1. SWOT analysis of the construction of China-Germany engineering alliance (developed by the author)

It can be seen that the establishment of the China-Germany engineering alliance has both advantages and opportunities as well as posing certain challenges. Those will be discussed in detail within the following section, presenting the results of the SWOT Analysis.

4.2 Organizational form

On the basis of joint cooperation, a combination of "top-down" and "bottom-up" organization can be adopted. Firstly, small-scale cooperation between schools can be formed spontaneously, so that a tacit understanding of cooperation can be established. After the development has stabilized, top-down management will be developed to bring it more in line with the standards. A contract that meets the interests of both parties should be formed in the co-operation to ensure that the co-operation between the two parties is in accordance with the law. In addition, in order to ensure international recognition of the co-operation, both parties need to achieve international consistency in the education system. In addition, English-medium programs can be offered to reduce language barriers. The partner institutions can also provide language services or assistance to ensure that communication is barrier-free. Establish a shared infrastructure platform and improve the system of mutual recognition of credits. It is also possible to expand joint training programs, give full play to professional advantages, create brand disciplines, and increase visibility. Finally, it is necessary to improve the supervision mechanism to ensure the implementation of the policy, and at the same time, it is necessary to receive the opinions of student representatives, enterprises, and other parties to improve the shortcomings in a timely manner.

4.3 Obstacles

4.3. 1 Financial obstacle

Obviously, overcoming long distances like between China and Europe requires financial resources. In order to ensure that the co-operative projects run smoothly, and that teachers and students are not affected by financial barriers, seed funds can be set up in the alliance to liquidly fund researchers who meet the requirements. Furthermore, existing scholarships systems could be expanded or new scholarships systems for deserved students and researchers to be set up.

4.3.2 Policy Orientation of Emerging Industries

The rapid development of emerging industries is inseparable from the policy orientation of each country. The rise of emerging industries will lead to a certain impact on traditional engineering. However, on the one hand, the alliance needs to continue to give full play to the advantages of traditional engineering disciplines and continue to give full play to the advantages of traditional engineering disciplines by driving scientific research cooperation with the advantageous disciplines; on the other hand, it is also possible to co-operate in the alliance to promote the development of emerging industries.

5. Conclusion

Through the case analysis of two alliances, The University of the Greater Region and TU9, the author draws a path to build the China-Germany engineering alliance. The basis for the construction of alliance was analyzed through SWOT analysis. Based on the case study, the organizational structure and obstacles of the alliance construction were analyzed, which have a positive impact on the China-Germany educational diplomacy and cooperation. However, this study lacks the interpretation of the policy, in the future research can be combined with the current foreign policy, improve the theoretical framework, promote the construction of the China-Germany engineering alliance, and actively develop education diplomacy to improve China's international influence.

Concluding this short analysis reveals that education provides a common ground for different cultures, with engineering providing a fertile soil for the future development of societies ever more shaped by sophisticated technologies. This SWOT analysis has revealed that global engineering-alliances are not an option but an urgency in an ever more connected world. However, in order to deploy the benefits of such alliances an appropriate context has to be set. This includes first of all getting aware of the respective foreign culture, becoming curious and eager to develop a common vision on the goals of this educational exchange. Furthermore, sufficient financial resources for mobility such as trained staff, speaking at least English is needed to overcome the language barrier. Eventually, the networks build up here, should build the cornerstone of an interdisciplinary, intercultural, and mutual confident corporation to shape the future. The research on engineering alliances reveals, that educational diplomacy through educational exchange provides the material for on the one hand building bridges among the people and cultures as on the other hand, establishing international academic networks build bridges into a future in a global world.

Through the cooperation and establishment of the engineering alliance, China and Germany can not only cooperate deeply in education, but also take this opportunity to promote the diplomatic career of the two countries. In addition, the talents cultivated in the engineering alliance with inter-cultural competence and professional qualities will also contribute to the development of engineering manufacturing in China and Germany. The author expects that a closer educational diplomacy can be established between China and Germany. If this model of cooperation is successful, it can also be extended to a wider region such as China with the European Union. In the future, more and more students will be able to learn professional knowledge and expand their horizons in the world. With the support of educational diplomacy, cooperation between countries can outweigh competition and contribute to the building of humanity within a community envisaging a shared future.

References

Cong, Xia (2017): "Research on British Council Education Association under the Perspective of Cultural Diplomacy." Shanghai International Studies University, no. 1;p. 230.

Li, Chen; Zhu, Liang (2018): "Exploration of Regional Economy-oriented University Union--Thinking Based on the Experience of European 'Big Region 'University Union." Research on Higher Engineering Education, no. 1;p.125- 127.

Liu, Zehao (2022). "Analysis of German public diplomacy's revelation to China." International Public Relations, no.150(18),p.22-24.

Nye, Joseph (2005): "Soft Power: The Means To Success In World Politics"Public Affairs,p.20.

Powell, Colin (2009): "Statement on International Education Week", p. 34-35
 available at https://2001-2009.state.gov/secretary/former/powell/remarks/ 2001/4462.html.

 Su,Shumin (2008): "Public Diplomacy and the Shaping of China's National Image." Teaching and Research, no.1, p.73-77.

Zheng, Lina (2021): "The practice and revelation of strategic management of German Polytechnic University Union." Modern Education Management, no. 1,p.121- 122.

Zhou, Guping; Liang. Han (2008): "Belt and Road Initiative and Educational Diplomacy." Comparative Education Research, no. 4(04),p. 3-9.

A Comparative Analysis of the Chinese and German Education Systems from a Chronological Perspective -- What Should be the Way Forward for Higher Education and Vocational Education in China Today?

CHEN Liming (陈梨铭) [1] */ CHEN Hongran(陈红燃)* [2] */ ZHOU Chao(周超)* [3]

Abstract

The demand for talents has changed in recent years as a consequence of China's economic and social transformation and development. Thus, the traditional Chinese educational system is not sufficiently adapted to meet this demand anymore. This has resulted in an imbalance between supply and demand on the job market and novel requirements for general higher education as well as vocational education. One of the numerous European nations with a more comprehensive educational system and exceptional economic growth is Germany. For the purpose of searching to elaborate on workable recommendations for the coordination of growth in higher education and vocational education in China in the new era, this paper analyzes the differences between the two based on the past experiences of the development of higher education and vocational education in Germany and China.

Keywords: Vocational Education, Higher Education, China, Germany

Introduction

Due to historical circumstances, China's educational modernization came late, and there are still many areas in which there is opportunity for improvement. The overall state of the job market in China is tense due to an imbalance between supply and demand, with graduates of vocational education programs facing discrimination in the workplace due to their academic credentials and higher education graduates facing criticism for their lack of real-world experience and difficulty finding employment. An unwelcoming "involution" of employment has resulted from both of these challenging predicaments in China. Looking abroad, Germany was a pioneer in the modernization of education, ingeniously incorporating many aspects of higher education and vocational education into the curriculum for students. Applied universities with distinct teaching departments that educate a wide range of students not only facilitate an efficient transfer from the classroom to the workplace but also acknowledge the need of students to get employment, particularly excellent employment.

In light of this development, this essay will examine in-depth the parallels and discrepancies between the educational systems of China and Germany across time, with the goal of identifying

---

[1] CHEN Liming(陈梨铭) is a Bachelor Student for Financial Management at the Chongqing College of Mobile Communication (重庆移通学院), Chongqing (PRC))

[2] CHEN Hongran(陈红燃) is a Bachelor Student for Sports Economics and Management at the Chongqing College of Mobile Communication, Chongqing (PRC)

[3] ZHOU Chao(周超) is a Bachelor Student for Financial Management at the Chongqing College of Mobile Communication, Chongqing (PRC))

This submission was supervised by Deng Jinying (邓锦莹),lecturer from the Chongqing College of Mobile Communication

workable solutions to the country's present employment issues. In this essay, higher education is described as instruction that follows the completion of upper secondary school and concentrates on cultivating academic aptitude and facilitating the growth of students' theoretical thinking skills. Practical skill development is given greater emphasis in vocational education. There is no degree difference between higher education and vocational education; they are basically two different types of education. In the following first a historic overview of the development of higher education in China and Germany will be given. After that, the next part will look upon the structure of the different system, with the third part focusing on a) potential career perspectives b) streamlining education and c) employability and market orientation. Eventually, this essay will end with a conclusion about potentials for learning from both systems.

I、 China and Germany before the Middle Ages

China has a long history of advancement in education. Ancient China's educational foundation was built during the pre-Qin period. Higher education at that point was mostly used for political purposes, and the majority of the students were the children of powerful families who learned military strategies and cultural knowledge. Educational requirements declined and private schools arose as a consequence of the social unrest that occurred throughout the Spring and Autumn and Warring States Periods, which had an influence on large families. The Guozijian, (Imperial College or Academy, the highest educational body in Imperial China), the top administration school, and nearby private academies helped shatter the aristocracy's monopoly on education by gradually popularizing education and reducing the enrolment criteria. The custom of providing "explicit" general education to the aristocrats and "implicit" vocational education to those in labor started to take shape at this point in time. Officials, peasants, laborers, and merchants were the main class bearers of vocational education throughout medieval society after the Han Dynasty, and it has continued to exist today in both school and non-school settings.[4]

The Church oversaw education in medieval Germany, which was ruled by ecclesiastical law. With the exception of church schools, there were hardly any secular educational institutions, and monks eventually held a monopoly on instruction that was more religious and theological in nature. Church schools were separated into three categories: monastic schools, episcopal schools, and diocesan schools .Urban crafts were produced by artisans who also apprenticed others to carry on their craft. Apprenticeships in the guilds were strictly divided into three grades, "apprentice-apprentice-craftsman," and they were also accompanied by the autonomy of the craft guilds. Up until the early 19th century, the tight division of apprenticeship education into "apprentice-apprentice-craftsman" and independent craftsmen's guilds went hand in hand.[5]

II. Modern China and Germany

The foreign affairs group established a number of academies in the 1960s as China learned from the West. The first connections between Chinese education and the outside world were made, marking the beginning of modern, structured higher education in China.[6] China's modern vocational education has undergone two transformations since the late Qing Dynasty. The transition from art apprenticeship education to vocational education took place in two stages, with the generalization of vocational education taking place in the second.[7] In contemporary China, higher education and vocational education are inextricably linked. Due to extensive research into related skills and educational reforms, vocational schools established by churches

---

[4]Xiao huayi,and Gong Jing, „The Development Process, Characteristics and Enlightenment of Vocational Education in Ancient China from the Perspective of Technology Inheritance", *Higher Vocational Education Exploration*,vol.22no.4July (2023),49-54

[5] Li Chao, „The Transition from Traditional Apprenticeship Education to Modern Vocational Education - the Example of Germany in the 19th century", Science and Technology of Chinese Colleges and Universities,2017

[6] Liu Jingkun,"A Review of the Development of Higher Education in Modern China", Journal of Southeast University(Phiosophy and Social Science,doi:10.13916/j.cnki.issn1671-511.2004.01.027

[7] Duan Lanyu. "The transmutation of vocational education in modern China,"2019.

and chambers of commerce in modern times have gradually evolved into comprehensive institutions. An example of this is the Zhang Jian-founded Nantong Textile and Dyeing Institute, which was formerly known as the "China Textile University" and is now known as the Tung Wah Group of Universities.

While higher education grew, vocational education was also established up in accordance with the need for specialized learning during the same period as the church's fall and the growth of new educational ideas in Germany. The University of Berlin in Germany is one of them and is considered to be representative. Humboldt proposed a perfect university model in his essay "on the internal and external organization of higher academic institutions in Berlin," which reads as follows: "colleges and universities to achieve the unity of research and teaching, the pursuit of academic freedom, education through science, the state of the overall supervision of the university and to give support to the university, the university has the right to regulate internal and academic affairs." The university is allowed to control its own internal and academic matters[8]

III. Contemporary China and Germany

The primary, secondary, and higher education systems in China and Germany are similar in that both have universally mandated education at least through junior high school. However, there are significant differences in the timing of the education streams and the level of dissemination of vocational education.

(I) education streams

The early start of streaming, in which students are divided into the main secondary school, the practical secondary school, the grammar secondary school, and the comprehensive secondary school at the end of primary school, is one of the most distinctive features of the German educational system. The majority of students in grammar secondary schools continue their education at the university level; the majority of students in substantive secondary schools continue their education in a dual or full-time vocational program after graduation. Comprehensive secondary schools include the other three types of schools, so they cannot be generalized. Students at major schools face more challenges, such as the fact that many are unable to enroll in vocational education and must enter the transitional system or the transition system, having to enter the transition system (Übergangssystem) after completing their studies.[9]

At the middle school level, there is a small-scale streaming process where students with good grades and good family backgrounds continue their education in regular high schools in China, while others opt to go directly to employment or secondary vocational education, which includes secondary specialized schools, technical schools, and vocational senior high schools. On the contrary, senior secondary schools' stream on an enormous scale. Students are split into undergraduate and university specialties based on their performance on college admission tests.

(II) Educational qualifications and the employment conundrum

According to data published public by China's Human Resources and Social Resources Security Bureau, the country would rely on a potential of 11.58 million college graduates by 2023, up from 950,000 in 2000.[10] On the contrary, the advantage that a degree may provide to getting a job has diminished due to the high rise in college graduates.

---

[8] Wilhelm von Humboldt, Schriften zur Politik und zum Bildungswesen, in: Werke, Bd. 4, hrsg. v. Andreas Flitner und Klaus Geil, Stuttgart 19934, S. 255ff
[9] Li Jun, and He Duoming, „Influence of Education Structure on the Interaction between Social Stratification and Education --Comparative Investigation of China Germany and America", *International and Comparative Education*,no3.(2017),1
[10] Ministry of Human Resources: http://www.mohrss.gov.cn/SYrlzyhshbzb/dongtaixinwen/buneiyaowen/rsxw/202307/t20230711_502716.html, last modified July 11,2023

Undergraduates in China's educational system are considered not as professional like experts for professions demanding a high degree of practical operation, and they are not as competitive as master's and doctorate students for positions requiring a low threshold of academic qualifications. While undergraduate education places a greater emphasis on the acquisition of theoretical knowledge, specialist education places a greater emphasis on the development of students' practical hands-on skills and workplace education in order to prepare students for future employment. As a result, even though specialist education is slightly less academically rigorous than undergraduate, it is still simple to find a job with a higher salary. As reported in Wisdom Recruitment's "2023 Survey Report on Employability of College Students," 45.7% and 47.5%, respectively, of the fresh graduates from the 2022 and 2023 undergraduate classes received job offers, while 49.4% and 54.4%, respectively, of the fresh graduates from the 2022 and 2023 junior colleges performed. [11]

The "dual system" approach has been widely applied in vocational education in Germany, and it has been progressively expanding since the 1970s in higher education. The Dual System has contributed to the modernization and expansion of higher education in Germany as well as the preparation of professionals and applied researchers who are well adapted to the nation's economic, social, and technical advancement. All Länder that are implementing the "dual system" in higher education have acknowledged its benefits, and the number of projects they are working on expands the following year.[12]

Table 1: Development of the "dual system" in German universities and colleges in the Länder, 2004-2016

YEAR	2004	2005	2006	2007	2008	2009	2010	2011	2012	2013	2014	20
Baden-Württemberg	141	152	167	192	194	201	214	228	237	245	268	27
Bayern	21	24	28	48	55	62	67	125	154	172	303	32
Berlin	21	22	23	21	21	23	24	25	20	25	48	47
Brandenburg	4	4	3	3	3	4	3	2	4	7	14	23
Bremen	2	2	4	6	6	6	8	8	7	7	12	13
Hamburg	8	13	12	13	13	14	15	16	12	15	38	37
Hessen	40	45	50	66	70	74	68	65	66	75	125	12
Mecklenburg-Vorpommern	2	2	5	5	7	6	6	7	7	7	14	19
Niedersachsen	68	71	72	62	61	59	60	64	70	73	98	10
Nordrhein-Westfalen	86	93	112	112	114	113	156	171	157	183	287	31
Rheinland-Pfalz	8	9	12	12	12	13	12	21	25	31	69	81
Saarland	6	6	8	9	9	9	11	9	9	10	17	17
Sachsen	52	51	58	65	69	71	72	77	79	82	98	98
Sachsen-Anhalt	2	2	5	9	10	10	11	13	14	24	35	34
Schleswig-Holstein	21	19	19	14	14	15	16	15	15	25	32	39
Thüringen	30	30	30	29	29	32	33	33	34	33	47	48

[11] China Daily: https://tech.chinadaily.com.cn/a/202305/05/WS6455ae37a310537989372f2d.html , last modified May 5,2023

[12] Xue Simin, and Dong Xianhui, „Current status and characteristics of the development of the "dual system" of higher education in Germany",doi:1001-7518(2020)09-0612-07

Total	512	545	608	666	687	712	776	879	910	1014	1505	1592

The top three states in terms of beginning salary for graduates are Baden-Württemberg with the University of Heidelberg, Bavaria with the Technical University of Munich, and Hessen with the University of Frankfurt, according to statistics on the website karrierebibel.de.[13]

Table 2. Average income of students in higher education in the Länder of Germany

Bundesland	Einstiegesgehalt(Jahresbrutto)
Baden-Württemberg	47,768Euro
Bayern	47,393Euro
Berlin	42,873Euro
Brandenburg	42,751Euro
Bremen	42,796Euro
Hamburg	45,105Euro
Hessen	46,351Euro
Mecklenburg-Vorpommern	42,782Euro
Niedersachsen	44,171Euro
Nordrhein-Westfalen	44,736Euro
Rheinland-Pfalz	44,377Euro
Saarland	43,068Euro
Sachsen	38,407Euro
Sachsen-Anhalt	39,351Euro
Schleswig-Holstein	42,739Euro

The vocational curriculum clearly has a significant impact on students' salaries and earnings, whereas higher education institutions, with their dual education model, integrate theory and practice, allowing students to fully utilize what they have learned and improve their professional competitiveness. Eventually the last section will provide an outlook for some future lessons.

---

[13] Karrierebibel: https://karrierebibel.de/gehalt/,last modified July,2023

FUTURES THINKING:

The sea is full of rivers, and they lean on each other for strength. The dynamic development of education in the world cannot be separated from the mutual inspiration and strengthening of the advanced concepts and experiences of various countries.

I. Constructing a "dual system" program and a structure where businesses and schools play key roles in vocational education.

To support vocational schools in developing various forms of enterprise cooperation, such as order-based training, modern apprenticeship, industrial colleges, and group-sponsored training and Education, while also promoting the development of "dual system" programs in universities, using school-enterprise cooperation programs as the guiding principle, so as to encourage students to acquire information while participating in internships and operations at businesses, allowing them to get job experience and improve their employability.

II. Triage time is necessary to provide more accessible ascending routes.

In China, lower secondary school level streaming is more acceptable than primary school level streaming, in contrast to Germany where streaming is done at the elementary school level. The students themselves are first and foremost more mature for their age and have clearer thoughts about their future careers. Second, the majority of junior high school graduates are around 15 years old and have a better understanding of technology, which can make teaching less challenging. However, most technology cannot be learned quickly, so learning about three years before adulthood can not only help children develop their skills to the fullest, but also help to prevent child labor from developing.

The barriers between vocational and higher education will be opened up on the basis of streaming, supported by the digitalization of education and more accessible channels for upgrading academic qualifications.

III. Adherence to market orientation and promotion of employment

Keeping the "visible hand" of the government and the "invisible hand" of the market, forming a pluralistic pattern of schooling with the strong promotion of the government and the deep participation of social forces, and strengthening the nation with talented people. Bolster the government's position of leadership, boost financial support for both higher education and career training, promote public oversight, and significantly raise educational standards. Second, promote the operation of diverse schools, support the widespread and equal participation of social forces in vocational education through a unified access system, and promote social forces' involvement in the coordinated development of higher education and vocational education through the use of resources like capital, knowledge, technology, management, and other factors.

CONCLUSION:

These two data shows that the implementation of the German "dual system" model can indeed enhance the comprehensive ability of students in theory and practice, and the better the development of the dual system model in the region, the better the salary of graduates. China's "college entrance examination" mode is not only a compromise of traditional culture, but also the key point of the current employment difficulties. Therefore, if you want to reasonably link the current employment problems of college students, it is necessary for colleges and universities to actively carry out teaching reforms and cultivate the comprehensive quality of students. In this regard, the initiative of Chongqing College Of Mobile Communication is worthy of reference. Located in Chongqing, China, Chongqing College Of Mobile Communication is one of the first 37 pilot colleges of the Ministry of Education's University of Applied Technology Reform in China, with some of its educational concepts borrowed from the German "dual system" model. Chongqing College Of Mobile Communication focuses on the overall development of students' quality education, innovatively builds a unique talent cultivation model, focuses on school-enterprise cooperation, accurately meets the latest market demand for talents, emphasizes the promotion of students' innovation and entrepreneurship projects, and develops a linkage guidance system for students' career development and employment and entrepreneurship, and has been awarded the title of "Model Unit for Employment and Entrepreneurship of Graduates of Chongqing Colleges and Universities" for several times.

References

China Daily: https://tech.chinadaily.com.cn/a/202305/05/WS6455ae37a310537989372f2d.html, last modified May 5,2023,

Duan Lanyu. *"The transmutation of vocational education in modern China"*,2019.

Karrierebibel: https://karrierebibel.de/gehalt/, last modified July,2023

Li Chao, *„The Transition from Traditional Apprenticeship Education to Modern Vocational Education - the Example of Germany in the 19th century"*, Science and Technology of Chinese Colleges and Universities,2017

Li Jun, and He Duoming, *„Influence of Education Structure on the Interaction between Social Stratification and Education --Comparative Investigation of China Germany and America"*, International and Comparative Education,no3.(2017),1

Liu Jingkun,"*A Review of the Development of Higher Education in Modern China"*, Journal of Southeast University (Philosophy and Social Science)

Ministry of Education
http://www.moe.gov.cn/jyb_xwfb/gzdt_gzdt/s5987/202208/t20220820_654207.html, last modified August,20,2022

Ministry of Human Resources:
http://www.mohrss.gov.cn/SYrlzyhshbzb/dongtaixinwen/buneiyaowen/rsxw/202307/t2023071 1_502716.html , last modified July 11,2023

Wilhelm von Humboldt, Schriften zur Politik und zum Bildungswesen, in: Werke, Bd. 4, hrsg. v. Andreas Flitner und Klaus Geil, Stuttgart 19934, S. 255ff.

Xiao huayi,and Gong Jing, *„The Development Process, Characteristics and Enlightenment of Vocational Education in Ancient China from the Perspective of Technology Inheritance"*, Higher Vocational Education Exploration,vol.22no.4July (2023)

Xue Simin, and Dong Xianhui, *„Current status and characteristics of the development of the 'dual system' of higher education in Germany"*

IV. Educational Diplomacy trough intercultural exchange

From Related Intercultural Experience to People-to-People Bonds: Field Research into a Post-Pandemic Art Salon of European and Chinese Youths

LYU Yuan (吕远)[1] JIN Shengyuan (金圣沅)[2]

Abstract

Given the post-pandemic uncertainty of people-to-people exchanges between Europe and China, this essay investigates a recent Sino-European youth dialogue project, with a focus on a successful art salon of European and Chinese youths in Freiburg, Germany as the core event. Through field research, this essay examines the process and effects of the intercultural youth project and argues that the art salon, based on the interculturality between the local event organizer and the core audience, seems exemplary for a future Sino-European youth program. It is observable that the German context of extracurricular education and lifelong learning provides a favorable environment for the formation of youth groups with intercultural awareness, who are the potential target groups of Sino-European exchange activities. With appropriate occasions and prior preparations, an ideal Sino-European exchange activity can intensify the target group's Sino-European interculturality and transform their intercultural experience into people-to-people bonds.

Keywords: Sino-European interculturality, people-to-people bonds, youth exchanges, extracurricular education

Research Background and Question

The past pandemic witnessed exceptional restrictions on people-to-people communication between Europe and China. Despite the ongoing restart in many aspects, it still seems to cast a shadow over post-pandemic relations between the two societies. On the one hand, the recovery of bilateral official contacts in the politico-economic sphere is observable. For instance, French President Macron paid a three-day state visit to China and Chinese Premier Li Qiang made his first overseas trip since taking office to Germany and France this year; the Chinese harbor city Ningbo hosted the first post-pandemic China-CEEC Expo. On the other hand, people-to-people exchanges seem to be faced with uncertainties. Albeit the official willingness for dialogue, tourist entries into China and European countries are still far below the figures from 2019[3] .

The high-level China-Germany people-to-people dialogues starting from the last decade, for example, reflected bilateral attempts of governments and civil societies to promote mutual understanding; this dialogue however remains in the exploration phase today. People-to-people exchanges between Europe and China have been attracting academic attention in the recent

---

[1] *LYU Yuan (吕远)* is a PhD student at the at the Institute of Chinese Studies, Albert-Ludwigs University of Freiburg

[2] JIN Shengyuan (金圣沅) is a Master student at the School of Crafts at the China Academy of Art (中国美术学院) in Hangzhou (PRC)

Both authors contributed equally to this work. Special thanks are due to SHI Xuanyang for his indispensable contribution to the fieldwork.

[3] This resulted from a limited number of visas issued for citizens on both sides as well as other reasons.

decade. Ever since the EU-China High-Level People-to-People Dialogue was established as the third pillar of bilateral partnership in 2012, an increasing number of studies have been conducted on public diplomacy in Sino-European relations.[4] Both the diplomatic role of people-to-people interactions in PRC history and its contemporary salience began to receive investigation.[5] Nevertheless, considering that people-to-people bonds are fostered through education, media, sport, youth exchanges, etc., contemporary Sino-European youth exchanges are still under-researched. Previous research in this field focused on the transnational history of Chinese and European youths' experiences in Europe and China, respectively, in the twentieth century.[6]

Against this background, this essay investigates a recent Sino-European youth dialogue project conducted in Freiburg, Germany, and focuses on a successful art salon at the University of Freiburg as the core of this project. Given the current situation mentioned above, such Sino-European youth dialogue and positive feedback generated therefrom are still rare in recent times. Based on field research on this intercultural project, this essay highlights its process and multiple effects and explores inspirational ideas for future dialogues between European and Chinese youths. This essay addresses the following questions: *How can the European audience's interest in Chinese culture be awakened and deepened and what principles can be applied when designing relevant intercultural programs?*

2.   Methods and Specifications of the Fieldwork

The fieldwork was conducted in Freiburg, Germany, which is a university city located in the border triangle of Germany, France, and Switzerland. The campus and urban space of Freiburg have been immersed in a long tradition of humanities and cultural crossings, enriched with intercultural youth activities. The recent youth dialogue project i.e., the focus of this essay is directed by the local intercultural platform *Chinesischer Kulturverein e.V.* (Chinese Culture Association, hereafter CKV) and supported by its long-term cooperation with a local German Kung Fu school named *Wu Xing Kung Fu Zentrum Freiburg* (hereafter the Kung Fu school).[7]

Registered as a student group at the University of Freiburg and a non-profit association in Germany, the CKV was established by local Chinese students in 2019 and continues to absorb Chinese students in this region who are interested in Sino-European communications.[8] The Kung Fu school in Freiburg has been in existence for over a decade, attracting locals (mostly Europeans) interested in Chinese martial arts.[9] As a complement to school and college education, the Kung Fu school provides local students with an option for extracurricular education;[10] apart from students, local intellectuals form an essential part of its membership, including teachers from local education institutions. In other words, both the CKV and the Kung Fu school play an active role in the German landscape of lifelong learning and intercultural education system and their long-standing cooperation is inspirational for future educational exchanges between Europe and China.

This research employs the methods of participant observation and interviews, which enable the gathering of both insiders' perceptions and participants' interpretations of the intercultural activities. Through the platform of the CKV, the authors participated in the project organization and took the rare opportunity to experience the whole process, closely observe the audience's

---

[4] For instance, see Burnay et al. 2014 and Hong 2014.

[5] See Wang 2016 as a review and analysis of this topic.

[6] For example, see Bailey 1988 and Levine 1993 as historical studies on Chinese youth in France during the Chinese revolutions in the early twentieth century; see Graziani 2017 and 2018 for Sino-European youth interactions during the Cold War.

[7] According to the two organizations' records, their formal cooperation started in 2019, while informal exchanges among some Chinese and German members of the two date back to 2016.

[8] See https://mp.weixin.qq.com/s/qzr-YDR4C1aO3si0m3R4Fw.

[9] See https://www.kungfuzentrum-freiburg.de/.

[10] This applies to students at different levels of education, such as half-day education at German elementary schools and college education with relatively flexible schedules

response during various activities, and engage in discussions with participants. The research focused especially on the art salon at the University of Freiburg besides other related activities.

3.　　　Process and Results of the Investigation

The intercultural project was held between the end of June and early July 2023, when two young artists from China were invited to display traditional Chinese calligraphy and ink paintings to an audience in Freiburg and communicate with them. This research analyzed three different types of intercultural art events. Firstly, a traditional type of exhibition was held in the form of an art salon. Secondly, several pieces of art were displayed in students´ dorms. Eventually, a performance on the street was conducted. Those had different impacts on the audience, revealing new insights for conceiving intercultural encounter events. In the art salon on June 22, there was an exhibition of videos and tangible copies of artworks under the theme "Chinese Culture-Kung Fu." [11] Toward the end of the salon, a special on-site performance allowed the audience to get up close and personal with ink paintings, and the attendees were also encouraged to take home some artworks from the on-site performance as a complimentary gift.

The salon accepted over ten European participants, mostly young students, and locals enthusiastic about Chinese culture. Among these were the trainer and trainees from the Kung Fu school. Throughout the event, the audience displayed great interest and appreciation towards the cultural exhibition and Chinese art. The visitors from the Kung Fu school were the most enthusiastic and appreciative, actively communicating with the Chinese artists on the spot. After the event, they even treated the Chinese artists to a Chinese dinner at a local Chinese restaurant and invited the artists to their school for further discussions.

It is noteworthy that the Chinese artists and event organizers of the CKV visited the Kung Fu school three times in total, as an introduction to and continuation of the salon. During the initial visit, the artists displayed some paintings, elaborated on the idea of "Chinese Culture-Kung Fu," and expressed their wish to present those paintings as gifts. Gradually, the idea of "Chinese Culture-Kung Fu" made sense to the European Kung-Fu practitioners at the school, and the trainer gladly helped mobilize his pupils to participate in the salon. During this period, it was observable how the locals' interest in Chinese culture was awakened or strengthened in response to the concept of "Chinese Culture-Kung Fu." This visit could be viewed as a rehearsal for the upcoming salon. The Kung Fu school served as a starting point to identify the potential audience in Europe for the event.

During the second and third visits following the success of the salon, the members of the Kung Fu school held two informal meetings with the Chinese artists to discuss "Culture-Kung Fu" and traditional Chinese paintings in further detail. At those meetings, the artists gifted a batch of paintings to the trainer and manager of the Kung Fu school, who immediately arranged for all the trainees present to take group photos with the Chinese paintings and expressed interest in visiting China in the future. Apart from the salon, the artists held other people-to-people cultural exchange activities in Freiburg such as live shows for college students at a student apartment (attended by 2-3 students) and an on-site performance for the general public at the city center. These two activities had limited outcomes compared to the salon. The live shows at the student apartment only achieved rudimentary results, such as presenting the artworks and taking group photos, but failed to stimulate further interest in Chinese culture among the participants. The activity at the city center had barely any attendees.

---

[11] The term "Chinese Culture-Kung Fu" refers to Chinese traditional fine arts such as painting and calligraphy. "Culture-Kung Fu" is contrasted with the concept of "Kung Fu" or "Combat-Kung Fu" in the Western context, which refers to traditional Chinese martial arts. However, similar to "Combat-Kung Fu," "Culture-Kung Fu" reflects the original meaning of the word "Kung Fu" in the Chinese context, which implies long-term training and on-site adaptability, and is a reinterpretation of the word "Kung Fu."

4.   Discussion

During their journey in Freiburg, the Chinese artists conducted three types of intercultural activities in an experiential style. All three encouraged audience engagement via live presentations of traditional Chinese paintings and calligraphy but generated contrasting effects. The art salon at the University of Freiburg received positive and persistent feedback, paving the way for further cultural exchanges at the Kung Fu school. The small-scale art presentations at the student apartment attracted temporary attention. The public art performance in the city center was poorly received. Despite the similar style of all three experiential activities, what made the art salon stand out? Three points of analysis are presented below:

First, the target audience made a significant difference in the outcomes of the intercultural activities. Considering the main topic of Sino-European cultural exchanges, the art salon found a highly selective group as the core audience i.e., local youth and intellectuals from the local Kung Fu school with a deep interest in Chinese culture. It benefited from the long-standing cooperation between the CKV and the Kung Fu school that laid a solid foundation for the event. Although the other two activities had almost identical themes, they paid little attention to audience selection.

Second, the occasion mattered. The salon was held at the University of Freiburg, utilizing the campus environment to gather young students and encourage an exchange of ideas. It provided a perfect opportunity to expand the reach of the event to a broader audience besides the core audience. However, the locations of the other two activities were relatively unsuitable in this regard, due to either a lack of facilities and atmosphere or an overly complex composition of the crowd, resulting in difficulties in targeting the right audience.

Third, prior preparations were essential. Before planning the salon, the organizer had long-standing communication with members of the Kung Fu school. Through this process, the organizer captured the interest of this core audience and developed corresponding topics, experiential sessions, and strategies for interpretation. In contrast, the other two activities were organized without clearly designed themes or preparations in advance.

Based on the analysis above, such cultural exchanges cannot be effective when the intended audience have unrelated experiences and share few common perceptions of the main topic with the organizers. In the art salon event, the relevant cultural experiences enabled interactions between the Chinese artists and the European audience, further deepened by occasions and prior preparations for dialogue; hence, this event can be referred to as an exemplary intercultural exchange of relevant experiences, resulting in people-to-people bonds.

5.   Conclusion

The investigated intercultural project served as an experiment focused on enhancing future Sino-European youth exchanges. The art salon involving European and Chinese youths, in particular, generated inspiration to design such programs in the future. Without a doubt, "people" are at the center of people-to-people communication. To be specific, a selective group with a deep interest in certain intercultural topics can effectively enhance the interactions in such activities; as an intended core audience, this group can affect other participants and even determine the general atmosphere. In the German context, extracurricular education and lifelong learning can be good spheres for the formation of and communication among youth groups with intercultural awareness that is shaped by intercultural experiences. By employing such core groups, various Sino-European exchange activities can be designed to intensify intercultural interest and understanding of experiences related to people-to-people bonds.

When such core groups are secured, it is crucial to determine the venue and organizer of such intercultural activities. Generally speaking, the solution to this question should be adapted to local conditions. A prospect can nonetheless be envisioned to take place in a public space such as a multifunctional room at a local college or school, which is familiar to youth groups and accessible to locals who may have a relevant interest. Based on the experience discussed above, local NGOs with a background in education seem to be good organizers of such envisioned events for intercultural encounters. The form of such activities can be taken as a seminar, a workshop, a salon, or any other possible options suitable to the subject of the planned activity. Depending on how curricula are designed in a given school or region, the envisioned intercultural event can further, in a close or relatively loose manner, be related to the local school education.

In addition to the principle and outlook mentioned above, the following methods of prior preparation and atmosphere building were highlighted in the fieldwork: To begin with, the experience of an event should be encouraged before it can be analyzed. Taking that the audience's perceptions constitute the foundation of their understanding, ordinary culture-themed preaching and discussion may simply produce intercultural stereotypes. It thus comes first to encourage relevant personal experience. Moreover, visible, and tangible artifacts can be used for the crystallization of abstract cultural concepts, e.g., traditional Chinese ink paintings. This step will not only reduce the abstractness of cultural elements but also satisfy the participants' expectations of experiencing original and authentic elements, thus laying the foundation for further dialogue. Furthermore, the methods of interpreting cross-cultural and local contexts must be determined. For instance, the concept of "Culture-Kung Fu" corresponded with the familiar notion of "Kung Fu" for the Western audience and was strengthened by local Kung Fu practitioners' interest in and understanding of Chinese culture. Last but not least, some kind of souvenirs should be arranged.

Taking the art salon as an example, the participants were encouraged to choose on-site artworks produced during the event as complementary gifts. This approach fostered their sense of involvement and strengthened the role of "artifacts" as carriers of the experience. Building on this besides taking the target group into account, a multisensory approach has to be considered.

References

Bailey, Paul. 1988. "The Chinese Work—Study Movement in France." *The China Quarterly* 115: 441–461.

Burnay, Matthieu; Hivonnet, Joëlle; Raube, Kolja. 2014. "Soft Diplomacy' and People-to-People Dialogue between the EU and the PRC." *European Foreign Affairs Review* 19 (SI): 35-55.

Graziani, Sofia. 2017. "The Case of Youth Exchanges and Interactions Between the PRC and Italy in the 1950s." *Modern Asian Studies* 51 (1): 194–226.
———. 2018. "China's Communist Youth League, Transnational Networks and Sino–European Interactions in the Early Cold War." In *Europe and China in the Cold War*, edited by Janick Marina Schaufelbuehl, Marco Wyss, and Valeria Zanier, 108-133. Leiden and Boston: Brill.

Hong, Natalie Yan. 2014. "EU-China Education Diplomacy: An Effective Soft Power Strategy?" *European Foreign Affairs Review* 19 (SI): 155-171.

Levine, Marilyn A.1993. *The Found Generation: Chinese Communists in Europe during the Twenties*. Seattle: University of Washington Press.

Wang, Shichen. 2016. "China's People-to-people Diplomacy and Its Importance to China-EU Relations: A Historical Institutionalism Perspective." *Journal of China and International Relations* 4: 1-19.

Fostering a transformative future: Advancing educational exchanges between Europe and China

Lorraine Lin (林悦莹)[1]

Abstract

The best way to understand a different culture and their perspectives on the world is to meet people from different cultures. According to the famous contact hypothesis, meeting people from another culture supports debunking stereotypes and fostering intercultural understanding. This is a critical skill for an ever more globally interconnected world. Simultaneously, educational diplomacy provides a valuable tool for improving international relations between countries. Therefore, this contribution is split into two parts. The first part will discuss new ways of creating and harnessing the potential of intercultural encounter programs. After that, the second part will elaborate on this groundwork for a potential outlook on the power of educational diplomacy. Putting those ideas into a European-Chinese context, the conclusion of this contribution argues that education exchanges have a tremendous potential to promote mutual understanding, encourage creativity and much more in the age of globalization.

Keywords: Educational Exchange, Intercultural Skills, Educational Diplomacy

---

I ADVANCING EDUCATIONAL EXCHANGES BETWEEN EUROPE AND CHINA

Introduction

Education exchanges between Europe and China have a tremendous potential to promote mutual understanding, cultural enrichment, and creative partnerships in the age of globalization. The first part of this essay examines how exchange programs are created, how to spark people's interest in other people's cultures, how educational diplomacy might be used more effectively, and how a new paradigm in international and global education is evolving. After that, the second part will apply those ideas to the spheres of educational diplomacy, revealing the implications for those programs on the global level.

a) Development and Evolution of Exchange Programs

In the future, exchange programs between Europe and China are expected to develop rapidly. The development of internet platforms and technological breakthroughs have made it possible to collaborate virtually and communicate efficiently. By utilizing these resources, universities can create hybrid exchange programs that mix virtual and in-person components. Even at periods when travel is restricted, this strategy improves accessibility, increases participation, and fosters cross-cultural contacts.

For instance, the European Union's Erasmus+ programme has promoted strong educational collaboration and allowed thousands of students to pursue their studies overseas. A reciprocal

---

[1] Lorraine Lin (林悦莹) is a scholar of International Relations with a graduation from the Marymount International School London (UK)

flow of students would result from the program's expansion to include relationships with prestigious Chinese universities, promoting intercultural dialogue and knowledge exchange.

Thanks to several important variables, exchange programs are expected to grow significantly in the upcoming year. Immersive virtual experiences made possible by technological breakthroughs will eliminate geographic restrictions and increase access to exchange possibilities. Students may participate in real-time conversations, cultural immersion activities, and team projects via virtual platforms, resulting in a more inclusive and adaptable exchange programme model.

Interdisciplinary exchange programs will also become increasingly popular, emphasizing the fusion of many academic fields, and encouraging holistic learning. These programs will develop well-rounded individuals with a global perspective and flexible abilities by enabling students to pursue a variety of academic subjects. Additionally, a stronger emphasis on research partnerships and professional internships will give students real-world learning opportunities that connect theory and practice, improving their employability and encouraging cross-cultural understanding.

Awakening and Strengthening Curiosity

Developing interest in and excitement for one another's cultures requires a diversified strategy. First, by including cultural competence training in the curriculum, students may get familiar with both areas' rich customs, history, and morals. Second, intercultural seminars, language classes, and cultural orientation programs help promote empathy while creating respect for variety and encouraging meaningful interaction.

Institutions should plan immersion activities like study trips, internships, and service-learning initiatives to foster curiosity. These events allow students to interact with residents, see historical sites, and participate in actual cultural practices. For instance, by working with the Northwestern Polytechnical University of Xi An and the European Guanxi project, the Institute for a Greater Europe (IGE) may promote collaborative initiatives that inspire students to collaborate, share ideas, and become immersed in both areas' rich cultural diversity.

Educational institutions and exchange programme planners can employ a variety of tactics that inspire and develop an interest in and excitement for the culture of the host country:

a.   **Pre-departure Cultural Orientation**: Students can participate in thorough cultural orientation programs before beginning an exchange programme. These programs offer information on the host nation's culture, history, language, and customs. In addition, students may build a foundation of knowledge and comprehension via interactive sessions, language lessons, and intercultural seminars, kindling their curiosity and fostering a sincere interest in the host culture. One example of an exchange program, especially involving European and Asian cultures, to help students understand both cultures can be the LSE BSc International Relations and Chinese program[2] , which enhances students' cultural experience by embracing British and Chinese culture. Similarly, the Dual BA Program between Sciences Po (France) and Peking University (China)[3] immerses students in French and Chinese cultures. By studying in France and China, students can understand cultural dynamics and engage in collaborative efforts focused on international policy and cultural exchange between Europe and China.

---

2 Science, London School of Economics and Political. "BSc International Relations and Chinese." London School of Economics and Political Science. Accessed November 18, 2023. https://www.lse.ac.uk/study-at-lse/Undergraduate/degree-programmes-2024/BSc-International-Relations-and-Chinese.

3 Sciences Po. "Dual Degree with Peking University." Paris School of International Affairs. Accessed November 18, 2023. https://www.sciencespo.fr/psia/academics/dual-degrees/peking-university.

Additionally, another exchange program called the Dual Degree Program between the Graduate School of Public Policy[4] (GraSPP) at the University of Tokyo and Kings College London[5] plays a role in deepening understanding and cooperation between Japan and European countries, contributing to improved policy-making processes and diplomatic relations.

1)   *Immersive Experiences*: Providing immersive experiences is crucial for igniting interest and zeal. Students may directly experience the spirit of the host culture through cultural immersion activities, including trips to historical sites, taking part in regional festivals, and being involved in the local community. These interactions enable interpersonal communication, offer chances to use the local tongue and give insight into cultural norms and values. An example is the ASEF, also known as the Asia Europe Foundation[6], which actively promotes understanding and cooperation between Asia and Europe through a range of cultural exchange initiatives. They organize events such as youth summits, cultural festivals, and artist exchanges to provide participants with experiences. These experiences include opportunities for community engagement and participation in festivals across Asia and Europe. Another platform called EAHEP (EU Asia Higher Education Platform)[7] focuses on strengthening collaboration in education between Asia and Europe. It supports activities like exchanges, study tours and internships that allow students to fully immerse themselves in the culture and academic life of the host country, whether in Europe or Asia. These programs play a role in enhancing students' cultural fluency while fostering relationships.

2)   *Cross-Cultural Collaborations*: Collaboration between pupils from various backgrounds encourages inquiry and solidifies cross-cultural ties. Students may engage in meaningful discussions, challenge preconceptions, and understand multiple viewpoints thanks to joint projects, group assignments, and cultural exchange activities. For instance, developing buddy networks that link native and international students may build a strong network, promote cross-cultural dialogue, and deepen interpersonal understanding. The ASEM Education Process, which stands for Asia Europe Meeting[8] (ASEM) is an initiative, between European countries in the field of education. It aims to foster cultural understanding and academic partnerships through activities such as student conferences and joint research projects. The ASEM Education Process helps break down barriers, promote respect, and facilitate learning opportunities by bringing together students from both continents. Another platform that promotes collaboration is the United Nations University[9] (UNU). Global Seminars. These seminars occur in Asia and Europe and bring together students and professionals from diverse cultural backgrounds—the UNU Global Seminars focus on addressing issues through learning, research, and dialogue. Participants work together on group projects while engaging in discussions that challenge their perspectives, leading to an appreciation of cultures and viewpoints.

3)   *Reflection and Dialogue:* Fostering curiosity requires creating environments encouraging thought and open discussion. Students can process their experiences, pose questions, and share ideas during the exchange programme. In addition, students are encouraged to explore the complexity of many cultures via moderated conversations and intercultural dialogues, which fosters curiosity, empathy, and a drive to learn more. The Classroom Network of the Asia

---

[4] The University Of Tokyo. "MA-Level Double Degree Programme with King's College London." GraSPP, July 15, 2021. https://www.pp.u-tokyo.ac.jp/en/news/2021-07-15-30716/.

[5] London, King's College. "War Studies Signs New Partnership Agreement with University of Tokyo." King's College London. Accessed November 18, 2023. https://www.kcl.ac.uk/news/war-studies-signs-new-partnership-agreement-with-university-of-tokyo.

[6] Asia Europe Foundation. "Bringing Asians and Europeans Together." Asia-Europe Foundation (ASEF), n.d. https://asef.org/.

[7] EU-Asia Higher Education Platform (EAHEP). "University Directory Worldwide." www.university-directory.eu. Accessed November 18, 2023. https://www.university-directory.eu/index.html.

[8] The Diplomatic Service of the European Union. "Asia-Europe Meeting (ASEM) | EEAS Website." www.eeas.europa.eu, n.d. https://www.eeas.europa.eu/eeas/asia-europe-meeting-asem_en.

[9] Knowledge to Transform the World. "United Nations University." Unu.edu, 2020. https://unu.edu/.

Europe Foundation[10] (ASEF ClassNet) encourages collaboration and meaningful conversations among students and teachers from Asia and Europe. This platform serves as a means for learning, offering discussions and face-to-face dialogues where participants engage in conversations about global issues, cultural diversity, and personal experiences. Moreover, The Global Liberal Arts Alliance[11] (GLAA) is another platform bringing together individuals from European and Asian backgrounds. These seminars involve discussions, workshops and moments of reflection that provide a space for students to reflect on their experiences and exchange ideas while exploring both cultures. The main goal of these seminars is to cultivate mindedness and foster a curiosity-driven approach to understanding different cultures.

Conclusion:

Future exchange programme development has enormous potential to promote intercultural understanding and forge enduring ties between people from different cultures and nations. Exchange programs may develop into transformative experiences that foster interest and zeal for the host culture by embracing technological breakthroughs, adopting multidisciplinary approaches, and emphasizing immersive encounters. Students may develop a genuine understanding of many cultures and become global citizens prepared to tackle complex global issues via thorough cultural orientation, immersive activities, cross-cultural cooperation, and support reflection. Thanks to these initiatives, exchange programs will continue to thrive, building people's understanding and helping to create a more connected and peaceful world. Those potentials will become concrete with the second part on education diplomacy.

II   UNLEASHING THE POTENTIAL OF EDUCATIONAL DIPLOMACY AND EMBRACING A NEW PARADIGM IN GLOBAL EDUCATION

Introduction

Having presented several suggestions for the development of innovative educational exchange programs, those ideas will be applied to the sphere of diplomacy. Promoting cooperation, understanding, and sustainable development through educational diplomacy has significant potential at a time of interconnection and global issues. The following paragraphs analyze the possibility of educational diplomacy and the newly developing approach to international and global education that gives students the knowledge and outlook necessary for a world that is fast changing.

a)   The Potential of Educational Diplomacy

Building bridges and strengthening international connections are possible through educational diplomacy, a potent instrument. Educational diplomacy promotes cross-cultural communication and knowledge sharing through building academic alliances, collaborative research initiatives, and faculty and student exchanges. Its promise goes beyond academics since it advances social, scientific, and economic progress.

The Confucius Institutes, which have effectively promoted Chinese language and culture worldwide, are a noteworthy example of educational diplomacy. A balanced exchange that fosters curiosity, understanding, and long-lasting relationships may be achieved by growing the influence of these institutes in Europe and creating reciprocal platforms that enable European languages and culture in China.

---

[10] ASEF CLASSROOM NETWORK (ASEF CLASSNET). "ASEF Classroom Network (ASEF ClassNet)." Asia-Europe Foundation (ASEF). Accessed November 18, 2023. https://asef.org/programmes/asef-classroom-network-asef-classnet/.
[11] Global Liberal Arts Alliance. "Global Liberal Arts Alliance – Member Institutions." Liberal Arts Alliance. Accessed November 18, 2023. https://liberalartsalliance.org/.

Additionally, educational diplomacy is essential in tackling world issues. For example, collaborations between Chinese and European institutions might concentrate on technical innovation, public health, and sustainable development. Educational diplomacy may lead to creative ideas and help create a wealthier and more peaceful world by merging knowledge, sharing resources, and using different views.

Educational diplomacy is a potent catalyst for forging long-term alliances and improving cultural understanding. Faculty exchanges, academic conferences, and joint research initiatives facilitate collaboration and information transfer. These programs encourage international communication and gap-closing while fostering trust and cooperation. Economic potential can also be found in educational diplomacy. For example, China's Belt and Road Initiative and Europe's robust research and innovation environment provide opportunities for academic partnerships that can promote technical improvements, sustainable development, and economic progress.

b)   The New Approach to International and Global Education

The new international and global education strategy must give pupils the tools to deal with challenging global issues. The importance of cross-disciplinary learning, cultural awareness, and problem-solving skills should be highlighted.

Universities can create combined degree programs that incorporate the knowledge of Chinese and European institutions, encouraging a collaborative atmosphere. These initiatives promote cross-cultural collaboration among students as they develop creative answers to common issues.

Additionally, encouraging entrepreneurship, innovation, and sustainable development in the classroom helps prepare pupils to face global concerns. Encouragement of intercultural cooperation and the ability for students to work together to solve real-world problems are two benefits of cross-cultural student-led initiatives, such as social entrepreneurship projects or sustainable development campaigns.

A trend towards comprehensive, interdisciplinary learning and a concentration on developing adaptive abilities are part of the evolving international and global education paradigm. This method gives pupils the skills they need to prosper in a world that is changing quickly.

First, multidisciplinary education enables students to work beyond conventional disciplinary boundaries and address challenging global issues. Students get a thorough grasp of complex topics and a systems-thinking approach by combining many study subjects, such as science, humanities, and social sciences.

Second, the new strategy for global education requires cultural competency. Students need to learn empathy, respect for cultural variety, and how to deal with subtle cultural differences. Students are given the tools to accept diversity and create inclusive settings via interactions with classmates from other backgrounds, study abroad opportunities, and cross-cultural partnerships.

Thirdly, the new strategy strongly encourages creativity, problem-solving, and critical thinking. Students will be encouraged to engage in project-based learning, put their knowledge to use in real-world situations, and hone their entrepreneurial abilities. This gives them the tools to tackle complex global problems and support sustainable development.

Additionally, technology is essential to the new strategy for global education. Students may interact with classmates worldwide, access materials, and participate in debates across cultures thanks to digital tools, virtual collaborations, and online learning platforms. This digital component makes it easier to collaborate internationally and offers a more comprehensive and accessible education.

Conclusion:

Educational exchanges between Europe and China have enormous potential for establishing ties, increasing cross-cultural understanding, and encouraging creative partnerships. We can create a transformative future where students from both regions engage in meaningful exchanges that benefit individuals, institutions, and societies by embracing technological advancements, encouraging curiosity, utilizing educational diplomacy, and adopting a forward-thinking approach to international and global education. Furthermore, creating exchange programs with virtual and in-person components will guarantee that educational exchanges remain robust and inclusive, allowing students to interact across cultures despite physical obstacles.

Curiosity may be sparked and strengthened through focused programs that immerse pupils in the varied cultural landscapes of Europe and China. In addition, students can receive first-hand exposure to various cultural practices and historical sites by including cultural competence training in the curriculum and setting up immersion activities like study trips and internships. These life-changing encounters will cultivate sincere respect for the diversity and distinctiveness of one another's cultures, inspiring curiosity and zeal that goes beyond superficial knowledge.

Educational diplomacy as a diplomatic tool has great promise for improving overall bilateral ties between Europe and China. Educational diplomacy may close gaps, build trust, and promote discussion on shared global concerns through encouraging partnerships, collaborative research initiatives, and academic conferences. Students and young scientists are empowered to explore novel ideas and communicate insights through collaborations like the European Guanxi initiative and the Northwestern Polytechnical University of Xi An, creating long-lasting relationships that cut across cultural and geographic borders.

Beyond academic boundaries, the new approach to international and global education must give students the tools to deal with complex global concerns. Students may successfully navigate the interconnected and fast-changing world by embracing interdisciplinary learning, encouraging cultural sensitivity, and promoting problem-solving abilities. Joint degree programs may give students a thorough education that combines various viewpoints and skills by utilizing the assets of European and Chinese universities. Additionally, incorporating entrepreneurship, innovation, and sustainable development into the curriculum gives students the tools to be agents of change and advance the global community.

In conclusion, there is much room for mutual development, cultural enrichment, and joint innovation in future educational interactions between Europe and China. Implementing these suggestions enables young people to develop into global citizens who can influence a more diverse, interconnected, and affluent world.

Building Bridges, Bridging Cultures: The Power of Exchange Programs and Educational Diplomacy

Sofie Serrer[1]

Introduction

In an era of accelerating globalization and interconnectedness, the landscape of education and cultural exchange is undergoing a profound transformation. As we peer into the future, it becomes increasingly evident that exchange programs, cultural diplomacy, and the very essence of global education are evolving to meet the demands of an ever-changing world. This essay explores the exciting developments and possibilities on the horizon, delving into questions that will shape the future of educational and cultural exchange. From the integration of technological advancements to the cultivation of curiosity and enthusiasm for diverse cultures, from the power of educational diplomacy to the emergence of innovative approaches in global education, an attempt is made to understand how these dynamics will reshape the way we learn, connect, and engage with the world.

Technology as Enhancement, Collaboration on Global Issues:
The Future of Exchange Programs

To answer the question of how exchange programs will develop, one has to consider three major areas of interest:

First, with the rapid advancement of technology, exchange programs are likely to embrace virtual and augmented reality platforms, enabling students to immerse themselves in cross-cultural experiences without physical travel (Barbosa & Ferreira-Lopes, 2021; Pandey, 2018). This will expand access to exchange opportunities and foster global connections. As shown by Habib (2023), implementing a comprehensive digital infrastructure can especially increase education access in war-torn areas, a fact that may become of increasing importance these days.

Second, future exchange programs may prioritize collaboration with a wide range of educational institutions, including non-traditional partners, such as think tanks and student-led-initiatives, to offer a broader array of cultural experiences and perspectives (Zhu & Yang, 2023). This will enrich the exchange experience and encourage cross-disciplinary learning.

Third, exchange programs may increasingly focus on global challenges, for instance, climate change and inequality (Rizvi & Beech, 2023; Martel & Goodman, 2022). This approach will instill a sense of global citizenship and encourage students to contribute to solving real-world problems.

---

[1] Sofie Serrer is a member of the Institute for Greater Europe. During her studies for International Business and Economics she has acquired several international working experiences from different internships in Southeast Asia foremost Malaysia.

Holistic Learning: Strengthening Curiosity and Inspiring Cultural Understanding

To foster cross-border collaboration among different partners, as addressed above, first, curiosity and enthusiasm for other cultures have to be awakened and strengthened. Among the most obvious possibilities here are cultural exchanges and events. Organizing cultural exchange events, festivals, and language exchanges within educational institutions can create a vibrant atmosphere of cultural celebration. Such activities encourage interaction, inspire curiosity, and facilitate understanding among students from different cultures. Encouraging students to participate in such immersive experiences, allows them to engage first-hand with the traditions, language, and customs of other cultures. Additionally, interdisciplinary studies are also known to ignite students' curiosity. This can be achieved both, through curricular and extra-curricular elements of intercultural education (Al-Maamari, 2016). An idea would be to incorporate elements of other cultures' history, arts, and literature into curricula. Thus, a holistic approach could provide a deeper understanding and appreciation for other cultures, foster further curiosity and spark enthusiasm for learning more.

The Power of Educational Diplomacy

When delving into the questions above, the potential of educational diplomacy should be considered. Educational diplomacy is generally known as a process where education and cultural exchange are used as tools to promote mutual understanding, cooperation, and positive relationships between different countries and their people. It involves fostering global connections, sharing knowledge, and creating opportunities for students and educators to learn from and collaborate with individuals from diverse cultural backgrounds. The goal of educational diplomacy is to build bridges of understanding and friendship among nations through educational activities, promoting peace and cooperation on the international stage. Thus, educational diplomacy fosters international understanding and has the power to facilitate peaceful dialogue on global issues.

Additionally, educational diplomacy enhances a country's soft power by displaying its educational institutions, cultural heritage, and values, as discussed for instance by Hong (2014), Knight (2022), and Peterson (2014). It attracts students, scholars, and professionals from around the world, thereby increasing a nation's influence on the international stage.

Consequently, investing in educational diplomacy can yield long-term benefits, as researched by Batey (2013), Khan et al. (2020), as well as Sustarsic and Cheng (2022). Students and scholars who experience a positive and enriching education abroad often maintain lasting connections with the respective host country. This contributes to building sustainable diplomatic ties and networks.

Three approaches to international and global education

Thus, what is the new approach to international and global education? As broad as an all-encompassing answer might be, this essay focuses on three aspects. Firstly, there is interconnectedness. The new approach to global education against the background of what has been outlined above emphasizes interconnectedness, recognizing that global challenges require collaborative solutions. It promotes cross-border partnerships among educational institutions and encourages students to engage with diverse perspectives. Tarozzi (2023) goes even further and actively calls for assigning a global perspective a central role in education. Additionally, he stresses the importance of balancing hope and idealism with a realistic approach to education and globally prevailing issues.

Secondly, global education now focuses on developing students' global competencies, such as intercultural communication (Sabet and Chapman, 2023), critical thinking (Barell, 2003), and consequently adaptability. These skills are crucial for navigating an increasingly interconnected world.

Thirdly, virtual learning platforms and digital resources will increasingly be employed to facilitate global education. This relates directly to the discussion presented above, where education is considered to receive significant enhancement through implementing a comprehensive digital infrastructure. Such an approach democratize access to education and enables students to connect with peers and experts from different parts of the world.

Conclusion

As we look into the future, it becomes abundantly clear that exchange programs, cultural diplomacy, and the very essence of global education are poised to embark on an evolution that mirrors the dynamism of our ever-changing world. This essay has embarked on a voyage of exploration, delving into questions that are destined to map the future landscape of educational and cultural exchange. From the integration of technological advancements, symbolized by virtual platforms, to the cultivation of curiosity and enthusiasm for diverse cultures, from the influential role of educational diplomacy to the emergence of innovative paradigms in global education, the endeavor has been to unravel how these transformative dynamics will redefine our pathways to learning, connecting, and engaging with the world.

In the realm of exchange programs, a future that embraces technological advancements, broadens collaboration to encompass a rich tapestry of diverse partners, and rallies our collective efforts towards addressing pressing global challenges has been envisioned. These shifts could not only indicate an era of inclusivity and accessibility but also instill in students a profound sense of global citizenship, empowering them to contribute to real-world problem solving.

The journey towards fostering cross-border collaboration depends on awakening and nurturing curiosity and enthusiasm for other cultures. Cultural exchanges, immersive experiences, and interdisciplinary studies offer key portals to mutual understanding and appreciation. These gateways create vibrant avenues for interaction, inspiration, and cultural understanding among students from diverse backgrounds. The holistic approach of including elements of other cultures into curricula ensures that curiosity remains a driving force, propelling students to delve deeper into global diversity.

On the topic of educational diplomacy, this essay explored how education and cultural exchange are powerful tools for promoting mutual understanding, cooperation, and international relationships. It is evident that educational diplomacy possesses the transformative power to bridge divides and facilitate peaceful dialogue on global issues. Furthermore, it is a beacon of a nation's soft power, influencing global perceptions by displaying its educational institutions, cultural heritage, and values. The investments in educational diplomacy have far-reaching effects, as it nurtures lasting connections and networks that can serve as a foundation for sustainable diplomatic relations.

As this exploration concludes, a new approach to international and global education can be sighted. It's a path illuminated by interconnectedness, where education embraces a global perspective and seeks collaborative solutions to our shared challenges. It is a journey of developing global competencies and equipping students with the skills needed to navigate our interconnected world. Lastly, it is a future where virtual learning platforms and digital resources democratize access to education, bridging continents and cultures.

In essence, the future of education and cultural exchange is built from a combination of technology, collaboration, curiosity, and diplomacy. It is a vision where borders blur, minds open, and the world becomes a classroom without limits. The journey into these future promises not only greater diversity in global education, but also a more connected and harmonious world.

References

Al-Maamari, S. (2016). Education for connecting Omani students with other cultures in the world: The role of social studies. *International Review of Education*. https://doi.org/10.1007/s11159-016-9577-2

Barbosa, M. W., & Ferreira-Lopes, L. (2021). Emerging trends in telecollaboration and virtual exchange: a bibliometric study. *Educational Review*, 1–29. https://doi.org/10.1080/00131911.2021.1907314

Barell, J. (2003). *Developing more curious minds*. ASCD.

Batey, J. (2013). Education diplomacy: Global diplomacy awareness developed through Short-Term international internships. *Childhood Education, 90*(1), 77–80. https://doi.org/10.1080/00094056.2014.872524

Habib, M. (2023). Digital transformation strategy for developing higher education in conflict-affected societies. *Social Sciences & Humanities Open, 8*(1), 100627. https://doi.org/10.1016/j.ssaho.2023.100627

Hong, N. Y. (2014). EU-China education diplomacy: an effective soft power strategy? *European Foreign Affairs Review, 19*(Special Issue), 155–171. https://doi.org/10.54648/eerr2014026

Khan, M. M., Ahmad, R., & Fernald, L. W. (2020). Diplomacy and Education: A Systematic Review of literature. *Global Social Sciences Review, V*(III), 1–9. https://doi.org/10.31703/gssr.2020(v-iii).01

Knight, J. (2022). Differentiating Knowledge Diplomacy from Soft Power and Cultural, Science, Education and Public Forms of Diplomacy. In *Springer eBooks* (pp. 113–125). https://doi.org/10.1007/978-3-031-14977-1_9

Martel, M., & Goodman, A. E. (2022). The Future of International Educational Exchange is Bright. *Comparative & International Higher Education, 14*(2). https://doi.org/10.32674/jcihe.v14i2.4036

Pandey, U. C. (2018, January 1). *Opportunities for educational diplomacy in South Asia*. http://www.asianjde.com/ojs/index.php/AsianJDE/article/view/236

Peterson, P. M. (2014). Diplomacy and Education: a changing global landscape. *International Higher Education, 75*, 2–3. https://doi.org/10.6017/ihe.2014.75.5410

Rizvi, F., & Beech, J. P. (2023). Volume 1: Globalization and the Shifting Geopolitics of Education. In *Elsevier eBooks* (pp. xxiii–xxvi). https://doi.org/10.1016/b978-0-12-818630-5.02001-7

Sabet, P. G. P., & Chapman, E. (2023). A window to the future of intercultural competence in tertiary education: A narrative literature review. *International Journal of Intercultural Relations, 96*, 101868. https://doi.org/10.1016/j.ijintrel.2023.101868

Singh, B. P., Kaur, J., Sen, R. K., Singh, B., & Chattu, V. K. (2021). The Double Whammy of Pandemic and War: A Systematic review of India's education diplomacy to address educational inequities in Afghanistan. *Education Sciences, 11*(10), 651. https://doi.org/10.3390/educsci11100651

Sustarsic, M., & Cheng, B. (2022). Public diplomacy and exchange programs at a secondary school level: Alumni experiences. *International Journal of Intercultural Relations, 87*, 119–130. https://doi.org/10.1016/j.ijintrel.2022.01.012

Tarozzi, M. (2023). Futures and hope of global citizenship education. *International Journal of Development Education and Global Learning, 15*(1). https://doi.org/10.14324/ijdegl.15.1.05

Zhu, K., & Yang, R. (2023). China's engagement with Southeast Asia in higher education. In *Elsevier eBooks* (pp. 666–672). https://doi.org/10.1016/b978-0-12-818630-5.01060-5

Educational Diplomacy between Europe and China

Andżelika Serwatka [1]

Abstract

This essay seeks to delve into the concepts surrounding EU-China cooperation, highlighting both its challenges and past mistakes. A theoretical dispute between Fukuyama with "the end of history" and Huntington with "a clash of civilization" serves as theoretical bedrock. A primary focus is placed upon advocating for the integration of educational diplomacy that encompasses the values inherent to both cultures. The objective is to facilitate a deeper understanding of these values, thereby emphasizing the significance of overcoming inherent biases. Additionally, this essay strives to identify potential shared values, with a particular emphasis on the pursuit of common global objectives (if work for common, global good can be named as value).

Keywords: China, UE, Europe, cooperation, digital, Fukuyama, Huntington, common goal

Introduction

The 21st century is characterized not only by great ideas but also by significant challenges. The world has become highly globalized, bringing us numerous advantages such as easier commuting and the exchange of knowledge and ideas. However, this globalization has also led to growing disparities between the affluent and the marginalized. Fukuyama has discussed the potential end of history, but in reality, human history is entering a new phase. We confront global issues that necessitate coordinated solutions on a worldwide scale. Simultaneously with different cultures coming closer, bringing different and contradicting cultures together can either imply an increase of corporation due to common goals or an increases conflict and competition due to diverging cultural understandings and visions for the future. That also raises the question, which was posted once by Samuel Huntington, if are we just on the verge of the war between cultures?

In other words, if instead of developing transcultural understanding are we not getting to the point where one civilization will oppose the other? And after all what we mean when we use term "civilization"? We talk about bringing east and west together, bringing our cultures and civilizations together, but is not the term "civilization" itself wrong? Dipesh Chakrabarty in his work "The Crises of Civilization" is arguing that the idea of "civilization" was used as a way to justify colonialism. In that view "civilisation" is something that is distinguishing one better society from the other barbaric one. In other words, term "civilisation" implies hierarchical dominance one over the other. That is also why Chakrabarty explores later the relationship between civilization and humanism, asking whether they are fundamentally oppositional or if one is a subset of the other. Having in mind hierarchical connotations of the term "civilisation" the famous "clash of civilisations" clearly appears as a strive for global dominance.

It is also important to explore one more concept, which was trying to define the future of mankind – so called "the end of history". In the 21st century, we can safely say that the thesis presented by Fukuyama in *"The End of History and the Last Man"* was incorrect. The anticipated

[1] *Andżelika Serwatka is a Master Student of International Relations at the University of Lodz (Poland)*

culmination of history, understood as the progression of ideas culminating in the universal establishment of Western liberal culture, did not materialize. And maybe for the good, as Fukuyama's concept could potentially be construed as an ambitious plan of eradicating diversity to achieve global tyranny of singular system, wherein uniformity in behavior and thought is prevalent.

Basically, what we can observe through the lens of Fukuyama's words is the ultimate belief in the almost messianic mission of the Western world (especially the US). Fukuyama regarded Western values as the universal ones – he presupposed them *a priori* as the values that would best serve the world. However, as we can see, he was mistaken regarding the end of history, and similarly, he also was mistaken about the necessity of Western value-dominance over the rest of the world as a necessity to achieve something like "perpetual peace". It is exactly what postcolonial theories criticizes. Seeing western culture and western values (including the "flagship" value which is democracy) as ones should rule the rest of world is not a right stance.

The democracy is often seen as indisputable value. But what we mean when we say democracy? How does differ US presidential democracy from German and Polish or Swiss forms? Does it mean that democracy is a value itself? Or maybe it is just a system, which enables us to protect actual values better? And maybe it is just showing that we should stop serving systems (such as democracy, communism or other) and finally serve people and try to overcome real obstacles. I am not criticizing democracy itself. I am criticizing those who call themselves (without self-reflection but with a lot of bigotry) democrats. Who believe that just the word "democracy" is overcoming all global obstacles (and who often are totally rooted in their right wing, stereotypical thinking).

Fukuyama was wrong, but what if another thinker, Samuel Huntington, was he right in the *Clash of Civilization*? Because quite often the approach of western civilization is appearing as if they actually want that clash. Rather in contrast the west is not the only guilty one. The same can be said about China challenging the global system with its ambitions to take part in shaping globalization according to the Chinese visions for the future. Visions, which often challenge international law, which are criticized by some human rights activists and which by some are even seen as neocolonial movement (China's engagement as a new emerging development aid donor especially in Africa and South America – which is a subject of controversy). Just as a reminder, international law is enforced by the United Nations, an organization of which China is a member. In other words, China, as one of the most prominent members of the UN, agrees to certain rules, only to then challenge them continually. Here, the fragility of common values in an international system becomes visible.

General disagreements in understanding between east and west are only one of many challenges which are faced by China-Europe cooperation. Those two entities, while collaborating, come across very particular difficulties. Take, for instance, the 16+1 model, designed to enhance economic exchanges between Eastern Europe and China. However, this concept faltered not due to a lack of engagement but rather due to multiple misunderstandings. Primarily, the approach was centered solely on economic exchange and didn't prioritize the pursuit of shared values. Furthermore, China's approach to Eastern European countries was misconstrued. They perceived Eastern Europe as a block of post-communist nations that were still developing and had a history of foreign dominance. To clarify, China viewed Eastern Europe through an Asian lens, attempting to identify shared commonalities. This approach didn't progress because Eastern European countries perceived themselves quite differently. While indeed distinct from Western Europe, this part of the continent also acknowledges its European heritage. This example highlights just one instance of misinterpreting the values and perspectives of both side

Numerous other challenges exist, including differing stances toward Taiwan (which for instance resulted in Lithuania-China diplomacy crisis), disagreements on China-Russia relations, approaches to the conflict in Ukraine (with China displaying restraint) and attitudes toward the

United States (which often hinders EU-China trade, perceived as a challenge by the US). For all of that it is necessary to acknowledge perspectives of both sides and learn about our biases.

Educational diplomacy should teach us about those biases and how to overcome them Modern states are increasingly adopting new diplomatic strategies, and education emerges as an effective tool of soft power, especially after the collapse of the bipolar international order. Joseph Nye, the creator of the concept of "soft power" emphasizes that the ability to attract and co-opt, rather than coerce, is the key to success in world politics. Educational diplomacy might be a part of that strategy. Strategy, which is necessary if we do not want the Huntington's vision of clash of civilization become real. That also raises the question if our global society more strives nowadays for dominance one over the other or more strives for Kant's perpetual peace. Unfortunately, judging by policies of nowadays superpowers, the first one appears more likely.

For all above, that is why educational diplomacy and strengthening mutual understanding are so important. And we have couple of tools to do that. For instance, providing learning opportunities for students from abroad and allowing them not only to acquire knowledge but also to become ambassadors of their own cultures can lead to better transcultural understanding. Openness and eagerness to learn about "the other" and "the other culture" is crucial. Similarly cultural exchange programs can also play a positive role here. Bring people from different cultures together leads to breaking down cultural barriers, it promotes positive international relations and also creates environment of thought and value exchange.

Other key factor is establishing transnational education. Partnerships and collaborations between universities from different countries and globalizing higher education That can stimulate the exchange of knowledge and ideas and promote intercultural understanding. Creating joint think tanks would be also advised. Think tanks aiming not only fostering UE-China or European-China relations, but also with focus on global problems. The same can be said about summer schools for students and those who work in academic field. What is important is to ensure that those groups of students will be mixed and not homogenous. Aiming together to face global problems is a powerful tool of fostering transcultural relations. The real exchange begins when we let the interactions flows and let those interactions shape the new idea of cooperation. And we have a lot of problems to cooperate on. Especially when it comes to the field of working on sustainable development, gender equality, social inclusion, human security, AI and its future governance, pandemic, space governance, ecology, preventing superpower countries from engaging in conflict and working in conflict zones? Why does or could those not be our shared values?

Moreover, learning each other's languages can help with fostering international relations. Language, and language structures differ from each other, and it is also reflected by patters in which we think. Therefore, providing language training we also foster our better understanding and understanding of intentions. We also have to remember about possibilities which we are provided by virtual education. Although it is not as effective as experiencing foreign culture in person, it is still useful tool when it comes to enabling large numbers of people to gain the knowledge about foreign country and their culture. Digitalization is not only useful while exchanging information and knowledge. It is also a tool for socialization. E-sport is a good example of that. It is wildly known that sport diplomacy plays huge role when it comes to nontraditional ways of establishing state to state relations (take even example of Nagoya championship, in 1971 which was a starting point of so-called ping-pong diplomacy and resulted in visit of Nixon to China in 1972). But e-sport also can become such a medium (much cheaper and easily accessible medium). And if we are talking about digital technology, we can also mention use of certain apps. Not only those which would aim users who look for pen pal. But what if those apps and platforms would also enable artists to work hand by hand? What if European artists would be judged by Chinese jury and the other way round? Those people could also discuss together new ideas and methods for their particular work. Educational diplomacy is not only academic exchange. And the whole society should be engaged in that process.

Upcoming decades and years will be full of global challenges. We all should better cooperate on those topics academically and from grassroots perspective then just create more obstacles. We can quote here Sun Tsu: "He will win who knows when to fight and when not to fight". And at that moment of history, we need to stop fighting each other and focus on other, greater hindrances, building a common vision for our common home as mankind.

Europe-China Educational Exchanges: Bridging Epochs and Cultures

Joel Christoph [1]

Introduction

The crimson hues of the Beijing sunset served as a poignant backdrop to one of my most memorable experiences at Tsinghua University. It was during an intimate gathering organized by our professors to foster dialogue between European and Chinese students. A Chinese peer eloquently quoted Victor Hugo: "To learn to read is to light a fire; every syllable that is spelled out is a spark." This not only left me in awe of his linguistic prowess but also symbolized the harmonious synthesis of European literature in Chinese academia. Such moments were commonplace at Tsinghua, reflecting the deep-rooted connection between European and Chinese educational exchanges.

This bond, nurtured over decades, has blossomed into a profound relationship between two ancient civilizations, each rich in history, culture, and knowledge. Yet, as the world rapidly transforms, driven by technological advancements and shifting geopolitics, so does the nature of these educational exchanges. Now, more than ever, it's imperative to re-envision this relationship. The aim of this essay is to explore and propose innovative visions and ideas that can redefine the future trajectory of educational exchanges between China and Europe. By delving into this narrative, I wish to shed light on the multifaceted avenues through which Europe and China can collaboratively lead the next chapter of global education.

1)   Historical Context and Current Scenario

The tapestry of educational exchanges between Europe and China, rich in its intricacy, can trace its roots back to the times of the Silk Road. This ancient trade route, while primarily economic, also saw the beginnings of educational and cultural exchanges, symbolized by figures such as Marco Polo. Their stories whispered of a China rich in knowledge, awaiting exploration by the inquisitive European mind.

Fast-forward to the 20th and 21st centuries, and these exchanges have taken on more formal and structured forms. Europe's ivy-clad universities welcomed thousands of Chinese students, eager to immerse themselves in a fusion of traditional European education and modern pedagogical techniques. Concurrently, China's educational establishments, in their magnificent juxtaposition of ancient tradition and cutting-edge innovation, became a beacon for European students desiring a different educational perspective.

---

[1] *Joel Christoph* is a PhD Student in Economics at the European University Institute (EUI) in Italy. He is also a Bretton Woods 2.0 Fellow of the Atlantic Council and a Dahrendorf Fellow of Oxford University. Joel completed degrees in economics at the EUI, Barcelona School of Economics and University College London. He also studied political science at Tsinghua University, where he was a Young Ambassador for the Carnegie Endowment for International Peace, as well as a Youth Delegate from the Global Alliance of Universities on Climate to the COP United Nations Climate Change Conference

On a personal note, I recall my semester in Jiangsu, where I was part of an exchange program during my undergraduate studies. The classroom, with its blend of European and Chinese students, was a microcosm of collaborative learning, mutual respect, and a confluence of diverse perspectives. Outside the classroom, interactions ranged from sharing meals that bridged the culinary divide to joint projects that merged European design with Chinese craftsmanship. The experience was illuminating, emphasizing that knowledge has no boundaries and cultures can coalesce beautifully when given the right platform.

Beyond the personal and the academic, these exchanges between Europe and China hold significant diplomatic and societal implications. Education serves as a non-threatening medium to bridge misunderstandings and foster camaraderie. As students return to their homelands, they carry with them not just academic knowledge, but also a nuanced understanding of another culture. In a world often rife with political complexities, these individual ambassadors of goodwill, equipped with firsthand experience, play a pivotal role in fostering positive diplomatic relations. Moreover, the intertwining of Europe and China through education sows the seeds for future collaborations in business, technology, and global policymaking.

In essence, the historical context of educational exchanges between Europe and China lays a foundation that is profound and promising. While the modalities and nuances of these exchanges have evolved, their importance in cultivating mutual respect and understanding remains paramount, serving as a beacon for international cooperation in an increasingly interconnected world.

2)   Future of Exchange Programs

As the world stands on the precipice of a new era, educational exchanges between Europe and China are poised to undergo a transformative evolution, shaped by global shifts, technology, and the dynamism of international relations.

To begin with, global trends point towards a more interconnected and interdependent world. The rise of the gig economy, remote work, and international collaborations implies that the next generation would require a multifaceted understanding of diverse cultures. Hence, the exchange programs of the future may not just be about traditional study but also encompass internships, research collaborations, and entrepreneurial ventures.

Technological advancements, particularly in the realm of virtual reality, augmented reality, and AI-driven platforms, are set to redefine the essence of these exchanges. Imagine a scenario where a student in Berlin attends a lecture in Beijing in real-time, through a virtual classroom, feeling as if they're physically present. Or where AI-driven language translators break down language barriers instantaneously, fostering seamless communication.

However, it's not without challenges. The most pressing issue might be the digital divide. Not every student has access to the latest technology or high-speed internet. During my own virtual exchange seminar last year, a few Chinese counterparts faced connectivity issues, underscoring the need for technological equity. Overcoming this requires collaborative investments in infrastructure and ensuring that programs are designed with inclusivity in mind.

Moreover, changing international relations, affected by economic policies, trade wars, or geopolitical tensions, can cast shadows on the smooth execution of exchange programs. It is essential for academic institutions to stay apolitical, emphasizing the core mission of education and mutual understanding. Close collaborations between European and Chinese educational bodies, backed by governmental support, can help in navigating these choppy waters.

Given the current global circumstances, especially the aftermath of the COVID-19 pandemic and its implications on travel and physical gatherings, the potential for virtual or hybrid exchanges has never been more apparent. While the pandemic posed challenges, it also accelerated the adoption of online learning platforms. A hybrid model, where students engage in both virtual and physical exchanges throughout their program, might be the new norm. This ensures continuity in learning, irrespective of global disruptions, while still preserving the essence of physical, cultural immersion.

In conclusion, the future of Europe-China exchange programs is not just about crossing physical borders but transcending digital, cultural, and psychological boundaries. By harnessing technology, being adaptive to global trends, and placing emphasis on mutual understanding, the next chapter of these exchanges promises to be as enriching as the illustrious chapters of the past.

## 3)	Awakening Curiosity & Strengthening Enthusiasm

At the core of any successful exchange program lies an innate curiosity about the unknown and a fervor to understand the myriad intricacies of another culture. This mutual enthusiasm, if nurtured correctly, can significantly contribute to the broader vision of unity, understanding, and collaboration between Europe and China.

First and foremost, sparking interest often begins with dispelling myths and preconceived notions. An innovative approach would be to leverage digital storytelling platforms, allowing students from both sides to share glimpses of their daily lives, debunking stereotypes. A "Day in My Life" video series, for instance, can offer raw, unfiltered insights into the lifestyles, challenges, and aspirations of young individuals, making the distant seem familiar.

Joint cultural events can serve as powerful instruments to further this cause. Picture a "Europe-China Cultural Fest," a week-long event hosted alternatively in European and Chinese cities. It could feature European students performing Peking opera or Chinese students orchestrating a rendition of Beethoven's classics. Such initiatives not only foster appreciation but also cultivate a sense of shared heritage. Furthermore, introducing courses that amalgamate European philosophies with Chinese wisdom, or exploring the intersections of European Renaissance art with Chinese dynastic art, can provide a rich, intertwined curriculum.

Beyond the classroom, real-world exposure is invaluable. Organizing village homestays, where students immerse themselves in local customs, or urban explorations, which highlight the modern ethos of bustling cities, can cultivate deep-seated understanding. My own experience of participating in a traditional tea ceremony in Hangzhou taught me more about Chinese values of patience, respect, and harmony than any textbook could.

Finally, we must recognize the instrumental role of educational diplomacy. At its heart, this concept marries education's transformative power with the strategic aim of diplomacy: fostering peace and mutual respect. Through shared academic research projects, policy-making simulations, or even debates on global issues, students can grasp the nuances of international diplomacy. By understanding another's viewpoint, not as an adversary but as a fellow global citizen, they lay the groundwork for future collaborations that are not just diplomatic gestures but genuine gestures of friendship.

In summary, curiosity and enthusiasm are not mere by-products of exchange programs; they are the lifeblood. By intertwining innovative ideas with traditional methods, and underpinning it all with a diplomatic mindset, we can awaken a shared passion for discovery and cement an unbreakable bond between Europe and China.

4)   **New Approaches to International & Global Education**

The contours of international education are rapidly shifting, sculpted by modern pedagogies, technology's omnipresence, and the ever-growing need for global collaboration. As Europe and China stand on the cusp of a renewed era of educational exchanges, embracing these novel approaches becomes imperative.

Contemporary pedagogical methods, like project-based learning and experiential education, emphasize real-world application over rote memorization. Imagine a curriculum where a European student collaborates with a Chinese peer to design a sustainable urban space, borrowing elements from both European and Chinese architecture. Such endeavors not only cement academic concepts but also foster intercultural competence, teaching students to navigate diverse perspectives and arrive at harmonious solutions.

Technological tools are the linchpins of this new educational paradigm. Platforms like Massive Open Online Courses (MOOCs) democratize access to knowledge, enabling a student in rural China to learn from a European maestro, and vice versa. Augmented Reality (AR) and Virtual Reality (VR) tools can transport students to simulated environments such as a bustling Shanghai market or a serene Tuscan countryside. Those places are facilitating cultural immersion without the constraints of geography.

Collaborative platforms, on the other hand, are redefining the essence of teamwork. Digital whiteboards, cloud-based project management tools, and real-time translators eliminate barriers, ensuring that collaboration is seamless, productive, and rich in diversity.

These innovative approaches yield manifold benefits. From an educational standpoint, they usher in a holistic learning experience, melding theory with practice, and individual effort with collective endeavor. More importantly, they cultivate global citizens individuals who are not just proficient in their domains, but also empathetic, adaptable, and keenly aware of the world's interconnectedness.

In conclusion, as the tapestry of international education becomes more intricate and vibrant, the threads binding Europe and China must remain robust and resilient. The advancements in pedagogy and technology are not mere tools; they are bridges , bridges that span cultural chasms, linguistic barriers, and historical divides. It is incumbent upon us, the torchbearers of this new epoch, to traverse these bridges with an open heart and an insatiable curiosity. For in the dialogue and collaboration between Europe and China lies the promise of a brighter, unified future, where knowledge knows no borders, and understanding is the universal language.

Interpretation of the Concept of "Aphasia" under the Discourse Theory of Foucault

ZHOU Zhi-jun (周祉骏)[1]

Abstract

Originally a linguistic or medical concept, aphasia was introduced into the field of literature and is now one of the commonly used terms in literary criticism, widely used in the study of literary theories such as Marxism, feminism and postcolonialism. Foucault's "discourse" theory discusses the essence and influence of discourse and the relationship between discourse and power. From the perspective of "discourse" theory, although there is no relationship between "aphasia" and "discourse" from the source, we can find the common ground between "aphasia" and "discourse" theory, that is, centering on power, using discipline and order to clarify the relationship between "other" and "self".

Keywords: aphasia, Roman Jacobson, metaphor, metonymy, Foucault, discourse theory, power, CAO Shun-qing

1. The origin of the concept of aphasia
1.1. Philosophical Foundation

The proposal of "aphasia" is closely related to structuralism, "a structuralist theory provides the practical critic with a fertile ground for interpretative application" (Selden 2005, 73). Roman Jacobson, a Russian linguist, and one of the representatives of the Prague School, proposed the idea of binary opposition between metaphor and metonymy. It comes from the binary opposites of syntagmatic and paradigmatic relations of structuralist Saussure, that is, the activities of the language system are carried out on two axes, which are composed of the horizontal syntagmatic relationship and the vertical paradigmatic relationship. These two relation systems run simultaneously and restrict each other. The vertical axis refers to the mutual substitution of words bearing the same component in a sentence. The horizontal axis is the combinatorial relation of language symbols. Jacobson applied this idea to his own research, and believed that language has two dimensions, horizontal and vertical, and the difference between these two dimensions is related to Saussure's theory of language and parole.

In short, Saussure holds that the study of language must be divided into two parts. Jacobson inherited this idea and applied it into his own studies of linguistics and literary criticism.

1.2. Linguistic Foundation

As mentioned above, the term "aphasia" (speech defect) comes from the study of linguistics, or from the field of medicine. Jacobson noticed that "aphasic children appeared to lose the ability to operate one or other of these dimensions" (Selden 2005, 73). Jacobson divides aphasia into two types, "contiguity disorder" and "similarity disorder". The former implies "the inability to combine elements in a sequence" and the latter means "the inability to substitute one element for another." Patients with the former are unable to complete sentences, can only use simple

---

[1] ZHOU Zhi-jun (周祉骏) is a Bachelor student for German Studies at the Northwestern Polytechnical University Xi'an (PRC) (西北工业大学).

combinations of words and phrases, and lack of grammatical structure or have a confused grammatical structure. Patients with the latter disorder, despite of being able to fully express sentences, lack the ability to define and interpret, that is, to replace and choose words and other expressions. It is associated with a series of words such as synonyms, antonyms, or other substitute words, which the patient cannot express. Thus, we can see that people with aphasia do not lose the ability to speak but are unable to express themselves smoothly and in a way that are easily understood.

1.3. The Loanwords of Literary Criticism

Jacobson used these two types of aphasia in his book *Two Aspects of Language and Two Types of Aphasic Disturbances* (1987) to discuss the distinction between metaphor and metonymy in literature and between realism and Romanticism. The presence of "contiguity disorder" (Jakobson 1987, 95) leads to substitution in the vertical dimension, similar to metaphor, whereas "similarity disorder" causes the generation of sequences for the entire entity, as seen in metonymy. Jakobson proposed that typical speech patterns also have a tendency towards one or more extremes. He drew a parallel between this phenomenon and the genre of literature found in literature studies. The literary style is characterized by a preference for either metaphoric or metonymic language. The progression of history, from romanticism to realism to symbolism, can be comprehended as a shift in style from the metaphorical to the metonymic and back to the metaphoric. David Lodge expounds upon Jakobson's theory and employs it in the analysis of present-day literature. In his book *The Modes of Modern Writing* (1977), he asserted that modernism and symbolism possess metaphorical qualities, whereas anti-modernism embodies realism and metonymism.

2. Foucault's "Discursion-Power" Theory
2.1 Discourse Theory and Foucault's Discourse Theory

The concept of "discourse" was originally born in the field of linguistics, and the concept used by Saussure can be understood as the speech act of sound. For a long time, the concept of discourse gradually expanded from the field of linguistics to literature, philosophy, history, political science, anthropology and other humanities and social sciences, and derived a series of terms, such as philosophical discourse, historical discourse, political discourse and more on. The content of "discourse" explained by Foucault in different works has different dimensions of function. For example, *The Order of Things* (1966), *Madness and Civilization : A History of Insanity in the Age of Reason* (1961) describe the function at the dimension of world, and *The Archeology of Knowledge* (1969) shows the role of "language practice" or "statement" in the formation of discourse networks. The "discursion-ego" model in the first and second volumes of *The History of sexuality* (1984) and *Technologies of the Self* (1982). The following mainly discusses the "discursion-power" model in *Discipline & Punish: The Birth of the Prison* (1979) and *The Order of Discourse* (1970). All of these above can be summed up as Foucault's theory of "discourse".

2.2. Foucault's "Discursion-Power" Theory

Discourse is the result of power, and the consequence and product of power. For a long time, the traditional notion of power believes that power is realized by suppressing the subject, and suppressing the subject is regarded as the necessary condition for the operation of power. Initially, Foucault agreed with this perspective and highlighted the relationship between discourse and power in *The Order of Discourse*. "Discourse is not simply that which translates struggles or systems of domination but is the thing for which and by which there is struggle, discourse is the power which is to be seized" (Foucault 1970). But later he found that power has no more than a negative effect on the production of discourse: "It traverses and produces things, it induces pleasure, forms of knowledge, produces discourse. It needs to be thought of as a productive network which runs through the whole society body" (Foucault 1980, 119). Similarly, power can also produce discourse contrary to the subject, that is, deprive the subject of discourse and make the subject "rarefaction"(Foucault 198,:224) and "aphasia".

Discourse serves power, is a tool of power, and is used by power, which in turn produces and strengthens or resists and weakens power. Discourse functions as a means and tool of power operation within the scope of power. The generation of a great deal of discourse is achieved through the "discourse incitement" of people by the authorities, which forces people to confess their sexual experiences in confession, transforms them into discourse, and records and organizes and institutionalizes them in all areas of social life. As Foucault said in his interview, without language creation, storage, transfer and functioning, these power relationships cannot be established and strengthened. The reaction of discourse to power is reflected in the management and restraint of children's discourse by educational institutions, which forces children to accept normative discourse, such as the knowledge taught in school. At this time, the children are in a state of "aphasia". But discourse is not always in favor of power, and sometimes it turns against it. For example, the emergence of various discourses on homosexuality in the fields of psychiatry and literature in the 19th century strengthened the power and social control over the group. However, homosexual discourse became the basis for homosexuals to fight for equal rights. At this time, the homosexual community gradually walked out of the dilemma of "aphasia".

3. Conclusion

CAO Shun-qing is a famous scholar in the field of contemporary comparative literature and literary theory in China, and he has put forward a lot of theories with considerable achievements. In his article *Aphasia of Literary Theory and Cultural Pathology*[2], he put forward: "For a long time, Chinese modern and contemporary literary theories have basically borrowed a whole set of Western discourse and has been in a state of 'aphasia' in the expression, communication, and interpretation of literary theory. Since the 'shake off the fetters of the old conception' (traditional culture) in the May Fourth Period, traditional Chinese literary theory has been basically abandoned and studied only in the desks of a few scholars. On the contrary, what participates in the construction of modern Chinese literature is the colorful Western literary theories." Aphasia here refers to the inability to use native theories and discourse systems to explain and utter local literary phenomena. It can also be seen that there is still a long way to go for the construction of academic theories and discourse systems in countries with later development. Based on CAO Shun-qing's definition of "aphasia" and Foucault's "discourse-power" theory, "aphasia" in literary theory would be defined as: "As the result of the oppression of power, the subject cannot form and speak its thoughts, basic categories rules and disciplines in its specific cultural tradition and social history."

---

[2] The original title of the article and the following citations are in Chinese and English versions are translated by me. The original title of the article is 文化失语症与文化病态

REFERENCES

Adams H. & Searle L. (1992). Critical Theory Since Plato, Orlando: Harcourt Barce Jovanovich, 30-33

Cao S. (1996, March 9), Wenlun Shiyuzheng Yu Wenhua Bingtai[Aphasia in Literature Theory and Cultural Pathology] *Contention in Literature and Art*, 02, 50-58

Foucault M. (1981). The Order of Discourse (Ed.) Untying the Text: A Poststructuralist Reader (pp. 224) London: Routledge& Kegan Paul

Hall S. (2003). Representation: cultural representations and signifying practices. London: SAGE publications Ltd, 50

Jakobson R. (1987). Two Aspects of Language and Two Types of Aphasic Disturbances, in Language in Literature (Ed.) Krystyna Pomorska and Stephen Rudy (pp.114). Cambridge, MA: Harvard University Press

Selden R. & Widdowson P.& Brooker P. (2005). A Reader's Guide to Contemporary Literary Theory. Harlow: Pearson Education Limited, 73-74

Different Worldviews under Chinese and Germany Education Systems

ZHAO Pengyue (赵鹏越) [1]

Abstract

The contemporary education system in German and China are different. Those different education systems reflect distinctive worldviews and mold the corresponding values. This article follows the aim to dive into the cultural background of Chinese and Germany education system and elaborate on how the worldviews of Confucianism and German idealism have influenced their respective education system. As it will be shown, the education system based on these worldviews have also influenced the thinking patterns of students and their social ethos.

Keywords: education system, worldviews, Confucianism, idealism, social ethos

Introduction

Education foremost does shape different worldviews and consequently values of the public, and then affects the direction of development and the expression of civilization. Taking an example Prussia's educational reform had more or less given birth to the prosperity of German culture and academia in the early 20th century; after the reform and opening up of China, the reform of education oriented to modernization has led to the emergence of talents in various fields. After all, basically all countries that have entered the process of modernization have adopted a unified education model, which means Chinese, Japanese or American students all basically follow the same curriculum of knowledge from primary to higher education, they learn basic fundamental mathematics as well as Newton's physical law. The content doesn't refer any significant difference, but fundamental differences can be found in their essence, which reflects the features of spiritual culture.The first part of the essay concentrates on the contrast between Chinese and Germany educational systems; the second part analyzes the philosophical background behind the two educational systems and the third part provides the conclusion of this comparison.

1)   The education systems in China and Germany

1.1.The education system in China

From 1949 on, the Chinese government has launched several reforms in the field of education. When the country had been established firstly, as 80 percent of the population were still illiterate, education aimed to eradicate illiteracy (sǎo máng 扫盲). After 1978, the education system recovered from the impacts of political disruptions of the cultural revolution. Gradually the government established the compulsory education system and built a number of elite universities to serve the target of fostering economic development. In the past thirty decades, the universities have increasingly expanded the enrollments in order to promote equity, which makes it possible

---

for more people in less developed area to enter the college.[2] Nowadays the Chinese education system is structured as such. In China, a student usually attends primary school at the age of six and finishes compulsory education after nine years. Then students will attend an exam in order to entry senior high school, those who were not able to acquire an admittance probably will enter technical secondary school, which often lack approbation in society. After finishing senior high school, students will take part in national college entrance exam. If they aren't admitted for university, they will go to junior college, which likewise enjoys a lower societal reputation. Fewer students directly enter the job market after failing these two crucial exams. Entering a university is a prevailing thought among the population in China, those who don't enter the university are often facing social stigmatization being regarded as "loser" or "incompetent", emphasizing the importance of commitment to education within the Chinese society . Parents tend to let their children get higher degree after finishing their bachelor, this kind of cult on degree could be traced back towards many aspects of cultural background such as bureaucratic hierarchy. Here, the motive consisted of the higher hierarchy you reach, the more successful you are, providing better means for sustaining your family.[3]

After having presented the Chinese education system, the next section will present the development of the German education system.

1.2. The education system in German

In German, pre-school education is available to children from upon the age of three, but it is not compulsory, and parents can choose whether or not to send their children to kindergarten; children over the age of six must begin nine years of compulsory education, and after the fifth grade of primary school, pupils will choose to enter Hauptschule, Realschule or Gymnasium by examination. However, it has to mentioned that the education system in Germany is not convergent everywhere, with each federal country following its own slightly different system. The former two are six-year courses, of which the level of general secondary education is relatively low; nearly half of the students choose practical secondary schools, after which they can continue their studies in specialized schools (Berufsschule) and professional schools (Fachoberschule), and then can directly enter the job market, Gymnasium have a nine-year study period of the highest standard, and most students are admitted to higher education institutions after graduation. Higher education is divided into vocational colleges (Fachhochschule) and professional colleges (Universität), also known as the " Duales System" of German education. In German, students usually don't have to pay enormous efforts to enter the university, nevertheless facing fierce competition in fields like medicine, and the rate of dropout is high, especially in science and engineering subjects. People don't regard university as the only way out, different from in China, graduating from Fachhochschule can imply good future prospectives as well, those graduates can also find a job with considerable salary.[4]

Having contrasted the German and the Chinese education system, the next section will delve into the cultural and philosophical background for the evolution of those education systems.

---

[2]Kirby, William C (2014): The Chinese Century? The Challenges of Higher Education. *Daedalus.* Vol. 143, No. 2, Growing Pains in a Rising China (Spring 2014), pp. 145-156.

[3] Oyeniran, Rassidy (2017): Impacts of Reforms in Chinese Educational System *International Journal of Education.* Vol. 9, No. 1, pp. 30-28.

[4]. Welsh, Helga A (2010): Higher Education in Germany: Fragmented Change amid Paradigm Shifts. *Special Issue,* Vol. 28, No. 2 (95), pp. 53-70.

2)   Different culture backgrounds behind education

2.1.Chinese Confucianism and its impact on education

During the long process of dynasties, China has produced generations of famous thinkers, who were also involved in a wide range of fields in their respective eras, these great thinkers were often philosophers, writers, and politicians at the same time.

Throughout Chinese history, only Confucianism occupied the position of absolute authority in the ideological world. Confucius broke the restrictions of learning for a governmental position (xue zai guan fu 学在官府) and spread Confucianism to people, providing a mass foundation for Confucianism; in Han dynasty, Dong Zhongshu deposed Confucianism and officially made Confucianism the orthodox ideology of the state; Cheng Zhu Lixue deepened Confucianism and enriched the philosophical connotation of Confucianism. Although Confucianism has ceased to be the ruling ideology in modern times, the very essence is still enshrined in the thinking method in Chinese people's head and subtly affects the political, social, and cultural landscape.

Different from the western philosophy centered on reason and focusing on the search for knowledge, Confucianism is oriented to reality and is embodied in the paradigm of ethics: focusing on the application of practical methodologies such as interpersonal communication and governance. The theory of Confucianism emphasizes "great unification", that is, "wholeness" or "Integration", which is reflected in many aspects of daily life. It emphasizes "harmony", reconciles the contradictions between people and between countries, and allows the "parts" that are contradictory struggling to coordinate and compromise with each other so as to become a perfect whole. In political practice, it emphasizes the maintenance of the rationality of the existing order and supports the centralization of power and the social moral ideology under the monarchy.[5] Compared with the Western concept of "wholeness", the word "he"(和) can more accurately summarize the connotation of Confucianism. It implies the resolution of contradictions, different from the fierce confrontation between the contradictory two sides in Hegel's or Marxist's systems, the idea of harmony is aimed to overcome rigidity with softness, which accepts and reconciles different ideologies and views with a tolerable attitude. In the area of education, the philosophical thought of "he" is embodied in "indoctrination", the word indoctrination is quite Confucian: the subject as the teacher transmits knowledge to the student as the unenlightened object. Teaching means to effect; it represents a gentle and smooth transition, a process of gradually dispelling obscurantism.

Such worldviews end up leading to a meritocracy because of the lack of educational resource. To be "he" means to be taught and indoctrinated. As the indoctrination becomes a requisite, which means, it's the only way to be admitted by society, people tend to strive for better educational chance to prove that they are qualified to be a suitable part of the society. The consequence is endless and meaningless struggle within finite educational resource. Behind "he" hides a new religion, it exerts subtle influence on the cultural concept of Chinese people, the young people grow up with such edification and everyone pursues his own harmony in the society, which leads to endless involution in a society with limited social resource. Different from this school of thought the German way is based on the principle of rationality as the next section will show.

2.2.Germany Idealism and its impact on education

Rationality is the essence of Germany Idealism. It also reflects the stereotypes of Germans. Any Germanic philosophical product like Romanticism in German literature, Marxism, even the Third Reich's ideology all can be traced back to the roots of rationalism. Rationality (Vernunft) was first emphasized by French thinkers in the Age of Enlightenment: Everyone has the ability

---

[5] Smith, Craig A. (2017): Govern the Country and Bring Peace to all: The Crisis in New Confucian Education. *Control.* pp.171-176

to use their own reason to think, judge and act. In Germany, the idea of emphasizing rationality was carried forward. Kant defined enlightenment as the courage to use reason: people must dare to utilize their own mind instead of obeying authority. Reason is powerful, it can have the ability to solve various problems and finally reach the truth. Rationality is "seeking truth". People can obtain objective knowledge through reason, so reason is reliable and unquestionable.[6]

In the Age of Enlightenment, dissatisfaction with the church became more intense, and people began to pay more attention to the reality of their lives rather than the illusory God or the afterlife, and reason symbolized the existence of personal will. God is no longer the Creator, and man has become his own master. It is man himself who created everything in the world, not the indescribable and supreme existence. It is the rationality hidden in everyone's heart that drives human beings to act, think and create.

With the in-depth study of rationality, philosophers marveled at the omnipotence of rationality. Kant demonstrated the epistemological structure of human beings in the "Critique of Pure Reason": human beings' understanding of the world is their understanding of phenomena itself. And the real noumenon world behind the phenomenal world is judged as a world that human beings cannot know. The understanding of phenomena relies on the function of reason. Reason gives concepts to the world. Reason depicts the connections between phenomena and makes phenomena understandable to humans. In this sense, reason has gained the authority like a Creator. After all, common sense in understanding the noumenal world is doomed to fail, and the understanding of the phenomenal world is all the function of reason. From this, it can be concluded that it is reason that shapes what people can see and act. With the development of philosophy, Hegel raised reason to the level of ontology and regarded it as logic (logos). German idealism has been pushed to its top.

German culture is shaped by rationality centrism. On the one hand, it emphasizes the importance of rationality and individuals; on the other hand, it elevates rationality to its original height. The beautiful country envisioned by Marx was shaped by reason. All the beautiful visions in this utopia need to be coordinated, arranged, and perfected by an omnipotent reason. Reason brings everything within its own capabilities and can handle it properly. All contradictions are finally eliminated under rational arrangements. In education, the fusion of rationalism symbolizing the values of pragmatism, which contributes to the prosperity of vocational education and make university less important as that is the case in China. The society adjust itself to capitalism-oriented form, which underline the importance of ability and productivity instead of the reputation of the school or the difference of education background. The rationalism-oriented society may make many achievements in fields like economy and technology, but such pragmatism makes rationality a tool, which on the contrary damages the freedom of the individual.[7]

3)   Summary: Analysis and Prospects

Concluding this essay "He" and "reason" are both positive thoughts. But excessive rationality brings cold arbitrariness, and reason cannot predict the disasters brought about by its transgression because of its own limitations; Similarly, the framework of "wholeness" brings the suppression of the individual and the obliteration of particularity, which limits the development of individuality. Communication is the best way to bridge the gap between ideas, and in education, a field of development and the future, it is particularly important to clarify the birthplace of different ideas, because the process of mutual understanding between ideas can be deepened only through this way. When two different systems learn from each other, those can make great progress. Chinese may learn to be more pragmatic so that they can solve the current

---

⁶ Bowie Andrew(2003): German Idealism and early German Romanticism. *Aesthetics and subjectivity*, pp. 49-68.
⁷ Deissinger, Thomas (1996): Germany's Vocational Training Act: Its Function as an Instrument of Quality Control within a Tradition-Based Vocational Training System. *Oxford Review of Education*, Vol. 22, No. 3, pp.317-336

problems more effectively; German could try to treat things and people with more harmony in order to make the society more humane. The exchange of ideas is not only the exchange of theoretical details, but more importantly, mutual understanding on fundamental issues.

References

Bowie, Andrew (2003): German Idealism and early German Romanticism. Aesthetics and subjectivity, pp. 49-68.

Deissinger, Thomas (1996): Germany's Vocational Training Act: Its Function as an Instrument of Quality Control within a Tradition-Based Vocational Training System. Oxford Review of Education, Vol. 22, No. 3, pp. 317-336

Kirby, William C. (2014): The Chinese Century? The Challenges of Higher Education. Daedalus. Vol. 143, No. 2, Growing Pains in a Rising China (Spring 2014), pp. 145-156.

Oyeniran, Rassidy (2017): Impacts of Reforms in Chinese Educational System. International Journal of Education. Vol. 9, No. 1, pp. 28-30.

Smith, Craig A. (2017): Govern the Country and Bring Peace to all: The Crisis in New Confucian Education. Control. pp. 171-176

Welsh, Helga A. (2010): Higher Education in Germany: Fragmented Change amid Paradigm Shifts. Special Issue, Vol. 28, No. 2 (95), pp. 53-70.

V. Report on the Symposium

Report on the Symposium: Dialogue through education between Europe and China on the 23rd of September 2023

Stephan Raab

Traditionally educational exchange programs act as bridgebuilders between cultures. But what can be learned from the past for the future for the European-Chinese exchange and diplomacy? The first EU-China essay competition of the Institute for Greater Europe in corporation with its partners from European Guanxi invited young people to share their answers to this question.

A call to action –
The first EU-China essay competition on educational exchange

An old Chinese saying states: "三人行，必有我师(Sānrén xíng, bìyǒu wǒ shī) – In a group of three people, there will always be one person I can learn from." Building on that ancient wisdom, educational exchange has always served as an essential bridge builder between countries and cultures. Meanwhile, in earlier times, foremost at the early 20th Chinese students mostly travelled to Europe and the West, such as the renowned Chinese educationist Cai Yuanpai (蔡元培). Nowadays in reverse many young students from Europe are travelling to China to learn more about this country, culture, and its growing influence in global politics. Under the current challenges of globalization, diversification and knowledge-based economy, cultural and educational cooperation between China and Europe has broader prospects and more far-reaching significance. However new challenges shape this corporation.

Participants of the Symposium Dialogue through Education

In that context the Institute for Greater Europe in corporation with its partners European Guanxi hosted the first EU-China Essay Competition. Students and young professionals from Europe and China were invited to share their visions and hopes, innovations for promoting the future development of this exchange as well as contributing their personal intercultural experiences.

The organizers were very delighted, that such call met on a fertile ground. Many students from diverse regions in China and different countries in Europe contributed to this essay competition. Especially the diversity of topics discussed is very impressive, ranging from aspects of language learning, over research in cultural projects, new perspectives for design education, as well as innovative ways for learning languages, including even empirical research. Furthermore, many essays submitted even gave concrete proposal on how European and Chinese education system can learn from each other, searching to promote intercultural and future oriented education.

A platform for exchange of ideas- Symposiums dialogue through education

After the deadline, the Symposium "Dialogue through education between Europe and China", was held on the 23rd of September, with the great support of the Confucius Institute Freiburg. Having evaluated the high-quality and though-provoking essays from various disciplines, this symposium provided a platform for personal exchange of ideas and different worldviews. Furthermore, this symposium was enriched by many high-quality speakers from various disciplines, giving insights into their expertise.

After a short welcoming speech by Bernhard Koch, Vice-Director of the Confucius Institute Freiburg, the symposium was officially inaugurated. Here, a wide audience from China and Europe joined this very inspiring and thought-provoking day. As first speaker, Dr. Ute Heilmann, graduate member of the Postgraduate Centre for Chinese Studies at Heidelberg University, shared her experiences on the evolution of Chinese academia. After her graduation she had been active as Editorial Director Clinical Medicine at Springer Verlag in China and Asia, providing a deep insight into commonalities between European and Chinese academia.

As second speaker Dr. LI Jie, Associate Professor at the Northwestern Polytechnical University Xi'an and co-organizer of this project gave an insight into her research work on cognitive linguistics. Here, she emphasized the importance of seeing languages in a wider, intercultural context, where translation is not just a box of words to be transported to another language, but more like painting and art, taking the high importance of the intercultural context into mind.
Following this language learning, Stephan Raab, President of Institute of Greater Europe and co-organizer of this project, emphasized the synergies and intersection between diplomacy and comparative international educational research. He argued, that seeing international relations more through educational lenses provides a better understanding of the trajectory of a country, as education reveals visions for the future and memories of the past. Likewise seeing education more through diplomatic lenses helps to promote more awareness for global citizenship.

Furthermore, Dr. ZHANG Tao research assistant at the Institute for Sinology at the University of Heidelberg put a special focus on the importance of movies in language learning. During her presentation, supported by her personal experience as language teacher, she revealed that movies can provide a fruitful source and motivation for language learning in both ways.

After that, Ardita Osmani, research employee at the University of Duisburg Essen and member of the European Guanxi, showed in her presentation, that China has tuned from an educational emigration to an educational immigrant spot. Many students from abroad are now coming to China for pursuing their studies. This gave a special importance to educational diplomacy.

Building on that Stefan Pellech, founder of the Austrian Chinese Consulting Firm Sinotan, who had spent several years in China, attached to this, explaining the educational reforms taking place in China. Here, he emphasized, that education has to be thought in a wider context than schools, sharing his experiences of collaboration in the arts and cultural exchanges.

Eventually, the first part was concluded by Finn Stallbaum, employee at Youth in Europe. During his presentation he was sharing his personal experiences of going abroad. Here, he encouraged the participants to be open-minded and curious about such opportunities, motivating them to spend some time abroad, for gaining new intercultural experiences and growing with them.

After the award ceremony, handing out the prizes for the best essays, ZHAO Xiaodan, English Teacher from the Shanghai Caoyang Middle School, introduced into the second part with a talk about the practice of blended Learning in English teaching in junior middle school. Following on that, the participants were invited to share their ideas discussed within the essays. Here, especially SHUI Ting and LOU Li has to be thanked for their great hosting during the second part of this event.

Learning as mutual lifelong process for becoming global citizens

Concluding this interdisciplinary and intercultural project between Europe and China, education and curricula always gives insight into what a society and culture has learned from its past as well as sharing, what it has learned for the future. With education always striving for the future, this project gave proof about the fact, that young people in Europe and China are likewise open-minded and curious to learn from and with each other about their respective regions, their cultures, memories of the past and their visions and hopes for the future. We hope that this project can serve as a founding stone for a fruitful and prospective educational exchange between Europe and China, opening new worldviews and building bridges.